COMPARATIVE HISTORY OF SLAVIC LITERATURES

by DMITRIJ ČIŽEVSKIJ

translated by
RICHARD NOEL PORTER
and
MARTIN P. RICE

edited, with a foreword, by
SERGE A. ZENKOVSKY

VANDERBILT UNIVERSITY PRESS
1971

C

Students and External Readers

Comparative History of Slavic Literatures

FOREWORD

Many histories of Slavic literature have been written, but only a few of them (and none in English except the present work by Dmitrij Čiževskij) approach this subject from the vantage point of comparative literary history. Most surveys either treat each Slavic literature separately and chronologically or organize them along the lines of the traditional division of Slavic languages—into the eastern, western, and southern groups. Such an approach may be found, for instance, in the chapters dealing with literature in the *Handbook of Slavic Studies*, edited by the late Leonid Strakhovsky, a very useful book, but unfortunately out of date and out of print.

Professor Dmitrij Čiževskij's approach is very different, since he presents the development of Slavic literature against the background of succeeding literary periods, schools, and movements. In each period, he discusses first a literary era, determining its philosophic content, themes, and styles, and then studies the achievements of the Slavic peoples in the given period. Such an approach is certainly not an easy one for a person writing a literary history; it requires from the writer a profound knowledge of the evolution of European thought; an understanding of the general trends of European, especially Slavic, literatures; and, finally, a thorough command of the Slavic languages, since many important works by Slavic writers have never been translated. The author of the *Comparative History of Slavic Literatures* has all these qualifications.

The reader of this book should certainly keep in mind that the Slavic literatures have not always been interconnected in their development, that they have experienced the influence of two distinct types of European civilizations, and that several of these literatures have had long periods of stagnation or unproductivity owing to the invasion of hostile

powers or domination by foreign nations. In this respect, Slavic literatures differ greatly from such major European literatures as English,
French, and German, all of which had long centuries of continuous
growth and were never catastrophically disturbed.

As mentioned above, and as the reader will see in the present survey,
the Slavs at the dawn of their history sustained the impact of two major
divisions of European culture: the eastern Christian or Byzantine, which
was primarily Greek in its essence, and western Europe, which had its
roots in the civilization of the Roman Empire and later was influenced
by the Church of Rome.

All of the Slavic literatures came into being after Christianization,
which took place in the late ninth and tenth centuries. The first Slavic
nation that became converted to Christianity was the Great Moravian
state, located in the territory of present-day Czechoslovakia and
Hungary. Two Greek brothers from Salonika, Constantine, who later
became a monk and took the name Cyril, and Methodius came to Great
Moravia in 863 at the invitation of the Moravian Prince Rostislav. They
organized there the first Slavic Christian church, created an alphabet
adapted to the Slavic sound system, and translated the most important
liturgical books into a Slavic language, now usually called Church Slavonic, which was a Macedonian dialect familiar to the missionaries. This
Byzantine mission remained in Great Moravia for only a few decades
and was soon forced to leave the country under pressure from the
German princes and German Roman Catholic clergy.

In 865 the Bulgarian ruler Boris accepted Christianity from Byzantium.
From Bulgaria, the Greek Orthodox faith, as well as Byzantine civilization and Byzantine literary patterns, spread to most of the Balkan Slavs,
who accepted the language used by Cyril and Methodius for liturgical
and literary purposes. Another century and a quarter later, in 988 or 989,
the eastern or Russian Slavs also became converted by their prince,
Vladimir, to Eastern Orthodox Christianity. While most of the eastern
and southern Slavs became Christianized under the Byzantine rite,
Czechs and Slovaks recognized the authority of Rome; consequently,
their evolution was profoundly influenced by the western church and
culture. This western religious and cultural influence also penetrated from
the confines of the German Empire into the northwestern Balkans, where
the Slovenians and Croatians accepted the Roman rites. In this way, the
southern Slavs became culturally split into two distinct groups, despite
the fact that Croatians and Serbians spoke the same language.

At almost the same time that the Russians accepted Byzantine Christianity, their Slavic neighbors to the west, the Poles, also became Christianized, but the missionaries who converted them came not from the south or east but from the west, and they brought with them the Christianity of the Roman rite and the Latin tongue. Thus, toward the year 1000, one part of the Slavs—the Poles, Czechs, Slovaks, Croatians, and Slovenians—became members of the western community of the European Christian world and for a long period of time used the Latin language in the Church and in their writings. On the other hand, the Serbs and Bulgarians in the Balkans and the Russians in Eastern Europe became connected with the Byzantine or eastern Christian rites and for centuries experienced the profound impact of Byzantine cultural patterns. In their churches and in their literature they used the Church Slavonic developed for literary purposes by Cyril and Methodius, although this language later underwent some modifications under the influence of local dialects.

The Roman Catholic Slavs were, to a considerable extent, more fortunate than the Orthodox, since they never experienced any domination by Asian and non-Christian powers. Russia, to the contrary, was conquered in the thirteenth century by invaders from the east, the Mongols, whose control over Russia lasted some two hundred years and resulted in cultural stagnation and the considerable weakening of ties with other Christian lands. Slightly more than a century later, the Orthodox Slavs of the Balkans, the Serbs and Bulgarians, were overwhelmed by the Turks. This Turkish domination lasted for almost half a millenium and left a very considerable imprint on these countries, setting them back several centuries in their cultural and literary development.

The Roman Catholic Slavs were also conquered by foreign powers, but the conquerors were European. These conquests were, however, not as long-lasting or disastrous as those of Asian invaders of Orthodox Slavlands. The Slovenians never developed their own nationhood, for they early became a part of the "Holy Roman Empire of the German Nation," joining the Serbs and Croatians only in 1918 to create Yugoslavia. Croatians were dominated by the Hungarians from the eleventh century to 1915 but preserved their political and cultural autonomy. By the sixteenth century they had a fluorishing literature that clearly followed western, primarily Italian, patterns. The Czechs lost their independence in 1621 after the Roman Catholic Hapsburgs defeated Protestant Bohemia, and the Czech language was replaced by German in the schools and administration for more than a century, although in the middle of the eighteenth century it was reintroduced in the schools and a Chair of Czech was even created at the University of Vienna. In the nineteenth century the Czechs experienced a literary revival and in 1918, together with the Slovaks, rebuilt their own independent state.

A major calamity befell Poland in the late eighteenth century when the Polish state was partitioned among Austria, Prussia, and Russia. This partition did not prevent the further blossoming of Polish literature, however, and the nineteenth century became one of the most interesting and fruitful periods in Polish literary history. Like Czechoslovakia, Slovakia, Croatia, and Slovenia, Poland was able to regain its independence in 1918.

Conquest of the eastern Slavs by the Mongols had a disastrous effect on their national cultural and literary development. Although Mongol domination persisted only in the northeastern part of Russia, the western Russian lands, toward the turn of the fourteenth century, were conquered by Lithuania and Poland, and remained a part of the Polish-Lithuanian commonwealth for some 500 years. The Polish-Catholic influence had an overwhelming effect on the population of the western territories of the Russian Slavs. Thus, the Eastern Slavic dialects became differentiated and developed into three varieties: Belorussian in the northwest, Ukrainian in the southwest, and Great Russian in the east. To be sure, these terms, Belorussian and Ukrainian, became officially recognized and more or less universally accepted only in the twentieth century after the Russian Revolution, but their linguistic and cultural differences became evident as early as the sixteenth century.

The vicissitudes of the historical fates of the Slavic nations often prevented close intellectual and literary intercourse, even hindering personal contact and not infrequently resulting in interslavic hatreds and conflicts and fratricidal wars; we can easily identify numerous periods, however, when one Slavic nation was able to exercise considerable influence on others. Particularly powerful was the early impact of the work of Cyril and Methodius, and, thanks to their mission and their translations, Church Slavonic affected the literary languages of Bulgaria, Serbia, Russia, Belorussia and the Ukraine. From the eleventh century to the fifteenth Bulgarian and Serbian translators and writers left a considerable imprint on Russian writings, while some Russian literary works penetrated the countries of the Balkan Slavs.

The earliest writings of the Czechs were reflected in Russian literature of the eleventh and twelfth centuries, and somewhat later in Polish literature. In the sixteenth and seventeenth centuries Polish literary traditions were likewise reflected in numerous Russian works. In the sixteenth century, Russian emigres from Moscow were instrumental in the development of early Ukranian literature, and in the seventeenth century and early eighteenth century Ukrainian and Bielorussian significantly influences Russian letters. Finally, in the era of realism, Russian literature produced powerful echoes in most Slavic lands; these trends and interrelations have been studied with particular acumen by the writer of this book.

The author of the present volume, Professor Dmitrij Čiževskij, hardly needs any introduction to students and professors of the Slavic languages and literatures. He has taught at more than a dozen Slavic and west European institutions; from 1952 to 1956 he was on the faculty of Harvard University, and he is widely known among Slavicists. Professor Čiževskij's publications number more than a thousand items in ten or fifteen European languages and include several dozen books on Slavic philosophy, intellectual and spiritual history, and literature. His erudition is almost proverbial. At the present time he teaches at the Universities of Heidelberg and Cologne.

The translation of *Comparative History of Slavic Literatures* was done by two Slavicists, Professor Richard Noel Porter of Vanderbilt University, who translated the first part, and Mr. Martin Rice of the University of Tennessee, who translated the second part. This may explain some accidental inconsistencies in style and punctuation. In a very few cases I have taken the liberty of adjusting the original text to the needs and academic habits of American readers. In some instances I have added explanatory footnotes, for which I am solely responsible and which, for the sake of identification, are clearly marked as editor's additions. Finally, I have updated Professor Čiževskij's bibliography, including some recent publications, especially American and English works.

Serge A. Zenkovsky
Vanderbilt University

CONTENTS

Comparative History of Slavic Literatures

PRELIMINARY REMARKS

In each chapter I give a number of quotations, some of which appear only in translation. They have been chosen to convey an idea of the stylistic peculiarities of the works of a period, and many are also of interest for their content. The texts do not, of course, represent equally all the Slavic literatures. The smaller literatures, such as White Russian, Lusatian, and Macedonian, have been treated as stepchildren; but there was not space to present them more fully. Prose works, especially modern ones, would also have required quotations too long for the scope of this book; and I have had to rely on the interested reader to turn to translations, which are becoming more and more numerous.

I have treated in more detail those questions to which in my opinion not enough attention has been paid. The dates of some writers may be found in the tables that precede each chapter. I have not increased the number of names for fear of overburdening the attention and memory of the reader.

The bibliography contains only selected works, particularly newer ones, that give further bibliographical references. Only the list of surveys of the individual literatures and of essays dealing with the basic problems of this book has been presented more completely. Since literary histories, especially older ones, often fail to deal satisfactorily with questions of style, reference to these works has been made only so that the reader may use the bibliographies to find more specialized works. The inclusion of a work in the bibliography of this book does not necessarily mean that I agree with the opinions of the author. Many newer works have been included in the bibliography mainly because they direct attention to neglected facts or because they raise new problems and seek to solve them.

I have not been able to deal at length with the development of literary languages, treatment of which may be found in several works on Slavic linguistics. Below is the information that one may need to read the Slavic texts in this book.

′ over a vowel designates the stressed syllable. In Czech and Slovak it also indicates the length of the vowel.

′ or ˇ over a consonant and ′ after the consonant indicate the palatalization of the consonant (cf. French gn).

y = ы is a dark *i* sound spoken with the tongue far retracted. But in Czech and Slovak it is equivalent to *i*.

c is *ts*, *č* is *ch*, *š* is *sh*, *ž* is *zh*, *x* is *kh*.

Peculiarities of the individual languages:

Russian: *e* initial or after vowels = *ye* and otherwise palatalizes the preceding consonant. ь indicates the palatalization of the preceding consonant.

Ukrainian: и = *y* (see above), г = *h*, є = *ye*.

Bulgarian: *â* = a dark vowel.

Serbo-Croatian: *ć* is a palatal *ch*, *đ* or *dž* a palatal *dzh*.

Polish: *ą* is a nasal vowel similar to the French *on*, *ę* a nasal vowel similar to the French *in*, *ó* = *u*, *i* between a consonant and a vowel indicates the palatalization of the preceding consonant. *ż* = *ž* (see above), *cz* = *ch*, *sz* = *sh*, *rz* = *ž* or *š* (depending on the phonetic environment); *ł* is a hard *l* close to the bilabial *ṷ*.

Czech: *ě* is *ye* ('e); *ů* is a long *u*; *ň*, *ď*, *ť* or *ń*, *n'*, *d'*, *t'* are palatal *n*, *d*, *t*; *ř* is a peculiar sound—*rž*.

Slovak: *e* palatalizes the preceding consonant, *ä* is distinguished from *e*, *ô* is a *uo* diphthong, the sign ′ indicates the length of a vowel and of vocalic *r* and *l*.

I

INTRODUCTION

1. The comparative history of Slavic literatures has attracted the attention of scholars for only a few decades. Too early, before specific problems could be adequately dealt with, fundamental questions were raised as to the possibility of such a field and the necessity for it. In the discussion that followed, the views expressed were not always scholarly, and some arguments were extraneous. The proponents of a comparative treatment of Slavic literatures have, of course, sometimes emphasized too much the unity of the Slavs and the closeness of their ties. But there are valid pedagogic and practical reasons for the necessity of our field, and considerable arguments have been brought to bear against doubts of its possibility.

2. "Slavistics" or "Slavic philology" is becoming increasingly prominent as a subject and field of research in the universities of America and Europe and in other parts of the world. But there is a possibility that instead of the broad and diverse "Slavic world," only the "Russian world" may be studied and that from it misleading conclusions may be drawn about the culture of other Slavic peoples, who in many ways belong to different traditions.

There have almost always been among the Slavs certain parallel currents, the same ones that have run through the great intellectual unity of Europe. Although parts of the Slavic world are on the edges of this intellectual unity, the ties that link them with the West are far more important than those that link them with the East. This is evident in all the Slavic languages, which do have numerous borrowings from Oriental languages, but borrowings that pertain mainly to material culture and only occasionally to intellectual culture or government. The common intellectual history of the Slavs, who were Christianized at almost the same time, in the ninth and tenth centuries, has tied them intimately to the Christian world. Beginning with the Bible, Christian literature has contributed substantially to the spiritual and intellectual vocabulary of the Slavic languages.

Russian is a good example. It is the language of the easternmost Slavic people, a people that was subjugated for two centuries to an Oriental empire. Let us take words that are used frequently in everyday life (the words here are from Turko-Tartar, Mongol, Finno-Ugric, and such "Oriental" Indo-European languages as Persian):

"mattress" *tjufjak;* "shoe" *bašmak;* "belt" *kušak;* "dressing gown" *xalat;* "sofa" *divan;* "tea" *čaj;* "porcelain" *farfor;* "pantry" *čulan;* "fur coat" *šuba;* "winter cap made out of camel hair" *bašlyk;* various articles of clothing worn primarily by peasants: *kaftan, armjak, tulup;* "woman's dress" *sarafan;* headgear: *kolpak, papaxa;* agricultural buildings: *saraj, ambar;* "hut" *kuren';* "market" *bazar;* various materials: "velvet" *barxat,* "damask" *kamka,* "red calico" *kumač;* the names for the colors of horses, of various precious stones, and for obsolete weapons: "quiver" *kolčan,* "dagger" *kinžal,* "saber" *šaška,* "bludgeon" *kisten',* "whip" *nagajka;* words of different meaning such as "fist" *kulak,* "dog" *sobaka,* "fetters" *kandaly,* "plague" *čuma;* the names of some foods; but few words that pertain to intellectual culture or government: "money" *den'gi,* and *altyn* "three-copeck piece," "postal service" *jam* (archaic but still preserved in *jamščik* "coachman," "custom house" *tamožnja,* "translator" *tolmač,* possibly *tovarišc* "comrade"); some words of this group have a negative connotation: "crowd" *vataga,* "nomadic camp" *tabor,* "horde" *orda;* some are even words of abuse: *karga* "hag," *balbes* "lout," *busurman* "unbeliever." [1]

Other Slavic languages have fewer and often different Oriental borrowings.

But the word *tovarišč* (Czech *tovaryš,* Polish *towarzysz,* Slovenian *tovâriš,* etc.) is common to all the Slavic language groups.

Many borrowings from Germanic languages belong to the same groups as the words above, but Germanic words pertaining to the state are far more important. Among them are

knjaz' "prince," *kral'* or *korol'* "king" (the word is simply the name of Karl der Grosse, Charlemagne), *myto* "toll," "customs"; even before

---

1. It should be noted, however, that many of these words no longer belong to everyday vernacular Russian (editor).

the Slavs had been Christianized they had borrowed from the Germans such words as (I shall give only the modern Russian form; for more information on the borrowings see Max Vasmer): *cerkov'* "church," *pop* "priest," *krest* "cross"; the names of weapons: *meč* "sword," *šlem* "helmet," *bronja* "armor"; and numerous words pertaining to material culture: *xudožnik* "artist" (originally "artisan"), *steklo* "glass," *plug* "plow," *bljudo* "dish," *kotel* "kettle," and even *xleb* "bread" (in the sense of a loaf of bread, in contrast to bread in the form of flat cakes, which were already known), *izba* "room," now "peasant house" (Polish also "chamber," *izba handlowa*, "chamber of commerce"), *xyža* (now usually *xižina*) "house," etc. There were also misunderstandings; for example, the Gothic word for "elephant" came to mean "camel" among the Slavs.

But much more numerous and culturally more significant were the borrowings from Latin and Greek, depending on the religion of the Slavs who were borrowing. In Russian one finds, for example, these words taken from Greek:

The names of the months, such words as *arap* "Negro," *aromat* "aroma," *krovat'* "bed," *fonar'* "lantern," *korabl'* "ship," *kad'* (now also *kadka*) "tub," *višnja* "cherry"; words pertaining to the church are particularly numerous: *ierej* "priest," *angel* "angel," *apostol* "apostle," *evangelie* "gospel," *episkop* "bishop," *monax* "monk," *ad* "hell," *demon* "demon," *Pasxa* "Easter," *ikona* "icon," *monastyr'* "monastery," *gramota* "reading and writing" and by extension "document."

There are also loan translations, literal translations of the semantic components of a word from one language to another, such as *pravoslavnyj* "orthodox" (*slava* = δόξα, "doctrine").

The Catholic Poles were closer to the West and borrowed many words from Latin, including church and legal terms:

atrament "ink," *termin* "boundary," *prezes* "chairman," *trybunal* "court," *tytul* "title," *kwestja* "question," *racja* "reason," "sense," *sens* "sense," *koncept* "plan," *kanclerz* "chancellor," *lektor* "reader," *lament* "complaint," *medytacja* "meditation," *deklarować* "to declare," *elekcja* "election," *kmieć* "peasant," "fellow" (from the Vulgar Latin *comes*), and also such words as *leguminy* "vegetable," *burak* "beet," etc.

Among the loan translations is the name of the Polish state: *rzeczpospolita*, "republic."

One can often tell whether a word has come from Latin or Greek: the East Slavic *labirinf*, which was in use until the nineteenth century, corresponds to the Polish *labirynt;* "myth" is *mif* in Russian and *mit* in

Polish; the Russian *mitropolit* is *metropolita* in Polish, etc. Often the meanings of words are changed, sometimes in a curious way: from *paganus* (Latin and Greek) are derived the Russian *poganyj*, "unclean," and the Ukrainian *pohanyj*, "ugly."

We can sometimes reconstruct the migratory route a word has taken on the basis of its present phonetic form. The Czech *palačinka* ("pancake"—the word has recently made its way into German-speaking areas as the Austrian *Palatschinke*) must derive from the Rumanian *plăcintă* (as does the Southeast Ukrainian *placynda*), which comes from the Latin *placenta*, which in turn goes back to the Greek πλκουντα, the accusative of πλακους. The Rumanian *plăcinta* must have come into Czech by way of the Hungarian *palacsinta* (initial consonant clusters are impossible in Finno-Ugric languages and the Rumanian *pla-* becomes *pala-*, as in Hungarian Stefan becomes István.) The word is said to have come into Czech from Slovak around the turn of the century, a supposition that would also explain the part that Hungarian played, according to V. Machek.

Since the seventeenth century the influence of the vocabularies of the Slavic languages on one another has become more pronounced, and the vocabularies have become somewhat more uniform.

3. It is difficult to evaluate "quantitatively" the centripetal forces that draw the Slavic peoples together and the centrifugal forces that drive them apart. Among the centripetal forces is surely their linguistic unity and, to a lesser extent, their prehistoric heathen religious unity and the similarity of their customs and usages, which is still reflected in their folklore. Although these elements have been appreciated by many scholars, such as R. Jakobson, their significance has been considerably overestimated. It was only by neglecting the centrifugal forces among the Slavic peoples in the nineteenth century that Slavophiles or Pan-Slavists exploited the linguistic and dubious "racial" kinship of the Slavs for political purposes.

The centrifugal forces are strong. The first of these has been the struggle for political independence. Ever since the appearance of the Slavs on the historical scene there have been numerous conflicts between them, through the entire history of the Middle Ages, through the awakening of nationalism in the nineteenth century, and down to modern times. One has only to recall the Polish revolts against Russian rule in 1831 and 1863, revolts that continued the centuries-long tradition of warfare between the two peoples. The achievement of independence by the South Slavs in the nineteenth century brought immediate conflicts between them. After the First World War, in which Slavs fought on different sides, and after the formation of the new Slavic states, political quarrels soon broke out in the new states between Slavic majorities and Slavic minorities. One might almost conclude that the Slavs are incapable of living at peace with one another. Although the differences between Poles and Ukrainian and White Russian minorities, between Serbs and Croats, between Czechs and Slovaks are often exaggerated, they do exist; and they were more or less skillfully exploited by German National Socialist foreign policy.

From the earliest times the centrifugal forces have been augmented by historical events. Soon after the Christianization of the Slavs the Christian Church broke into Eastern and Western Churches; and in time the schism considerably affected the Slavs, who were joined in part with Constantinople—the Russians, the Bulgarians, and the Serbs, and in part with Rome—the Poles, the Czechs, and the Croats. After the schism, Church Slavonic lost its original meaning for those Slavs united with Rome, who now used Latin in their church and political lives. Phonetic changes in the various Slavic languages could scarcely have separated them as much as did the cultural orientation toward Constantinople or Rome. Although fifty percent of the words of the various Slavic languages are cognate, they often mean different things or belong to different levels of language, to the formal, everyday, or even vulgar levels, to the generally understood or specialized, and so on. Phonetically the Slavic languages differ from one another perhaps less than do the Germanic dialects (cf. *Zeit, Zit, Tid, Zik,* etc.). The Slavic languages had no *Lautverschiebung* or sound shift, but lexically they do differ considerably from one another. One can find similar examples of these differences between Swedish and Danish or between High German and Dutch.

Compare, for instance:

	Russian	Polish	Czech	Serbo-Croatian[2]
earth	zemlja	ziemia	země	zeml'a
water	voda	woda	voda	voda
sun	solnce	słońce	slunce	sunce
fire	ogon'	ogień	oheň	oganj (or vatra)
spring	vesna	wiosna	jaro	proljeće
day	den'	dzień	den	dan
morning	utro	rano	jitro, ráno	jutro

2. I have used Croatian forms for Serbo-Croatian.

	Russian	Polish	Czech	Serbo-Croatian
good	xorošij	dobry	dobrý	dobar
big	bol'šoj	wielki	velký	velik
one	odin	jeden	jeden	jedan
ten	desjat'	dziesięć	deset	deset
wind	veter	wiatr	vítr	vjetar

We are not concerned here with peculiarities of pronunciation in the various languages.[3] There are also many words with deviant meanings in the other Slavic languages:

Ukrainian has as variants for "good" *dobryj* and *harnyj; xorošyj* is rare and vulgar. For "big" Bulgarian has *goljam.* For the Russian *krasnyj, alyj,* "red," Ukrainian has *červonyj* and Serbo-Croatian, *crven.* The Russian for "to speak" or "to say" is *govorit',* the Ukrainian is *hovoryty, movyty, kazaty,* or vulgarly *balakaty;* the Polish, *mówić;* the Czech, *mluviti;* the Serbo-Croatian, *kazati, govoriti;* among Slovak dialectal variants is *hutorit',* similar to the Russian.

Moreover the same words in different Slavic languages may have different meanings. The Russian word *krasnyj,* "red," means "beautiful," "handsome," and the like in other Slavic languages.

The deviations in the table above are understandable. In Russian and Polish *rano* means simply "early." The Russian words for "good" and "great" have different meanings: *dobryj* means only morally good and *velikij* means "magnificent," "great," "important." The words for numbers and kinship, however, are usually identical.

It is more important to note that for concepts introduced later words often had to be borrowed or new words coined from Slavic roots, and this was done in different ways in different languages. The considerable differences in vocabulary that resulted from this make it difficult for a Slav to understand other Slavic languages. Here are some examples, among them words in everyday use. Lesser-used variants are given in parentheses.

	Russian	Polish	Czech	Serbo-Croatian
duck	utka	kaczka	kachna	patka, plovka, raca
floor	pol	podłoga	podlaha	pod, tavan, patos
hat	šljapa	kapelusz	klobouk	šešir, klobuk
man's jacket	pidžak	surdut, marinarka	kabat, sako	kaput

---

3. Cf., Russian *voda,* pronounced "vada," solnce, pronounced "sonce," etc.

	Russian	Polish	Czech	Serbo-Croatian
street	ulica	ulica	třída (ulice)	cesta, drum (ulica)
state	gosudarstvo	państwo	stát	država
feeling	čuvstvo (èmocija)	uczucie, poczucie	cít, pocít	osjećaj, cuvstvo
decision	rešenie	rozstrzygnięcie	rozhodnutí	odluka, presuda, rješenje
verdict	prigovor	wyrok	úsudek, ortel	sud, presuda
election	vybory	wybór	volba	izbor, biranje
newspaper	gazeta	dziennik	noviny	novine
magazine	žurnal	czasopismo	časopis	časopis
city	gorod	miasto	město	varoš, grad

There are also important differences in scientific terminology. Many words that appear in one Slavic language above occur in other Slavic languages with somewhat different meanings. For instance, *klobuk* in Russian means only a "monk's hood" or "cowl"; *deržava* means only "imperial orb" (*država* means "state" in Serbo-Croatian) and *sud* means "court" as an institution; as opposed to the Polish *wybór*, the Czech *výbor* means a committee that has been selected from a larger group or a selection from some material, as for example texts.

Variations among the languages have been promoted by culturally conditioned borrowings from neighboring languages, by the purism of some languages, such as Czech, and by the complete freedom in borrowing by some languages, such as Russian and Polish, by the maintenance of traditional linguistic elements, such as the Church Slavonic elements in modern and even in Soviet Russian, and the archaisms in Czech, or by a reliance on popular language in the literary language, as in Ukrainian or Slovak.

4. Folkloric elements in Slavic life—by folklore we mean tales, legends, songs, proverbs, and so on, as well as features preserved from old customs and usages—connect the Slavs not only with one another but also with other Indo-European and even non-Indo-European peoples. A unity of Slavs based on folklore is therefore illusory. A Czech may note the kinship of his folk tales with those of the Grimms as easily as with those of the Russians. Even when proverbs are the same among Slavs, they have often just been handed down in different ways from antiquity; in the West they have been translated or adapted from Latin, and in the East from Greek. One should not be misled by "local" coloring. Proverbs can hardly be taken as evidence of racial wisdom on the part of the Slavs.

"Haste makes waste" or "Eile mit Weile," for instance, simply renders the Latin "Festina lente." One should note, however, that borrowed proverbs are often somewhat altered.

Although "a dog on the hay," which he does not eat and does not give to others, has an exact Byzantine counterpart, "the tongue that can lead to Constantinople" is replaced in Russian and Ukrainian by "jazyk do Kijeva dovedët," "the tongue leads to Kiev," as in Russian. Many seemingly topical proverbs of local origin are in reality revised borrowings. One could take the Ukrainian proverb "z moskalem družy, a kamiń za pazuxoju derži," ("make friends with a Great Russian, but keep a stone ready in your shirt") to be a product of the historical experience of the seventeenth and eighteenth centuries. Actually it is borrowed from Byzantium, but the Byzantine proverb speaks of a dog, which has been replaced by *moskal'*, "Great Russian," in the Ukraine.

Many Polish proverbs by Rysiński (1618) and in Cnapius's dictionary (1632) were translated from Latin. J. A. Comenius's *Widsom of the Ancient Forefathers*, compiled between 1629 and 1633, contains translations from the German proverb collection of Sebastian Frank (1541). Other Czech collections were made by Sarnetius (Jakub Srnec, died 1586) and by Jan Blahoslav (see Chapter VII); a Slovak collection was published by D. Sinapius in 1678. All of these contain borrowings.

In the literary language, which is of particular importance here, a new centripetal force drew the Slavic literatures closer together, the stylistic unity of the literatures. Here too one must take into account the forces that worked against the tendency to converge, forces that amounted by and large to social differences, the lack of a powerful, traditional nobility among many Slavic peoples, the inadequate development of the bourgeoisie among others, the predominance of the clergy in cultural life, and finally the differences in the peasantry, a point to which we shall return.

5. Studies have shown that at various times among the Slavic literatures there have been striking similarities of style and theme, particularly in the romantic period but also in the classicist, and even, as has been recently demonstrated, in the baroque. Certain generalizations may be made on the basis of these findings. With the exception of short periods, at times not very productive, the Slavic literatures have followed the same course, although there have been important differences in the tempo of development. Periods of literary style do not begin and end simultaneously among the Slavic peoples.

There are many reasons for this unity of style. First of all, there is the fact, often overlooked, that the Slavic literatures are a part of the greater unity of Western literature, just as the Slavic peoples are a part of this Western unity—something that is even more often overlooked or denied. One must remember, therefore, that living together with other Europeans has had an effect on the intellectual life of the Slavs and on the Slavic literatures. But one should not think of this process as a purely external influence on the Slavs—purely external effects have been mostly unproductive, have appealed to weaker minds, and have not lead to appreciable results except where there was some native foundation on which to build. For instance, the romantic view of the world and the romantic literary style influenced the Slavs considerably because the "spirit of the time" (by which I mean intellectual culture as a whole) demanded. Previous developments had prepared the Slavs to accept romanticism and to regard the rejection of classicism as a necessity of the times.

In this way Slavic literatures have repeatedly been brought closer together. Literary affinities have overcome political and national differences. It was during the wars with Poland in the sixteenth and seventeenth centuries that Russia looked especially to Polish literature, directly and by way of Ukrainian and White Russian literatures. The same thing was true to a lesser extent during the age of romanticism when political relations between Poland and Russia could not have been worse. Even the Ukrainian nationalists, who zealously opposed both the Great Russians and the Poles, could not resist the literary influences of these peoples. They succumbed to Russian symbolism and futurism and to Young Poland, "Młoda Polska"—one often learns especially well from opponents.

Although Slavic literatures have not always influenced each other, they have at least developed in the same direction under the influence of European literature. But the instances of affinities between Slavic literatures are so numerous that one could not be a Slavist if one ignored them.

6. One should not overlook what is called, for want of anything better, "the Slavic consciousness," that is, the fact that there is a consciousness among Slavic peoples of a communality of language, culture, and even political interests. It would be quite unhistorical, however, to assign a common denominator to this "Slavic consciousness" for different peoples at different times. This "Slavophile" spirit has been objectively conditioned and subjectively motivated in different ways; it has assumed various forms and led to various results. It has often been a confessional consciousness—Catholic, Greek-Orthodox, or Protestant—and has had the missionary aim of excluding Slavs of a different faith from the unity of Slavs. Many Russian Slavophiles objected for a time to including Poles

in the unity of Slavs and saw in their dependence on Catholicism a betrayal of the Slavs—they had forgotten that Czechs, Slovaks, Croats, and Slovenes are also Catholic. At other times the Slavic unity was supposed to have social ("peasant peoples") or political ("anti-German") significance. "Slavophilism" has often served as a cover name for egoistic national interests and degenerated into empty rhetoric. This would certainly hold true of the Russian Slavophiles, whose older representatives, Xomjakov and the Aksakov brothers, might better be called "Russophiles," since they had only vague notions of the other Slavic peoples. But they were at least sincere. The second generation of "Slavophiles" included many men who saw in their ideology a convenient disguise for the imperialistic tendencies of Russian policy. The only genuine Slavophiles to be found at the time were among Slavists.

7. Methodological difficulties arise when we ask what aspects of a Slavic literature can and should be compared with corresponding aspects of other Slavic literatures. An answer to the question is suggested by the word "corresponding." One may consider works to correspond when they are written in the same genre and especially in the same style.

Literary history has demonstrated that the art of literature, like other arts, assumes different styles at different times. One has only to think of the treatises on classicism and romanticism or the discussions on the concept of realism. One can summarize the results of previous scholarship by saying that every period has its own style and that style is characterized by a complex of means of expression derived from a few stylistic principles. A style is, of course, often associated with an ideological attitude, as in the case of romanticism or of the classicist "Enlightenment."

The difficulties in characterizing styles are considerable. Scholarship has paid far too little attention to the features of individual styles in Slavic literatures. Scholars have been interested mainly in the content of literary works and have spent much energy in investigating "influences" and "borrowings."

8. In the development of literary styles there are tendencies that make it possible for us to view the history of literature as a meaningful process. It is easy to understand that change always represents a kind of turning to something different and that this change to something different can be a change to something opposite.

As in the history of art, there is in the history of literature a fluctuation between opposites; and it is the primary task of literary scholarship to characterize this fluctuation.

The two poles in the development of art were characterized by Wölf-flin, who contrasted the Renaissance and the baroque; Th. Spoerri applied the principle to literature to contrast classicism and romanticism. There are also studies of this kind in Slavic scholarship (Ju. Krzyżanowski).

One pole is characterized by the great value placed on serene, harmonious beauty, simplicity of composition, transparency of construction, limited, unobtrusive use of stylistic ornamentation, the attempt to frame a work completely, and an inclination to portray static situations. These are features of Renaissance art and of classicism. Opposed to this style is one that does not especially value harmonious serenity and does not consider the ideal of serene beauty in art to be the exclusive aesthetic quality to be striven for. This view is more interested in antitheses, the conflict of forces, and tension. It makes use of complex construction, even deliberate obscurity and mysteriousness, a murky association of component parts, and an overload of stylistic ornamentation—these features are emphasized. No effort is made to frame a work; on the contrary, incompleteness is valued, boundlessness, the "infinity of perspective," which is often achieved by external means (fragments as a poetic form). Dynamic character, anxiety, mutability are stressed. These features are characteristic of the baroque and of romanticism.

These styles were aware of the differences between them and Renaissance and classicism. Romanticism sensed its kinship with the baroque, and baroque literature was rediscovered by the romantics (such baroque writers as Jacob Boehme, Angelus Silesius, Calderon, Lope de Vega, Friedrich von Spee).

This alternation of opposite styles is not restricted to the four periods mentioned above. After romanticism came realism, which in many respects recalled the aesthetic ideals of the Renaissance and of classicism, particularly of classical Enlightenment. Later in opposition to realism there arose various schools of poetic naturalism, which was often called "neoromanticism" by its adherents and opponents because of its striking similarity to the romantic movement (for instance, Russian symbolism and the so-called "Młoda Polska").

The entire development of Slavic literatures can be presented as an alternation between two diametrically opposed styles (Ju. Krzyżanowski). On one side are such styles as Renaissance and classicism, which are in turn superseded by such styles as the baroque and romanticism. The pattern can be represented graphically as follows:

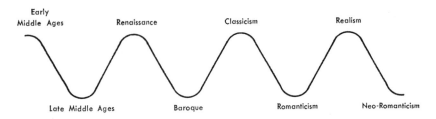

Like all schematic hypotheses, this working hypothesis can be misleading if certain facts are overlooked. There are difficulties inherent in this pattern, and these will be dealt with individually.

9. We shall return to specific questions in our discussion of the various literary periods. Here I shall only characterize briefly the difficulties that I have mentioned.

Like any periodization, this one can be applied successfully only if one remembers that no historical period can be placed in precise chronological boundaries. No century really ends with the turn of the century. Literary schools seldom appear with a program or manifesto, as has sometimes been the case in recent decades. Frequently these programs require years of preparation by "predecessors." In any case, no historical period begins on a certain day or in a certain year or decade. It is more difficult to determine approximately the end of a literary period. The "old" writers do not die off with the beginning of a "new era." Often they live on for decades; they seldom change and are apt to go on writing in their old style. There are also the many epigones of the old style, who are sometimes important. Baroque poetry lived on for a long time under the rule of classicism, actually to the beginning of the nineteenth century. "Incorrigible" romanticists wrote on together with the realists to the beginning of neoromanticism (several Russian writers). Russian realists were still influential after the appearance of the symbolists (or neoromanticists) and were able to win over writers who had been close to symbolism. A strict periodization cannot be satisfactory.

The periodization of literature is less applicable to a span of time than to the content of literary work. We will have done enough if we establish complexes that unite a number of literary works and their authors through properties of style.

10. In grouping intellectual material and in forming appropriate concepts for them one should not proceed as in forming scientific or mathematical concepts. It would be wrong to expect to find exactly the same features in all literary works that we group together stylistically and refer

to by a conventional name, such as renaissance or realism; it is not as though we were dealing with the anatomical peculiarities of a species of animal or the properties of a particular geometric figure, especially from a topological point of view.

Not all Gothic churches have the same characteristics. In dealing with works of art one must distinguish between "significant," "prominent," and "insignificant," second-rate objects. Works of the latter kind often have vague stylistic features that merely suggest a given style. Moreover, there are periods of style, such as the baroque and romanticism, that place particular value on originality, on the inimitability of works of art. One cannot find like characteristics for all ballads, even those of a given stylistic period, in the same way that one could for species of beetles and butterflies. The writer does not want merely to repeat what others have already done but to create something new. Works of cultural creativity are not determined by external, equalizing conditions of nature but by the creative will and the intention of the creator (we should remember that it was for this reason that Plato doubted the presence of "ideas" in these works of human creation).[4]

In literary scholarship, as in the other arts and social sciences, one must strive to form not concepts but "ideal types" (Max Weber). Concepts of this sort (if one can use "concept" in a broader sense) include not characteristics common to an entire group of objects but typical characteristics, which may be absent from many objects or present only in a small subgroup that includes the most significant objects. To create an ideal type of Gothic church, the characteristics of the Strassburg Cathedral are more important than those of a hundred small village churches. One should proceed in just this way in dealing with works of literature. The selection of typical features will depend, however, on an evaluation of them and a distinction between what is important and what is not (again, Max Weber).

This is the only way to order and arrange the materials of literature. Unless we approach literature in this way, we can offer at best a description of the materials; but we still would not have decided which of many features the description should include.

11. Familiarity with literary scholarship may give rise to doubts about the pattern of literary development suggested above. Besides the periods of stylistic development mentioned here, there are other concepts, such as rococo, Biedermeier, more recently mannerism, and others that are

4. See my remarks in the collection of articles *Nachahmung und Illusion* (*Munich, 1964*), *p. 202 ff.*

not generally recognized, such as sensibility, impressionism, or Literary Empire—a useless term in my opinion. Moreover there are works in Slavic intellectual and literary history that cannot be accommodated by our pattern, which was made on the basis of Western intellectual history —a typical example is the Hussite "Pre-Reformation." It did produce a certain style of its own (R. Jakobson) that we must take into account.

Most of the styles mentioned above, however, can be fitted into our pattern—and not merely in order to vindicate the pattern—quite naturally as transitional periods. Mannerism represents a transition from Renaissance to baroque style, rococo a courtly form of late baroque; Biedermeier was also called postromanticism; impressionism is an aspect of late realism or a forerunner of modern literature, as, for instance, symbolism; Literary Empire is an arbitrary and dispensable designation for a group of Russian romantics. Later on we shall deal with other forms of transitional literature.

In any case our pattern can now be expanded somewhat:

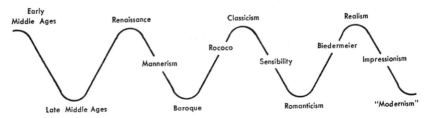

Apart from transitional styles there are often individual writers or works that do not fit into this pattern of literary development or into any other. Here one is usually confronted with writers of great importance. One of the best examples is Dostoevskij, who lived in a period of literary realism and was in many ways connected with it, but who would not have liked to call his own work "realistic." Another example of a literary individualist who broke with his time is the Pole Cyprian Norwid, a contemporary of the romantics. There are also cases of writers who followed one literary school, often for quite a long time, and then more or less decisively turned to another school. One thinks, for instance, of the many romantics who later turned to realism (although it is doubtful that Gogol' should be included among them).

12. On the basis of comparative studies that have been made, one might ask whether all or even some stylistic features are limited to a given time or whether the most important properties of style are eternal and change but little from age to age. One might call various literary works baroque, even classical works such as the tragedies of Seneca or

the satires of Persius; one may speak of the impressionism of late Gothic or the baroque and of impressionism as a tendency within symbolism, not merely as a transitional step between realism and symbolism. Romanticism may be viewed as an eternal mode of style within various other styles. The portrayal of realism throughout literary history has been studied by Erich Auerbach; and individual features, devices of style, and forms of expression have been examined in different stylistic periods by E. R. Curtius.

One must admit that there are eternal, recurrent devices of style, individual tropes and figures, individual metaphors, at least in Western literature, such as light as a metaphor for knowledge, the sea as a metaphor for human life and the historical process, plant and book as symbols of the world. But these "eternal" elements of poetry serve different functions and appear in different forms in different stylistic periods. An example is enumerations, or "catalogues" as E. R. Curtius calls them, which are associated with "chains of words" in prose and verse. These chains of words have been said to be especially typical of baroque style, although this is perhaps not accurate. It is easier, certainly, to employ them in a heavily ornate baroque work; but they are nevertheless one of the eternal devices of style, as E. R. Curtius has convincingly demonstrated. In classicism they have a different structure and function from those in baroque.

In renaissance and classicist literature catalogues are generally meaningfully constructed enumerations of related objects, but in baroque and modern literature the function of catalogues is often to surprise the reader by a juxtaposition of unrelated objects. Baroque sermons include such lists, full of disorder, often ironic; and lists can be found in the works of poets, satirists, even philosophers (see J. A. Comenius's *Labyrinth*). The structure of the lists changes and betrays their "baroque" character. Later these chains of words and short sentences, grotesquely colorful, surprising, and often quite long, were reintroduced by the romantics.

Puškin sees Moscow this way:

Sentry boxes flash by, women, boys, shops, lanterns, palaces, gardens, monasteries, Bukharans, sledges, vegetable gardens, merchants, hovels, peasants, boulevards, towers, Cossacks, pharmacies, fashionable stores, balconies, the figures of lions on gates, and swarms of daws on church crosses (*Evgenij Onegin*, VII, 38).

Gogol' uses catalogues to describe the activity on the main street of St. Petersburg, Nevskij Prospekt (*Nevskij Prospekt*, opening passage).

Other devices of style, such as hyperbole and individual images and symbols, undergo a similar change. If one were to compile the metaphoric expressions for the moon in different periods, one would find that metaphors or similes are graphic or sentimental, as are expressions and epithets about the moon. The neoromantics, on the other hand, have attempted to create strikingly unusual images of the moon.

In eighteenth-century and early nineteenth-century verse the moon is simply "candlestick" or "candlestick of the night." Later it becomes a witness of love scenes or of sadness and grief. It is the "friend of those who grieve," a "witness of unhappy life" in folklore, and above all a "sickle" or a "disk."

Modern poets view the moon differently. One reads of "the cold horns of the moon," "the running moon" (even in Puškin "the moon slips through the rolling fog"), "the slow moon," "the dying sickle." The moon is the queen (*luna*—feminine), not only of the night, but of human destiny. It shines like "a cloud," it is "always drunk." One finds all of this in the Russian symbolist V. Brjusov.

Or the moon is "mysterious," "enchanted," "bewitched." The sickle is "glowing red," the moon is "a golden cup," "our queen" or at least "sibyl and enchantress"; it gives rise to weird ideas: it is "the face of a faithless girl," a "ghost from a fairy tale," "the dead eye." One finds all of this in the like-minded poets Brjusov and K. Bal'mont.

The sickle is also "silver" or even "green." It is "the bright sickle in the harvest field of night." The moon is "a weird lantern," "the heavenly gold coin," or "the heavenly Pierrot." It is "the bent finger" and "creeps" or "rises out of the tall grass like the red shield of a hero." One finds this in the Russian Symbolist A. Blok.

In the postsymbolist poet S. Esenin, who was familiar with futurism, one finds countless images and symbols for the moon, which is only occasionally called "sickle." He sees the moon as "an egg," "a hat," "a comb" that cards the clouds, as "a piece of cheese," "a loaf of bread" (*kovriga*) or as "a round cake baked by the Mother of God" (*kolobok*), a "shepherd's horn" or a vessel, also in the shape of a horn, from which drops of oil are poured. If the sky is "a bell," the moon is "the clapper" (*jazyk*); and finally the moon is "a golden hill." Esenin also likens the moon to animate beings. It has "horns" with which it can "butt the clouds," but it is "a lamb with curly fur" that "frolics in the blue grass." It is "the red goose," lies in the cradle—perhaps the halo around the moon—like a child. It is "a sad horseman" and even "a seal"—the moon reflected in water.

The very gifted modern Polish poet Julian Tuwim poses a problem that he thinks can be solved, to connect the moon with the concepts and images from a list of seventy-five words, all of which begin with "a." The beginning,

amfora, anioł, alkoholik	i.e. amphora, angel, alcoholic
archimandryta, as, akolit	archimandrite, ace, acolyte
August, asceta, apostata	Augustus, ascetic, apostate
albatros, Abel, akrobata	albatross, Abel, acrobat
aktor, angora (kot), abażur	actor, angora cat, lamp shade
agorafobik, Azef, ażur	agoraphobic, Azef, openwork
arlekin, azbest, alpinista	harlequin, asbestos, mountain-climber
augur, Akiba (Ben), artysta	augur, ben Akiba, artist
arbiter, adept, akademik	arbiter, adept, academician
Aladyn, Andersen, alchemik	Aladdin, Andersen, alchemist
Adonis, arcybiskup, arbuz	Adonis, archbishop, watermelon
adjutant, almaviva, Argus	adjutant, Almaviva, Argus
apokryf, Alibaba, aster	apocrypha, Ali Baba, aster
albinos, Alfons, alabaster	albino, Alphonso, alabaster

At the end of the list is the melancholy observation, "and it is still a long way from A to Z." With a lively imagination one can easily use all the words here, or almost all of them, as metaphors for the moon.

13. One should keep in mind that despite their kinship with Western writing the styles of the Slavic literatures have a particular quality all their own. Perhaps these differences can best be explained by accounting for their origins.

a. First of all, the propagators of literature play an important role. For a style to have a courtly character there must be a flourishing court, and it is understandable that the courtly rococo style is represented predominantly by Russian and Polish literatures. On the other hand, in places where literature was supported mainly by the clergy there is a religious or scholarly character to the writing, as in Old Czech or Old Russian literatures. Romantic literature was not vigorously promoted by the clergy, and Byronism found no support or was opposed, as among the Slovaks.

b. One must remember that periods in Slavic literature have been affected by many literary and extraliterary events that the West did not experience. There are gaps in the Slavic literatures that divide periods into two or more phases. This was the case in Russian literature of the baroque, which is divided into two different phases as a result of Peter's reforms around 1700, particularly his reform of the language. The literature before Peter I had been propagated mainly by priests and monks, and worldly works were often thought to be of secondary importance. After Peter I there was a considerable decline in religious literature; Polish and Ukrainian elements in the literature give way to German, Dutch, and French. Poets and the mood of the reading public preferred French precious literature, Fénelon, and the German late baroque (J. Chr. Günther) to Polish baroque and Marini as he was transmitted by the Poles. Russian classicism was similarly divided into two phases by the linguistic reforms of N. M. Karamzin around 1790. The period began with close imitations of French classicism and ended with imitations of bourgeois classicism, as in the novel, considerably altered by Russian social conditions. Among other Slavs, particularly among the Poles, romanticism was divided into two phases by political events. The dividing line is the revolt of 1831, which became a focal point for literature. Polish romanticism considerably influenced other Slavs, who borrowed from it everything but the characteristically Polish radical nationalism "Messianism."

c. There are also times when politics come before literature: the defeat of the Czechs at the battle of White Mountain in 1620, the Tartar invasion of Russia in the thirteenth century, the subjugation of the South Slavs by the Turks in the fourteenth and fifteenth centuries, Josephinism and tolerance in Austria in the eighteenth century, the Napoleonic Wars in Poland and Russia, the retarded liberation of the serfs in Russia in 1861, the casting off of Turkish rule in the Balkans, particularly after the war of 1877, the Russian Revolutions of 1905 and 1917, the political effects of the First and Second World Wars. Even in apparently peaceful times, as in the reign of Nicholas I in Russia (1825–1855) or in the Metternich-Bach period in Austria (1815–1848), literature was affected, not necessarily by clear stands that poets took but by the fate of the poet and of those close to him and by the subtle mood of the time.

14. Finally, we must deal with certain prejudices that attach to Slavic literatures.

First, as we have already suggested, Slavic literatures do not merely trail along behind the literatures of the West—and here I am not thinking just about such major figures, as Gogol', L. Tolstoj, and F. Dostoevskij, who cannot be thought simply to have been following Western models.

More important, borrowings from Western European literature often appear in concentrated form in Slavic literatures. In dealing with influences one should remember that thoughts and forms from the West have often been intensified by the Slavs and developed into something new in literature, even if these transformations have at times been "unimportant." An example of this is the Russian naturalist realism of the 1860s. And Karl Marx cannot, of course, be held responsible for the further development of Marxism by Lenin and Stalin as Russian Marxists well understand when they refer to "Marxism-Leninism" or "Stalinism." Among Western thoughts that were "intensified" were many philosophical ideas that affected literature such as Russian Slavophilism (F. Stepun) or the ideas of the "Russian Feuerbach," Černyševskij (who also borrowed freely from Ludwig Büchner). There are also lesser known episodes in Slavic literary and intellectual history, such as the Polish anti-Trinitarianism with its intensified idea of tolerance. There is the idea of Moscow as the Third Rome (fifteenth and sixteenth centuries), which is a development of rather primitive and not very effective Byzantine and Bulgarian ideas. There is the intensified form of Wycliffism in Hussitism (fifteenth century) and more recently the intensification of romantic thought in Polish "Messianism" and Russian anarchism, by which I do not mean political anarchism, which was not very effective in Russia, but the ideological anarchism of Count L. Tolstoj and Prince P. Kropotkin.

On occasion, Slavic literature has anticipated Western literature. This was the case in the Hussite pre-Lutheran Reformation of the Czechs and is perhaps today the case in the Communist socialism of Russia.

15. Finally we should mention that as one gets to know Slavic literary and intellectual history, one should not trust blindly the opinions of Slavic literary and intellectual scholarship. One should not, as some Soviet literary historians recently did, view Dostoevskij and the symbolists as existing outside the mainstream of the "great realist literature." One should not overlook the fact that in the decisive early years of his development (1890–1904) Gor'kij was much closer to Russian symbolism than to the epigones of realism. One should not view Comenius as an "enlightener" and a forerunner of present-day pedagogy and intuitive instruction. Other literary and historical matters are distorted by Slavic literary scholarship, which is of course well informed but often tendentious.

Unfortunately, the biased and tendentious judgments of some leftwing and Soviet critics on Russian poets and literary trends are often accepted abroad at face value, even though these critics are politically, socially, philosophically, and personally prejudiced. An example is the well-known critic V. Belinskij, whose errors of judgment are countless. At the end of the nineteenth century the judgment of A. Skabičevskij was taken to be authoritative. Apart from his philosophical bias he was totally blind to the artistic values of literature, but he is still read in the West, especially in the United States.

Not even literary scholarship can always be taken at face value. The propagator of Western romanticism at the beginning of the nineteenth century, V. Žukovskij, has been declared a sentimentalist *sui generis*, not a romantic, mainly on the strength of a biography of him by A. Veselovskij, which is less important in evaluating Žukovskij than his own works. The closer one comes to our own time, the more biased and tendentious judgments are. The most significant representative of Russian prose in the twentieth century, Andrej Belyj, is dismissed in most Soviet literary histories with a few vapid sentences. The leading futurist V. Majakovskij is celebrated as a Communist poet, and the importance of his futurist poetry, even for his later works, is glossed over. The fact that B. Pasternak belonged to the futurist movement is subtly denied because in the USSR and among Russian emigrants futurism is said to have been out of keeping with the times.[5]

16. One should emphasize that although the West Slavs maintained a considerable linguistic and intellectual cohesion, despite their ties with Byzantium and Rome, a part of the South Slavs, particularly the Bulgarians and Serbs and some Croats, had in addition to a cultural tradition of their own many ties with non-Slavic peoples whose culture was in many respects different from that of Western Europe: the Rumanians, Hungarians, post-Byzantine Greeks, and the Moslem Turks.

The Bulgarians have preserved little from the Turko-Tartar, pagan "proto-Bulgarians" from whom they got their name. But their centuries-long dependence on the Ottoman Turks (fifteenth to nineteenth centuries) left deep linguistic and cultural traces. This Ottoman influence is also important among the Macedonians, Serbs, and some Croats and Slovaks. Some of these peoples even accepted Islam and still adhere to it.

The influence of the Turko-Tartars (Crimean Tartars and Ottoman Tartars) on the Poles and Ukrainians was relatively slight but should not be overlooked. One should also allow for the influence of the Finno-Ugric tribes and Volga Tartars on the Great Russians, a subject that has not been sufficiently treated (see bibliography in G. Vernadskij).

The Slovaks and a part of the Croats were for a long time under the rule of the Hungarian kingdom. Although various factors, such as the

5. I emphasize this by way of warning the reader against accepting either my views or the views of "authoritative" textbooks or scholars without having first investigated the original materials for himself.

national languages, the use of Old Czech as a church language by the Slovaks, and the presence of a German population with strong cultural traditions, mitigated against the influence of the Magyars, one must still take the Hungarian influence into account (see Chapter VII, 10).

The fate of the Rumanians living among the Slavs is also connected with the Turko-Tartars and the Magyars, but the Rumanians had a different relationship with the Balkan Slavs and Hungarians. This relationship, which continued until recently, has scarcely been explored. The Slavs, especially the Bulgarians, appear for a time to have influenced the Rumanians more than they were influenced.

All these problems have been dealt with in separate useful studies, but a full treatment of the questions raised here is still in the distant future. I hope that such a general work as the present one will be of value as a first step toward a synthetic study.

II

THE BEGINNINGS OF SLAVIC LITERATURE

1. The origins of Slavic literature are connected with the Slavic religious mission of 863. Two Greek brothers from Thessalonica, the learned philologist Constantine and his older brother, the monk Methodius, were sent to Moravia in answer to a request made by Prince Rostislav to Emperor Michael III of Byzantium. Moravia had already been partly converted to Christianity, and it was the task of the two brothers to carry on missionary work in a Slavic language intelligible to the people. The brothers knew the Old Bulgarian or Old Macedonian dialect spoken around Thessalonica. Constantine's great achievement was the creation of an alphabet that is still occasionally used in parts of Catholic Croatia and is called Glagolitic.[1] It is not certain whether this alphabet was an imitation of the Greek minuscule script, supplemented by letters from Oriental languages, or whether its letters were simply made up. It is exceptionally well designed to render the sounds of Old Church Slavonic. It was in this alphabet that the first translations were made by the brothers, mainly by Methodius.[2] Constantine was not active for long in the Slavic mission. In 867 the brothers were invited by Pope Nicholas to Rome but were not received until late 867 or 868 by his successor, Hadrian II. Constantine took monastic vows, assumed the name Cyril, and in 869 died in Rome. Methodius was ordained a bishop. His further work

1. The relationship between the Glagolitic and Cyrillic alphabets remains rather obscure. Most contemporary scholars are inclined to believe that the Glagolitic was the original Slavic alphabet created by Constantine and was only later replaced by Cyrillic. See Chapter III, 2 (editor).

2. Information about the Slavic alphabets may be found in any textbook of Old Church Slavonic.

in Moravia was marred by disputes with the German bishops over his canonical status. He was even imprisoned for a time in Bavaria ("Swabia") and was released only after the intervention of the Pope. His later work consisted mainly of training priests and of translating. He was also able to extend his missionary work to a part of southern Poland. Methodius died in 885, and soon afterward his successor, Bishop Gorazd, and his pupils were expelled from the country. After considerable hardship, many of them found refuge in Bulgarian Macedonia, where they continued their work.

2. The language of the translations was based on Old Bulgarian and was certainly close to the Old Bulgarian dialect spoken in the native region of the missionaries. At the same time, the brothers probably used elements, particularly lexical, from the regions where they were working. This must remain a moot point since we do not have original copies of the translations and there are many lexical differences in the texts that we do have. The Slavic language used in the translations was at the time intelligible to all Slavs.

3. The translations made by the missionaries were mainly of religious texts, the liturgical books, the New Testament and large parts of the Old Testament (with the exception of the historical books), then Byzantine legal monuments-ecloga (*Zakonъ sudnyj ljudemъ*), the Nomocanon (*Kormčaja*), and also a Patericon, probably *The Words of the Holy Fathers* (N. van Wijk). The liturgy in use was probably the "Liturgia Santi Petri" (J. Vašica); the oldest Old Church Slavonic manuscript (tenth century) is a form of this liturgy and is preserved in the Glagolitic "Kiev Fragments." Other Old Church Slavonic texts are preserved in somewhat later redactions made in Bulgaria. One of the original works of the missionary period is the Saints' Life of Constantine and Methodius, presumably a translation from a Greek original. Constantine and Methodius were very likely the authors of two works: an Old Church Slavonic poem that served as a preface (*Proglas*) to their translation of the Gospels and was written in imitation of Byzantine syllabic, unrhymed poetry and a short hymn to St. Gregory of Nazianzus that was included in the vitae (saints' lives) of Constantine and Methodius. Remains of other theological works by Constantine and Methodius may be found in Old Church Slavonic vitae translated from the Greek or in later redactions of original narrations. Further fragments may be contained in various short texts from the missionary period that have been preserved only in copies. The authorship of the "Alphabet Poem" (see Chapter III) is contested. It is possible that even the Life (vita) of Methodius was written before the Slavic priests were driven out of Moravia.

4. The linguistic and stylistic accomplishments of the missionary period are interesting. Since few works survive in their original forms, we must limit ourselves to general observations. The works of the Slavic mission were written by educated Byzantines,[3] and the style is not primitive but highly artistic. This is a typical example of precocity that has been influenced from without, that will probably not survive long, but that may influence the later independent development of the language. (See other examples of this among the Slavic literatures in the following chapters.)

The translation of the Holy Scriptures is, of course, a touchstone of the translator's ability. The Slavic version was equally successful in rendering the language of the Synoptic, the philosophically colored language of the Book of John, the religious lyrics of the Psalter, and the pathos of the prophets. The language of original works, such as the Saints' Lives of Constantine and Methodius, is on an equally high plane. The report on the living conditions of the two brothers, the theological observations in Constantine's polemic writing—directed at the Byzantine opponents of icons, the Islamic Arabs, the Mosaic Khazars, and, during the mission, at the proponents of the view that divine services should be held only in the three "sacred" languages, Hebrew, Greek, and Latin—and finally the panegyric to the brothers are delivered on various stylistic levels; but all display artistry of expression and poetic ornamentation of language. The poems also seem perfect, although they are preserved only in later, partially corrupted versions.

Here are several examples. First, Constantine's arrival in Moravia:

But when he arrived in Moravia, Prince Rostislav received him with great honor, called pupils together, and gave them to him to be instructed. Soon the entire church ritual had been translated, and he taught them [the pupils] the matins, the hourly prayers, the midday prayer, vespers, the compline, and the mass. And as in the words of the Prophet, "the ears of the doves were opened" to hear the words of the Scriptures, and "the language of stammerers became clear" [Isaiah 32, 4]. But God had great joy in this, and the devil was full of shame [vita of Constantine, XV, 1-4].

In Venice, Constantine the Philosopher answered those who maintained that services should be held only in the three sacred languages.

Does not God let rain fall on all men equally? Or does not the sun shine on all men? [Mat. 5, 45]. Do we not all breathe the same air? And are you not ashamed to

3. Constantine was called "the Philosopher," which meant that he was a professor of the Constantinople "university" or theological school, although we do not know whether he actually taught there.

say that there are only three peoples, that all other peoples and tribes must remain blind and deaf? Say then, do you think God is weak, so that he cannot bestow [his gifts] on others, or jealous, so that he does not wish to? But we know many peoples who can write and who praise every god in his language. Everyone knows them: the Armenians, the Persians, the Abasgs,[4] the Iberians [in the Caucasus, that is, the Georgians], the Sugds[5] the Goths, Avars, Turses [? according to some manuscripts Turci, so "Turks"], Khazars, Arabs, Egyptians,[6] and many others. If you cannot learn from this at least allow the Holy Scriptures to judge [loc. cit., XVI, 4–9].

Or the eulogy to Methodius, who is likened to other pious men:

So he became like all of them and exemplified in every way: the fear of God, the observance of the Commandments, chastity, zeal in prayer and in holy works, the gift of strong and gentle speech, strong against adversaries, gentle to those who received his teaching, austerity, gentleness, compassion, love, long-suffering, patience. So he was everything in all [possible situations] so that he might win over everyone [based on 1. Cor. 9, 22] [Life of Methodius II, 3].

The apt use of quotations from the Scriptures is particularly striking. The following lines from the *Introductory Song* to the Gospel are an example.

> As the Prophets have proclaimed,
> Christ is coming to gather heathens
> because he is the light of the whole world.
> Behold, this has come to pass in this seventh aeon.
> For they said the blind will see,
> the deaf will hear the word of the Scriptures
> in order to know God, as is fitting.
> Therefore give heed, all you Slavs,
> because this is a message from God,
> a gift from God to those on his right hand,
> a gift to souls that will never perish,
> to those souls who will receive it.
> Matthew, Mark, Luke, and John
> teach all of us to speak.

5. There has been a recurrent theory that there was another Slavic system of writing before the Glagolitic alphabet. This theory is based on a passage in the Saint's Life of Constantine, who on his missionary journey to the Khazars in the Crimea received the Gospel and Psalter "written in Russian letters." The word, "rusьkymi," on which this

4. I.e., the Abkhases, a Caucasian people known to the Greeks since antiquity.
5. I.e., the Soghdians, once an Iranian people in Central Asia; their literary monuments extend over the first millenium A.D.
6. Who at that time were still predominantly Christian (editor).

hypothesis depends, could also be an error for "syrsькymi," Syrian, a language that Constantine, as an Orientalist, could easily read, as we know from his life. Although there is no specific proof of a pre-Glagolitic system of writing, the theory is still defended by Soviet scholars, by the Bulgarian Emil Georgiev, and by the Ukrainian I. Ohienko in Canada.

III

THE EARLY MIDDLE AGES

West Slavs (Czechs)

Saints' Lives (Wenceslas and Ludmila)
Translations of religious literature from Latin
(Works of Pope Gregory the Great, possibly saints' lives—
Vitus [?] and others)

Bulgarians

Sermons: Clement, Presbyter Kozma
Compilations: *Hexaemeron* of John the Exarch of Bulgaria
Translations: *Zlatostruj* of John Chrysostom, *Source of Knowledge* (*Pege gnoseos*) by John Damascenus, the Chronicle of Malalas, Hamartolos (?), the *Alexandreis*, an encyclopedic work
(the so-called *Izbornik* [Collection] of 1073)

Russians

St. Feodosij: Sermons
Metropolitan Ilarion: *Slovo* on Law and Grace
Nestor: Saints' Lives of Boris and Gleb and of St. Feodosij
Chronicles: The so-called Nestorian Chronicle (Kiev) and the
Norgorod Chronicle

Translations: Novels (*Digenis Akritas, Barlaam and Josaphat, Akir the Wise* [?]), sermons, historical works (*History of the Jewish Wars* by Josephus Flavius, Hamartolos [?]), *Izbornik* (Collection) of 1076

1. The forcible interruption of the Slavic mission in Moravia did not end Old Church Slavonic literature. On the contrary, it flourished in the next two centuries and in scope and to some extent in ideological importance surpassed all contemporary Western European literatures written in the vernacular (V.. Jagić). Old Church Slavonic literature passed into neighboring Bohemia and stimulated original works. Refugees from Moravia came to Bulgaria, carried on missionary work, and laid the foundation for a new literary tradition, which was to reach its peak in the tenth century. The Christianization of the East Slavs toward the end of the tenth century brought with it Bulgarian and West Slavic Church Slavonic literature. Eventually original works were written by the Russians, particularly in the second half of the eleventh century.

2. The Old Church Slavonic literary language, which was intelligible to all Slavs, was no longer entirely uniform. We know from a tenth-century Glagolitic monument, the *Kiev Fragments*, that West Slavic already had significant phonetic peculiarities and the reflexes of the Proto-Slavic *tj, dj* that later became typical of West Slavic languages (see Bräuer, 17, p. 42). The oldest East Slavic (Russian) monuments show that in the eleventh century the nasals ǫ and ę (Ѫ and Ѧ) had completely disappeared in this region (see further, 5). An eleventh-century Old Church Slavonic monument of Bulgarian origin, a menaeum or a collection of saints' lives and sermons for the month of March, the *Codex Suprasliensis*, contains many occasional phonetic deviations from the oldest form of Old Church Slavonic, among them the confusion of the two nasals, which were now pronounced alike.

Moreover, there were already phonetic dialectal differences within Bulgarian, between East and West Bulgarian, and in East or Russian Slavic, as between the language of the Kiev and Novgorod monuments. There were, of course, also lexical differences between the dialects. Unfortunately these differences have not been adequately studied.

Although the West Slavs continued to use the Glagolitic alphabet, its use in Bulgaria, which had close cultural ties with Byzantium, was less practical. As a consequence, a new alphabet was devised, closely akin to the sound system of Glagolitic and based for the most part on letters of the Greek alphabet, which was well known in Bulgaria. The Greek letters used were the simpler majuscules. Letters for the sounds not represented in Byzantium, including *b*, since Greek β by then stood for a *v* sound, were taken from Glagolitic and altered considerably or were simply invented. This alphabet is now called "Cyrillic." We shall continue to use this designation, which has become traditional, even though it was originally applied to Glagolitic. We know from a Russian manuscript that Glagolitic was still called Cyrillic in 1043. Glagolitic was still used for a time in Bulgaria, especially for liturgical books, and was also familiar to the East Slavs, as we know from the occasional use of Glagolitic letters in Cyrillic manuscripts and from short insciptions on the walls of old buildings and from graffiti.

Almost all West Slavic and many Bulgarian monuments survive only in later manuscripts, for the most part preserved by the Russians. To a large extent even the East Slavic Church Slavonic manuscripts come down to us in later manuscripts, some from as late as the sixteenth to eighteenth centuries. The relative freedom with which the orthography and at times words were changed often makes it difficult or impossible to determine the origin of works for which we have only later manuscripts (see 6).

3. West Slavic monuments come from Bohemia. It was once believed that the Slavic liturgy that had been brought there from the Slavic mission and that had been forbidden by the Vatican in 1094 had been a "delicate plant" (V. Jagić), preserved mainly or exclusively by the Sázava monastery in Bohemia. It has since been shown that the Slavic liturgy was more widespread. On thirteen pages of the *Kiev Fragments* there is a liturgical formula connected with the "Liturgia Sancti Petri," that is, with the Western Church liturgy created for services in the vernacular (J. Vašica). The Bulgarian author Presbyter Kozma was familiar with the use of this liturgy in the second half of the tenth century. The Eastern Church liturgy was also known in Bohemia. Only four pages of a Bohemian eleventh- or twelfth-century Glagolitic manuscript have been preserved, the so-called Prague Fragments. We do not know whether Cyrillic was also known in Bohemia: the only evidence is a later Cyrillic entry in a tenth-century manuscript in a library in Moravia (Rajhrad).

More important are the lives of the Czech saints Princess Ludmila and Prince Václav (Wenceslas), preserved in later East Slavic and Croatian manuscripts. The short life of Ludmila was intended for the Slavic *Synaxarion,* which the Eastern and Balkan Slavs used to call a *Prologъ,* collections of short lives, tales, and sermons arranged by the days of the year. Wenceslas is the subject of three Lives (vitae): a brief *Synaxarion* Life, the "first" Life, in Croatian, Ukrainian, and Great Russian versions, and the "second" long Life, a considerably expanded translation of the Latin Wenceslas Life by Humpold, bishop of Mantua. The Church Slavonic version of this is preserved in Russian copies. The knowledge of historical persons and events, geography, and Western Church festivals attests to the source of the original works and of the translation of Bishop Humpolds' Lives as well as to the additions from Bohemia. The same themes are dealt with in many Latin vitae from Bohemia, and these works are especially important for the study of Bohemian Old Church Slavonic monuments. There were certainly translations from Latin at the time in Bohemia, especially the works of Pope Gregory the Great. Further translations of Western saints' lives and of prayers that mention saints unknown in the Eastern Church, among them the patron of Prague, Saint Vitus, cannot be said for sure to have been made in Bohemia. Croatia, especially Aquileia, is a possible origin.

Old Church Slavonic did not pass out of use all at once in Bohemia. Proof of this is the Old Church Slavonic glosses, well over a hundred of them, in Latin script in a manuscript of the dialogues of Gregory the Great, the "Prague Glosses," and also the Old Church Slavonic glosses (122) in Latin script in a Latin Gospel, the "Vienna Glosses." These two groups date from the eleventh or more likely from the twelfth century and were probably written from memory. Apparently there were still clerics who knew Old Church Slavonic.[1]

It is possible that the old Czech hymn "Hospodine, pomiluj ny!" is of Old Church Slavonic origin (R. Jakobson).[2]

4. Bulgarian literature flourished along with the Bulgarian state, especially under Tsar Simeon (893–927). Most of the Old Church Slavonic monuments—the Gospels, the Psalter, a prayer book—that had originated during the Slavic mission were translated and revised. Theological and liturgical works were written, but unfortunately most of these are preserved only in smaller manuscript fragments or in East Slavic copies. Undoubtedly the various saints' lives and Apocrypha and probably other Paterikons were included in this Bulgarian literature. At the same time there were various new translations: a large collection of sermons by John Chrysostom (*Zlatostruj*), a Byzantine Chronicle by John Malalas, which contains much information on antiquity, the *Physiologus* (the so-called first version), a geographical and cosmographical work by Cosmas Indikopleustes, and works that may be called novels, such as the *Alek-*

---

1. It should be kept in mind that after the departure of Methodius and his disciples from Bohemia in 880, Latin replaced Slavonic as the liturgical language in Czech lands. Only in the monastery of Sázava was the Slavonic liturgy preserved until 1097 (editor).

2. "Hospodine, pomiluj ny!" remains preserved in a fourteenth-century manuscript but was probably written in the eleventh century. Its language is Old Czech but includes several Old Slavonic words (editor).

sandreis and the Greek version of the famous Oriental didactic novel known by the Arabic name *Kalila and Dimna* and ultimately derived from the Indian *Pañčatantra* (the Slavic title, patterned on the Greek, is *Stefanit i Ixnilat*). That these translations were in part pedagogic is attested by an encyclopedic collection dedicated to Tsar Simeon and preserved in a Kievan copy of 1073 (*Izbornik 1073 goda*).

This collection contains a short rhetoric by the Byzantine scholar George Choiroboskos. Various tropes and figures are dealt with and illustrated; the Greek names of them are allegory, metaphor, catachresis, metalepsis, hyperbaton, anastrophe, synecdoche, syllepsis, onomatopoeia, pepoiemenon, antonomasia, metonymy, antiphrasis, periphrasis, ellipsis, pleonasm, epanalepsis, exoche, hyperbole, enigma, antapodosis, prosopopoeia, paradigm, irony, sarcasm, scheme, and hysteron proteron.

We know of individual writers in Bulgaria at the time and have work by them. Among the students of Methodius were Clement of Ohrid (or "Veličeskij"; died in 916), who wrote many sermons, and Constantine of Preslav, who wrote sermons and a teacher's Gospel and revised the "Alphabet Prayer," an alphabetic acrostic that may have originated during the Slavic mission. A contemporary of Tsar Simeon, John the Exarch of Bulgaria, made two large compilations, which include original parts: the *Hexaemeron* (*Šestodnev*), a large work dealing with the six days of creation and drawing on the corresponding Greek works, especially the *Hexaemeron* of Basilius the Great, and the *Nebesa* (*Heavens*), a free reworking of the *Source of Knowledge* by John Damascene. In John the Exarch one finds polemical writing against the Bogomils, a dualistic sect that reminds him of the Manichaeans. Along with sermons on other subjects Kozma the Presbyter, who wrote in the second half of the century, left sermons directed at the Bogomils. The writings of these heretics are known to us only through later manuscripts and through folklore.

There were, of course, also anonymous works. The Saint's Life of Bishop Naum of Ohrid and a work by the Monk Xrabr, a pseudonym, on the Slavic alphabet are particularly worthy of note.

5. Bulgaria was overcome by Byzantium as the East Slavs were being Christianized. Although much of the early history of the Eastern Church is uncertain, there can be no doubt that the liturgy, the Bible, and the literary works came from Bulgaria. The movement toward literature in the East began under the Russian Prince Jaroslav the Wise of Kiev (1019–1054), who also appointed a committee of translators. From about 1036 there were further translations of church and secular works. Old Church Slavonic continued in use as the literary

language, but to some extent the peculiar development of sounds in the East distinguish works that originated there from works that were merely borrowed.

The most important characteristics of East Slavic are (1) the absence of nasals—as has already been mentioned (Ѫ as retained as the sign for Я), (2) different reflexes for the Proto-Slavic *dj*, *tj*, (3) a different treatment of the sound groups *-or*, *-ol*, *-er*, *-el* between consonants, (4) a different ending for the instrumental singular of the masculine and neuter *o*- declension. Lexical criteria, such as archaisms and words that appear only in East Slavic, are not very reliable for distinguishing characteristics (see 3 above).

Examples:

	Old Church Slavonic	East Slavic
1.	ѫ (ǫ), Ѧ (ę)	u, ja
	rǫka, męso	ruka mjaso
2.	št, žd	č, ž
	noštь, voždь	nočь, vožь
3.	-ra, la, re, le-	-oro, olo, ere-
	gradъ, mlatъ	gorodъ, molotъ
	brěgъ, mlěko	beregъ, moloko
4.	-omь, -emь	-ъmь, -ьmь
	Bogomъ, mečemь	Bogъmь, mečьmь

(cf. Chapter I and Bräuer, *op. cit.*).

It is significant, however, that scribes were often at pains to write genuine Old Church Slavonic and refrained as best they could from using East Slavic forms.

6. The East Slav or Russian translations included saints' lives, commentary on the Scriptures, the statute of the Studion monastery in Byzantium, several Apocrypha, the so-called second version of the *Physiologus*, the *History of the Judean Wars* by Josephus Flavius, several florilegia, and novels, like the two didactic works *Varlaam i Iosaf* (*Barlaam and Iosaphat*) and *Premudryj Akir* (*Akir the Wise*[3]), and the heroic *Devgenievo dejanie* (the *Digenis* novel known to us in Greek from the much later Byzantine epic tradition). It is not always possible to

3. It is not certain that the translation is of East Slavonic origin; it is possible that the translation was made from a Syrian original instead of Greek.

date translations exactly. Translations were made from Greek until the thirteenth century.

There are also original works by Russian authors. First, there is the Nestorian Chronicle, which continued to the beginning of the twelfth century and was only revised by the monk Nestor. The Chronicle was begun around 1036, although it reports on events back to the ninth century. The chroniclers included various old tales and even sagas, which had perhaps been passed down by word of mouth. Nestor was also the author of two saints' lives, one on the first abbot of the Kiev Crypt Monastery, Saint Feodosij, who died in 1073, and one on the princes Boris and Gleb, who were treacherously murdered in 1015 and later canonized. There is also a very poetic tale (*Skazanie*) of their martyrdom. Nestor's works bear witness to his knowledge of Western Slavic Literature, in particular of the first, second, and Humpold's *Wenceslas Life* and of a historical work that we do not know. Saint Feodosij himself wrote several sermons intended for monks. The Bishop of Novgorod, Luka Židjata, wrote two short catechetical sermons. The first Metropolitan of Kiev who was Russian and not Greek, Ilarion, is the author of a sermon or festive oration delivered around 1050 on *The Law of Moses and the Grace of Christ*. At the turn of the century the Kievan Prince Vladimir Monomax wrote several works that are still preserved, though with lacunae: these are the *Instruction* (*Poučenie*) for his children, a politically pointed letter to a hostile prince, an autobiography, which was perhaps part of the *Instruction*, and three prayers. Among works not mentioned here, most of them anonymous, some are significant for their form or content. Some of them are known to us only from the *Chronicle*, where works of all kinds were included, or from later compilations.

There were also compilations of translated works, among them the *Collection* of 1076 made in Kiev (*Izbornik 1076 goda*), which includes mostly short works translated from Greek (I. Ševčenko).

Under these circumstances, it is understandable that there are works to which one cannot ascribe a time and place of origin. The language of the extensive Chronicle by George Hamartolos (Slavic Amartolъ) is characteristic; one finds there South Slavic, East Slavic, and even West Slavic features. One is inclined to believe that the translation was a collective project, either by Prince Jaroslav's translation committee, mentioned above, or perhaps by representatives of various Slavic tribes working at the behest of Byzantium.

It is uncertain whether traces of Old Church Slavonic or of East Slavic terminology are to be found in the opening lines of the oldest Polish spiritual song, "Bogurodzica" (Mother of God). Neither do we know for sure the origin of a part of the oldest Slovenian monument, the "Freising Monuments": three sermons from the tenth century written in Old High German orthography. A. Isačenko has suggested that the texts come from Glagolitic works of the missionary period, a theory doubted by other scholars.

7. The works of the Slavic Early Middle Ages are stylistically uneven. Almost all the translations are more complicated than the original works, but they are not always stylistically successful, especially in later copies. For instance, the translation of the *Life of Saint Vitus*, the patron saint of Prague, is bad. But the translations of the sermons of John Chrysostom, of the Humpold Life of Saint Wenceslas, and of the *Digenis* novel (for which we have no model but only late Greek versions) are of a quality almost on a par with Byzantine works of the time.

Here is an example from the collected sermons of John Chrysostom, a Kievan manuscript of the twelfth century. The subject is the different kinds of men. The soul of a man involved in matters of the world is likened to a noisy fair, the soul of a pious man, to a beautiful landscape:

On the hillside the pure wind blows and bright rays of light shine. Here are clear springs and all manner of fragrant and lovely flowers and gardens with good fruit. . . . Here songbirds sit in the tops of the oak trees: nightingales and swallows and blackbirds, and they sing in harmony. And the east wind gently stirs the leaves and rustles the forest of oak. And the hilltop is covered with flowers, purple and red, white and green [*sic*]. And when the wind blows, waves form in the flowers, and no one there can get his fill of the fragrance or of the colorful scene. It seems to him that he is in Heaven and not on earth. And the water flows and swells over the rocks and splashes sweetly.

The original works are by no means bare of poetic ornamentation. Often they have adornments typical of later folklore: euphonic elements —there is alliteration, for instance, in Nestor's Chronicle—epithets, often of the "Epitheta ornantia" kind, and the use of proverbs and stock phrases.

Most characteristic of all are the simple "monothematic" and "monumental" compositions. Shifts in the text are immediately discernible through the concluding formula, "Let us go back to what we were speaking about before." But these writers were also capable of presenting their thoughts clearly and systematically and of making their points.

Let us take, for example, a legendary tale from the year 912 in the Nestor Chronicle. The subject is the death of Prince Oleg. The tale has a traditional motif, a misunderstood prophecy, and has many parallels, such as the much more complicated and less concentrated Scandinavian legend of Odd and his horse Faxi.

> And fall came and Oleg remembered his horse that he had had fed but had not ridden. For he had asked magicians and soothsayers how he would die. And a soothsayer had said to him, "Prince, the horse that you love and ride will be the cause of your death." Oleg bore that in mind and said, "I will never again ride him and will not see him again." And he ordered him to be fed but never again to be brought to him. . . .
> Four years passed after Oleg returned from his campaign against Byzantium. In the fifth year he remembered his horse, which according to the soothsayer would cause his death, and called the head groom and said, "Where is my horse that I commanded to be fed and cared for?" The groom answered, "He is dead." Oleg laughed and reproached the soothsayer and said, "What the magicians say is untrue. It is all a lie. The horse is dead and I am alive." And he ordered a horse to be saddled, "Because I want to see his bones." And he came to the place where the bare bones and the bare skull lay, and he got off his horse and said, laughing, "And is my death to come from this skull?" And he set his foot on the skull, and a snake rose out of the skull and bit him on the foot, and he grew sick and died. . . .

One notes here the brevity of the sentences, which are arranged paratactically, and the artistry of the tale—the action is consigned to dialogue, and the point of the tale, the resolution, is not revealed until the last sentence. There is also striking alliteration in this passage, as in many others. The author plays with words that begin with "k": *knjazъ* "prince," *konъ* "horse," *kudesnikъ* "magician," who is also called *volxvъ*, and *Kievъ*.

One of the many sermons will serve as an example of clear, simply developed thought. Here is a passage from the Presbyter Kozma. He maintains that people who own books (he has in mind, of course, the Christian literature of the time) should put them at the disposal of other people:

> You are rich and have all things in abundance, the Old and the New Testament and other books filled with excellent works and words of every kind. . . . Why do you bar men the way to salvation by hiding God's word from your brothers? If you have ever read in books that one should keep God's word from one's brothers, then these books deserve not to decay or be eaten by worms but to be burned by fire. . . . No, O man, do not hide God's words from those who wish to read and copy them but be glad that through you your brothers may be saved. For they [words] have not been written to be concealed in our heart or in a room. Do not bar the way to God's Kingdom to those who wish to enter. Do not bury the pearls of God in your avarice and greed. Do not put the burning light under the bushel. For the Lord has commanded us to put it on a candlestick so that all men will see the light of God. . . .

One frequently encounters stock formulas borrowed from translated literature; their sources range from the Bible to the battle scenes of Josephus Flavius and the picturesque heroic battles in the *Digenis* novel. The formulas are usually taken in rough form, and, as was usual in compiling at the time, were incorporated in their entirety before the writer returned to what he had "been speaking about before."

In the Slavic Early Middle Ages one finds many works of unusual artistic expression and composition. They either imitate skillfully their Greek, or in the case of the Czechs, Latin models or reflect the "precocious" period of Slavic literature (see Chapter II, 3).

8. Ideologically one could characterize this literature as broadly optimistic. There is no contradiction or cleft between recently adopted Christianity and the life of the world. One is glad that one joined the Christian faith "at the eleventh hour." Even in religious literature there is no asceticism or animosity toward the world.

Vladimir Monomax emphasizes in his *Instruction* that one can be saved within the world:

> Our Lord has shown us how to overcome the enemy [devil]: one can escape his grip and deceive him by three kinds of good works—repentance, tears, and alms. God's commandment is therefore not difficult, my children, for by means of these three kinds of good works one can redeem one's sins and assure oneself of the Kingdom of Heaven . . . these works are not difficult. It is not necessary to live alone, to become a monk, or to fast, as some pious people do. One can obtain God's grace through small works as well.

One finds similar views in the religious literature, even warnings against exaggerated asceticism and "ascetic pride" in ascetic "good deeds" that one has performed. An example is the tale of the monk Isaakij of the Kiev Crypt Monastery, recorded under the year 1074 in the Nestor Chronicle.

It is of great ideological importance that by a reinterpretation of pre-Christian vocabulary and by the use of neologisms, especially loan translations from Greek, and foreign words, mostly Greek, the language was enriched and made into a suitable instrument for expressing new concepts and ideas.

It has been asked whether it would not have been better for the Slavs in the Eastern Church to have accepted Greek as the liturgical language, thereby putting at least a limited circle, the clergy, in direct touch with Byzantine culture and the culture of antiquity (A. Brückner). We cannot deal with this question in a purely historical work but must accept the decision of the Slavic mission as a matter of fact.

IV

THE LATE MIDDLE AGES

Russians

Cyril of Turov: Sermons, prayers, tales (twelfth century).
Paterikon of the Kiev Crypt Monastery
(beginning of the thirteenth century).
Epifanij the Wise: Saints' Lives of Saint Stefan of Perm and of Saint
Sergij of Radonež (fourteenth and fifteenth centuries).
Chronicles: Kievan (within the so-called Hypatian Chronicle,
twelfth century), Laurentian Chronicle (northeastern
principalities, twelfth and thirteenth centuries),
Novgorod and Pskov Chronicles.
Princes' Lives: Daniil of Galicia (in the Hypatian Chronicle,
thirteenth century), Alexander Nevskij
(Novgorod, thirteenth century).
Epic works: *Igor' Tale* (1185–1187), *The Tale of the
Destruction of Rjazan'* (thirteenth century).
Nil Sorskij (died 1506), Josif Volockij (died 1516).

Bulgarian

Metropolitan Evfimij of Trnovo (died 1393):
orthographic and stylistic reform.
Translations: Chronicle of Manasses
Grigorij Camblak (fourteenth and fifteenth centuries,
also wrote in Serbia and Kiev).
Konstantin of Kostenec (fifteenth century, also wrote in Serbia).
Paxomij Logofet (fifteenth century, wrote in Russia): author
and revisor of numerous saints' lives and other works.

Serbs

Lives: biographies of princes, kings, and monks written in the style of saints' lives—Simeon Nemanja by Saint Sava (1171–1235), Sava by Domentian and Teodosije (thirteenth century), Stefan the First Crowned, in part by Bulgarian authors.
The nun Evfimija: panegyric to Prince Lazar (about 1399).

Croats

Marko Marulić (1450–1524): Latin works and the Croatian *Judita*.

Czechs

Saints' lives in verse (after 1274).
Religious and secular lyrics, didactic and satirical verse.
Epics: *Alexandreis, Legend of Katherine.*
Dialogues: Mastičkář and others.
Translations: Marco Polo, Mandeville, and others.
Tkadleček (beginning of the fifteenth century).
Tomáš Štítný (1325–1400): several religious works and translations.

Poles

Latin Chronicles (fourteenth and fifteenth centuries).
Beginnings of religious writing (fifteenth century).

1. At the beginning of the Slavic Late Middle Ages a new style emerged, and Slavic languages drew further apart. This divergence was first brought about by a sound development in the languages: in the twelfth century the two reduced vowels ъ and ь underwent a change. They disappeared in final and weak position and in other cases became full vowels. In the old Slavic languages, which had originally been rich in vowels, a number of new consonant groups arose; and these were treated differently by each language. As a result, words began to sound different. A man who spoke one Slavic language was no longer readily able to understand another Slavic language. It is enough to illustrate the changes in the word for "bee" (for further information see Bräuer, I, p. 108 ff.):

Old Church Slavonic bъčela. After the disappearance of ъ the word becomes
Russian: pčela (regressive assimilation)
Ukrainian: bdžola (progressive assimilation)

Polish: pszczoła (supplementary articulation and regressive assimilation)

Czech: včela (facilitation of articulation)

Serbo-Croatian: čela (simplification of the sound group)

Slovenian: čebela (vocalization, or, better, secondary development of a vowel and metathesis)

Bulgarian: pčela (as in Russian)

Upper Sorbian: pčolka (like the Russian diminutive)

Lower Sorbian: colka (simplification and change in pronunciation)

Cultural differences among the Slavs resulted in different words for the same concepts. These words might already have been in use in the language or might have been coined, and in the course of history they often changed. The concept of the "state" will serve as an example. The following words were used:

Old Church Slavonic: carьstvo, carьstvije, kъnęžьstvo, kъnęženije;

Russian: knjažьstvo, knjaženie, carstvo, gosudarstvo;

Bulgarian: carstvo, carovište, carština;

Serbo-Croatian: carstvo, država;

Czech: mocnářství, stát, říše;

Polish: panstwo, cesarstwo, królewstwo, rzecz pospolita.

2. More important was the development in the twelfth century of a heavily ornamental style. Unfortunately the study of style in Old Slavic literature is not very far advanced. The Old Slavistic tradition contributes to this by calling literature as late as the seventeenth century "Old Russian" or "Old Czech" without taking into account stylistic changes that had taken place. Even within the literary period called the "Late Middle Ages," extending from the twelfth to the fourteenth or fifteenth centuries, there were stylistic developments that have not been classified according to period.

The study of style was encouraged by acquaintance with foreign theoretical works (compare Choiroboskos's treatise, which was later copied, Chapter II, 7; Latin poetics was also a source for the Western Slavs). The imitation of good models, translated or in foreign languages, was also important. And the epistolary guides, which have not been sufficiently studied among the Eastern Slavs, were of real significance.

The heavy ornamentation of Late Middle Ages works was thought to be as important as the content, and this style may be called "decorative" or "ornamental." I shall use these terms because stylistic decoration now acquired a value in its own right and sometimes so luxuriated that the content was neglected.

New elements of style occur especially in the often systematic symbolism since we now encounter for the first time in Slavic literature the view that "everything transient is a comparison." Significantly, the same images, symbols, and expressions were often used quite differently. And authors of this period did not hesitate to appropriate passages from the works of others. These passages were revised and incorporated in the new work so skillfully that it is now difficult to distinguish the borrowings. One quality for which this style strove was newness and originality. Old, borrowed texts were "improved" and made to fit the style of the times. In the course of revision the structure of the original work was often changed, and sometimes a new sense was given to the text. Frequently the work was not merely revised but was retold or adapted.

The quest for originality led to the creation of new genres and the mixing of old ones, and the result was an extraordinary variety of literature. Individual shading in style and content is much more apparent than before. These works are of special importance in studying the cultural history of the Slavs.

3. We have a number of literary works written in this period by the East Slavs and the Czechs. Bulgarian literature, especially its linguistic and stylistic reforms, influenced East and South Slavic literature. A considerable literature was being written by the Serbs and Croats as the Poles were first beginning to use the Slavic literary language, which was their own native language strongly influenced by Czech.

Among the East Slavs, the Chronicles were continued in the new style, and secular biographies were written, on Daniil of Galicia and Alexander Nevskij of Novgorod, both in the thirteenth century. Religious literature is represented by the sermon (Cyril of Turov, twelfth century), hagiography (the Paterikon of the Kiev Crypt Monastery, beginning of the thirteenth century), and saints' lives, the most important author of which was Epifanij the Wise, a brilliant stylist at the end of the fourteenth century. In the fifteenth century more lives of secular rulers appeared, especially in Moscow's rival city, Tver. The only examples of Old Russian epics still preserved are contained in manuscripts of this period. These works are the *Tale of Igor'*, written around 1185–1187—doubts as to its authenticity are not substantiated—and the *Tale of the Taking of Rjazan'*, written after 1240. The *Zadonščina* celebrates the first great victory of the Russian Prince Dmitrij Donskoj over the Tartars in 1380 and is merely an imitation of the *Tale of Igor'*.

In the fourteenth century Bulgarian literature acquired new importance for all Slavs who wrote in Cryillic. The Patriarch Evfimij of Trnovo introduced into the Bulgaria of the Šišman dynasty a reform in orthography that retained the old letters but adapted them rather arbitrarily to the sound changes that had taken place in Bulgarian. This reform was taken over by other Cyrillic Slavs although the rules were not appropriate to other South Slavic and even less appropriate to East Slavic languages.

Of particular importance was the arbitrary distribution of the letters ъ and ь; ъ was to appear within a word and ь at the end of the word. This arrangement was not historically correct and for the East Slavs was not phonetically correct. Moreover, the jotation of the vowels was to a large extent set aside, so that one wrote *sil'naa, mnogaa, rabotaa*, although the East Slavs said *sil'naja, mnogaja, rabotaja*. Under the stylistic influence of the Trnovo school, one began to coin new compound words, such as *xrabropobědnyj* and *krasnosmotritel'nyj*. Church Slavonic forms were preferred, and in Russian the East Slavic forms often gave way to Old Church Slavonic forms. One began to write *nužda* for *nuža, junoša* for *unoša, blago* for *bologo*, where previously one had used only East Slavic forms.

Even more important was the reform in style, that is, the consistent use of the contemporary heavily ornamental style, which lent itself particularly to saints' lives and panegyrics.

Grigorij Camblak, who died in 1419, wrote in the style of Evfimij in Serbia after 1393 and later in Kiev. The other Bulgarians, Constantine of Kostenec and Vladislav the Grammarian, wrote in Serbia, and the Serbian Paxomij Logofet wrote in Great Russia.

In Serbia biographies of the Serbian rulers and bishops were written, and in both cases the elements of secular and religious style were mixed (cf. especially the biographies of the Archbishop Sava, who died in 1233, and of King Stefan the First Crowned, who died around 1277, both of them from the royal Nemanja family).

After an interval in which all literature was written in Latin, the Czechs began in the last third of the thirteenth century to write a vernacular literature that reached its peak in the fourteenth century at the time of Charles IV. The first saints' lives in verse are preserved in long fragments and are mostly influenced by the *Legenda aurea*. They were followed by a number of religious and secular songs, the latter in part imitations of Western lyrics, and more extensive works, such as the verse *Alexandreis*, a fragment of more than 3,300 lines that represents almost

half of the work and was probably influenced by the *Alexandreis* of Ul-
rich von Eschenbach,[1] and later the extensive Verse Chronicle, which is
preserved in several manuscripts, was preceded by Latin chronicles and
in the seventeenth century was mistakenly attributed to a certain Dalimil. The *Legend of Katherine* deserves attention as an especially typical
example of the high style. Mention should be made of a group of alle-
gorical and satirical verses, the latter connected with Smil Flaška of
Pardubic (1348–1403). The range of Czech poetry is remarkable for a
small country.

Prose literature was also developing. There were a number of translations of the Bible, of which many manuscripts survive, and translations
of the Apocrypha, novellas, the autobiography of Charles IV, and, in the
learned literature, the *Travels of Marco Polo*. Besides translations there
were grammatical works and the dialogue *Tkadleček*, written after 1407
in imitation of the German literary argument *Der Ackermann aus
Böhmen*,[2] and especially the theological-philosophical works of a noble-
man, Tomáš Štítný, who lived from about 1335 to 1409. Štítný collected
or retold for his children a number of works from the church fathers and
medieval literature and raised the Czech literary language to a level that
was important to the subsequent "Czech pre-Reformation."

As has been mentioned, Czech strongly influenced the early stages of
colloquial and literary Polish (for more details see 11 below). Fragments
of sermons and verse are the surviving Polish monuments of the popular
speech of the time. Although the beginnings of Croatian verse can also be
traced to this period, the first significant works were written in Latin by
song writers in the fifteenth century. A notable author of the fifteenth
century is Marko Marulić (1450–1524), who wrote *Davidias* in Latin and
Judita in Croatian but who does not go beyond medieval stylistics and a
medieval view of the world. For the most part, translations of the usual
medieval repertoire go back no further than the fifteenth century.

4. It is characteristic of this period that authors felt free to adapt
other works to their compilations, that is, so to incorporate them that the
"seams" would no longer show (see Chapter III, 7). As a result, one can
usually tell borrowings only by their content. This is the case with the
East Slavic Chronicles, especially the magnificent Russian Hypatian

1. The original version was written in Greek. In the twelfth century, the French
cleric and poet Gauthier de Chatillon produced a versified Latin (in hexam-
eters) version that was later reworked into German and Czech versions (editor).

2. The form of both works is so peculiar that there is no appropriate term for
them today. Recent Czech criticism has used the vague word "composition."

Chronicle, which joined the Kievan Chronicle of the twelfth century with
the Galician-Volynian Chronicle of the thirteenth century and added the
three princes' Lives of Izjaslav II of Kiev (twelfth century) and Daniil of
Galicia and Vladimir of Volynia (thirteenth century). In the *Tale of Igor'*
there are reminiscences of earlier times, probably taken from older epic
works. There are similar borrowings in the saints' lives of Epifanij the
Wise or in the Serbian Life of Stefan the First-Crowned, where a long
addubitatio from the Kievan Metropolitan Ilarion has been incorporated.

5. The most important feature is the luxurious ornamentation of the
works, which at times seem to glitter with gold and precious stones and
remind one of colorful carpets.

We find in the tale of Daniil, the prince of Galicia who was called
"king" at the end of his reign:

In his army

were horses in masks and leather saddle blankets, and his regiments shone bril-
liantly, for their weapons glittered. And he himself rode . . . in the Russian
fashion, and the horse below him was a marvel, and his saddle was of burned gold
and his arrows and saber were trimmed in gold. . . . And his cloak was made of
Greek silk woven with gold and trimmed in flat gold lace, and his boots were of
morocco leather embroidered with gold (1152).

The frequent hyperboles are also decorative:

Stones fell from the towers like heavy rain . . . arrows fell like rain on the
city. . . . Spears and burning branches were hurled like lightning . . . and bodies
fell from the castle bridge into the moat like sheaves; the trenches were deep and
filled with bodies, and one could have walked over the bodies as though crossing
a bridge [ibid.].

Or the characteristics of a prince who in reality was rather powerless:

"He invaded the land of the Polovtsians, trampled the hills and ravines, mud-
died the rivers and lakes, dried up the streams and marshes" [*The Tale of Igor'*—
here the prince is practically a natural force.]

Long enumerations or chains of words and questions also serve as
decoration:

May this be protection, security, a bringer of victory, and help against enemies
visible and invisible for you and your descendants forever, a remedy against the
diseases of the body and the soul, a refuge and a bulwark, for your princes, a
sharp lance, for your soldiers, a shield of faith and a bold victory and a talisman
of peace in your life . . . ,

said Simeon in sending a cross to Stefan (The Life of Stefan the First-

Crowned). Epifanij the Wise and the unknown author of the Dalimil Chronicle are also fond of long word chains.

6. Metaphor is a particularly popular kind of decoration and, whether traditional or newly coined, serves various purposes. First of all, there are simple, stated metaphors or comparisons. The images in an Easter sermon by Cyril of Turov are of this kind. He compares Easter with spring:

> Today spring shines forth in its beauty and awakens the earth, and the gentle winds increase the fruit of the earth. And the earth that nourishes the seed brings forth green grass. The spring is the beautiful Christian faith, which regenerates man through baptism. The stormy winds are sinful thoughts, which are turned to virtues by repentance and which increase the fruit that benefits the soul. The earth of our being receives the word of God like a seed and brings forth the spirit of salvation, ever increasing it through the fear of God.

More typical are undisclosed metaphors. There are many of them in the sermons and saints' lives, and they also occur in the chronicles. In the epic works they abound. In the *Tale of Igor'* the battle is a feast or harvest, the bones of the dead are the sowing. The sermon is also a sowing, and the conversion of heathens to Christianity and virtue, the harvest. In the *Tale of Igor'* and in the chronicles gold and precious stones are metaphors for power. Various colors are metaphors for good and evil. There are frequent omens or foreshadowings, used metaphorically without explanation. Names of animals, like the traditional falcon, are metaphorical designations for principal characters. In the Slavic languages metaphors are particularly easy to form. The instrumental singular is polysemantic and can express either a comparison—"like" or "as"—or the real action of the subject of the metaphor.

In the *Tale of Igor'* we read, Prince Vseslav "ludemъ sudjaše, knjazemъ grady rjadjaše, a samъ vъ nočь vlъkomь ryskaše." This may be taken to mean that Prince Vseslav sat in judgment on men, ruled cities in his role of prince, and raced around at night in the guise of a wolf, or that he raced around at night transformed into a wolf. And after his escape Prince Igor' "poskoči gornastaemъ kъ trostiju, i bělymъ gogolemъ na vodu . . . i polete sokolomъ podъ mьglami." This may mean either that he sprang like an ermine into the rushes and like a white duck onto the water and flew like a falcon through the mist, or that he did these things having first been transformed into an ermine, a duck, and a falcon.

There are works that present whole series of metaphors without clarification. Among these are several Czech religious songs, probably from the fourteenth century. This will serve as an example:

Mistr Lepič

1. Slýchal-li kto práv při vieře
také divy od hrnčieře,
jakož tento mudrý, jenžto
nazývá se Lepič? Věz to:

2. Slepil velmi malú látku,
dal z nie dosti všemu sňatku,
anjelskému i rajskému,
vedle toho i zemskému.

3. Viz, kterým ji darem daří!
Šestera več v jednej tváři:
víno s medem, mléko s stredem,
a smetana s bielým chlebem.
. . .

6. Nemocné, trudné na stranu
sázej, krmieci smetanú,
biedné medem, slepé stredem,
daj pocestným vína s chlebem.

1. Has a true believer ever heard of such wonders performed by a potter as those performed by the wise man called "Lepič" [modeler, ceramist]? Know that: 2. He pasted a small piece of material together, gave to every station in life something from it, to the angelic, to the heavenly, and also to the earthly. 3. Behold, what gifts he gives them! Six things in one form: wine with honey, milk with virgin honey, and cream with white bread. . . . 6. Set the sick and weary aside and nourish them with cream, the poor with honey, the blind with virgin honey, give wine and bread to wanderers.

The metaphor, which is not disclosed, is of course that of God the potter (cf. Isaiah 29, 16; Jeremiah 18, 6; II Cor. 4, 7; Romans 9, 20 ff.). The second and third stanzas certainly refer to God's gift to mankind, especially to Communion and to the word of God (cf. the foods in I Cor. 3, 2; Hebrews 5, 12 ff.; I Peter 2, 2). The last line presumably alludes to both forms of communion that priests render.[3]

In the Russian literature of that era one finds similar metaphors, comparable perhaps to the Scandinavian "Kenningar."

7. Great stress is placed on the speeches of principal characters in many works of this period. In sermons, speeches appear to be used to enliven the subject matter, in chronicles, to emphasize and explain pragmatic connections, the motivations of the characters, and in hagiography,

3. *Parochus*, "priest," derives either from the Greek *párochos*, "innkeeper," "postmaster" (from the secret language used by early Christians; cf. also, *viaticum, ephod*—"communion") or from the Latin *paroecus* (Greek *pároikos*, "neighbor," "stranger") (J. Schröpfer).

to give expression to the inner life of the saint and of his adversaries. There are various ways in which speeches are developed, and one finds many forms of "erlebte Rede." Prayers are also stylized as speeches. Proverbs and proverb-like expressions were frequently used and in turn gave rise to the historical anecdote.

An example of a speech is this passage from a sermon by Cyril of Turov. A cripple is describing his condition to Christ at Bethesda:

There is no herb that can mitigate the punishment of God. My friends scorn me and the stench has robbed me of every pleasure. My neighbors are ashamed of me. Through my affliction I have become estranged from my brothers. Everyone reproaches me. I can find no one to comfort me. . . .

I would call myself dead—but my stomach wishes food and my tongue is parched with thirst. I think I am alive but not only can I not get up from my bed, I cannot even touch myself. I believe I am a corpse that has not been buried. This bed is my coffin. I am a dead man among the living and a living man among the dead. . . . I groan and sob, tortured by the pain of my disease, and no one comes to visit me. I have no possessions with which to pay someone to care for me. There is no one who would attend me without scorning me. . . .

And Christ answered: "Why do you say 'I have no one'? For your sake I became incarnate. I am generous and merciful. I have not broken the commandment of my Incarnation. For your sake I set aside the scepter of the Kingdom of Heaven and now go about serving mankind in this world. . . . For your sake I, who was incorporeal, became incarnate that I might cure men of all infirmities of body and mind. . . . I became man to make man God.

"Who serves you more truly than I? In order to serve you I made all living creatures. . . . And you say 'I have no one.' Who is more truly a man than I since I have not broken the commandment of my Incarnation?"

In the same sermon there is another dialogue, between the cripple, who has been healed, and the scribes. In other sermons by Cyril of Turov we find a complaint by the Mother of God, a eulogy to Christ by a man blind from birth, who has been cured, and eulogies to the Resurrection by the angels and saints.

There are also speeches and conversations in the Paterikon of the Kiev Crypt Monastery, in the Serbian biographies, and in the saints' lives of Epifanij the Wise. This art of "dramatization" occurs in almost all genres. In the epic *Tale of Igor'* we find it in the speech of the Kievan prince Svjatoslav, who urges the other princes to battle against the Polovtsians, in the lament of Igor's wife, who invokes the elements of nature to protect her husband and to return him to her from captivity, and in the grateful address of Igor' to the Donets after he has escaped.

Prayers within saints' lives and secular biographies take the form of speeches (Cyril of Turov left a whole collection of prayers), and entire works were written as speeches. The Old Czech *Tkadleček* is in the form of a law suit. The unhappy lover complains of the personified evil that has taken away his love. In the German source of the novel *Der Acker-mann aus Böhmen*, the complaint is directed at death; and the tragic pathos of the Czech version is therefore weakened.

The three imitations of laments in the Life of Saint Stefan of Perm and the eulogy to Saint Sergij of Radonež, both by Epifanij the Wise, are written in the form of vivid, highly ornate speeches, as are other imitations of laments in Old Russian and Old Serbian literature (such as the conclusion of the life of Stefan Nemanja).

The panegyrics of the period are also important. The nun Evfimija (about 1349–1405), a member of the Serbian ruling family, dedicated a panegyric and prayer to the Serbian Prince Lazar, who was killed in the Serbian defeat at Kosovo Polje in 1389. She called him a martyr and stitched her work in gold thread in his coffin. She is the first Slavic poetess whose name we know. Here are some excerpts from her brief work:

From your childhood on, new martyr, Prince Lazar, you were among the most noble men in the world, and the strong hand of the Lord showed you mighty and glorious among the rulers of the earth. You ruled over the land inherited from your father and made happy with all manner of blessings the Christians entrusted to you. With manly heart and a desire for piety you marched off to oppose the dragons and adversaries of God's Church, for you thought it intolerable for the Christians of your land to be ruled by Ismaelites. You were resolved that if you did not succeed, you would take leave of the transient heights of worldly rule, dress in the purple of your blood, and join the host of heavenly kings. . . . Do not now forget your beloved children, who have been orphaned by your death . . . for they are ruled now by Ismaelites, and all of us need your help. Therefore we beseech you to intercede for us with the Ruler of the universe for your beloved children and for all who serve them with love and devotion. . . . And since, as a martyr, you can trust in the Lord, bend your knees before the Ruler who crowns you and ask for long life for your beloved children, Stefan and Vuk. . . . Gather the host of your heavenly companions and beseech God who has exalted you. Tell Saint George, urge on Saint Demetrius, persuade Saint Theodore, take with you Saint Mercurius and Saint Procopius and do not leave behind the forty martyrs of Saint Seba-stian . . . come and help us wherever you are. Look down on my small offering and take it for much, for I have praised you not according to your merit but according to the ability of my poor mind. . . .

Proverbs and proverb-like sentences are a special device. They occur in the Old Russian chronicles, in saints' lives, in the *Tale of Igor'*, and in other places, for instance in Czech works, where we also find longer maxims.

The thirsty man reaches gladly for a drink, moisture is good for dry soil, the pious woman is dear to a man above all else [*Alexandreis*]. Coal often turns to fire that robs the rich man of his possessions. Worthy knight, look out for your name for there is nothing more precious than it. The good man does good for his people, the faithless man does not take care of his [Dalimil Chronicle].

8. As an ornament to the text, much euphony is now used in religious and secular literature. One finds alliteration and other sound correspondence. Sound is especially prominent in the *Tale of Igor'*: there are the sounds of nature—the voices of birds (each voice is characterized differently), cries of animals, the thundering and roaring of the earth—and of human life (songs, bells pealing, war cries, the groans and sobs of the wounded, trumpets). There are many instances of onomatopoeia. The trumpets sound:

truby trubjatъ　　　　　　　　tru-tru

or the stomping of horses' hoofs:

sъ zaranija vъ pjatokъ　　　　p-t-k
potoptaša poganyja　　　　　　pot-pt-po
polki poloveckija　　　　　　　pol-ki-pol-ki

(cf. Vergil's "quadrupedante putrem sonitu quatit ungula campum").

"Early in the morning on Friday they (Igor's warriors) trampled the heathen army of the Polovtsy."

In the *Tale of Igor'* we find an accumulation of words with the dark vowels "u" and "y" (ы) along with other euphonic effects: "Ne takoli . . . reka Stugna, xudu struju iměja, požrъši čuži ručьi i strugi prostre na kustu." Here there is repetition of the sounds: stu-u-u-stru-ju-u-ru-stru-str-u-u. The passage deals with the flooding of the river Stugna in 1093. "It was not this way with the river Stugna, which [otherwise] does not have much water but which was swollen by other streams and cast the boats [of the army] onto the bushes [of the shore]." The young Prince Rostislav is drowned in the flood, and we read farther on: "Unoši knjazju Rostislavu zatvori Dněprъ," "the Stugna barred young Prince Rostislav the way to the Dnepr," that is, it did not allow him to reach it. There are similar passages in the *Tkadleček*, such as, "Slyšav smrt synóv svých, trp ty také, Tkadlečku!" (s-y-s-rt-sy-s-y-tr-t-t-k-tk-k).

The natural environment of euphony is, of course, poetry. But there is no record of verse among the East Slavs and little among the South Slavs. We know nothing of the folk songs, but we have a number of Old Czech religious and secular poems. We find here the same abundance of euphony as in one of the oldest surviving religious poems, the "Ostrov Song," which deals with the "Logos" Christ.

We have noted here the recurrent sounds, especially alliterative, and syllables.

1. Slovo do svĕte stvořenie   s-ov-s-s-vo-enie
v božství schováno,   s-ov-áno
jež pro Evino z(h)řĕšenie   no-enie
na svĕt posláno.   s-áno

2. Dievcĕ dřéve porozenie   d-d-po-enie
jest zvĕstováno,   ov-áno
z Davidova pokolenie   d-ov-po-enie
božsky vzchováno,   ov-áno

3. ot nĕhože náše kršćenie   n-ná-enie
jménem nazváno,   na-ano
pro, drahé náše spasenie   pro-ná-enie
Židóm prodáno,   pro-áno

4. a pro náše vykúpenie   pro-ná-enie
na smrt prodáno,   na-pro-áno
jehož nám slavné vzkřiešenie   ná-enie
vesele dáno.   áno

Our marginal notes have not exhausted all the euphonic effects.

Translation: 1. Before the creation of the world the Word was concealed in the Godhead. Because of Eve's fall It was sent into the world. 2. Its birth was announced in advance to the Virgin. It was raised divinely from the family of David. 3. Our baptism is named after It; It was sold to the Jews for the sake of our precious salvation, 4. and sacrificed to death for our redemption. But Its glorious resurrection was given to us for our joy.

Some few Serbian poems have the same feature, as in this eulogistic epigram from the fourteenth century.

Slavi otbegnuv, slavu obrete, Savo   slav-ot-slav-o-t-s-avo
tamo otjudu slava javi se rodu   t-ot-slav-av-se-rod
Roda svetlost veri svetlost prezre   rod-svetlost-v-svetlost
tem že rodu svetilo javi se vsemu.   t-rod-svet-javi-se-v
Uma visota sana visotu sverže   uma-visot-s-visot-s
tem ubo uma više dobrotu stiže.   t-u-uma-vi-s
/Slavu/ slavi Save splete Siluan.   sl-v-sl-v-s-v-s-s

Translation: In escaping glory you have found glory, o Sava, there whence the glory of mankind appeared. The light of mankind despised the light of faith. A light appeared therefore to all men. The pinnacle of spirit has surpassed the pinnacle of worldly position, and you have obtained the blessings of the spirit. Siluan has made a crown of fame for Sava.

9. The subject matter of these works is quite varied. But in contrast to the literature of the Early Middle Ages there is here a division between the secular and sacred worlds, and writers on both sides of this dividing line are aware of the separation and at times painfully conscious of it. On

the one hand, the world is portrayed as exaggeratedly splendid and luxurious, as in the case of the small economically and politically ruined principalities in the Russian chronicles. On the other hand, there is the rigorously ascetic ideal of escape from the world and the total condemnation of the moral decay of the world. The successes of the Tartars in Russia and of the Turks in the Balkans contributed significantly to this pessimistic view, not only because Slavs had come under foreign domination, but also because the center of the Greek Orthodox Church, Constantinople, had fallen into the hands of infidels.

Among the Czechs there is a growing sense of national consciousness and nationalism (especially in the Dalimil Chronicle). In religious verse, poets tend to concentrate on serious theological problems, as do writers of theological literature in Latin. The Old Czech "Song of Kunigunda" contains a discussion of theological questions in poetic form. Old Czech songs are also concerned with historical problems. The two songs "On Truth" (*o pravdě*) picture "veritas exul," which can find no home on earth because of social contradictions and the decline of the Church. The division in the Western Church and the two popes, one in Rome and one in Avignon, also provide material for pessimistic lyrical reflection. On the other hand, Old Czech love songs with their abundance of pretty images recall the Minnesang of the fourteenth century (V. Černý).

The frequent expression *služba* "service to ladies" is reminiscent of courtly love. Love is portrayed hyperbolically and is made to appear more important than empire. The obstacles to love are recounted, the enemies who cause lovers to suffer. Separation and loss of a lover are dwelt on:

Mámt' já jednu paní,	I have a lady
tét' s věrú slúzím,	whom I serve truly,
pro nit' v túhách vadnu,	I long for her,
své srdce mařím . . .	I torture my heart . . .
Milost jíné nenie	Love is no different
nežli smrt druhá,	from any other death,
krátké utěšenie	its solace is brief
a věčná túha . . .	and its longing eternal . . .

Or,

Tajná žalost při mně bydlí
když' mi jie nelze vídati . . .
A secret sorrow dwells with me,
whenever I cannot see her . . .

Or,

> Zvolil sem sobě milú,
> ta tře mé srdce pilú . . .
>
> I have chosen for myself a love
> who scrapes my heart with a file . . .

Or,

> a mat' smutku přieliš dosti
> pro to smutné rozlúčenie,
> že s tebú býti lze nenie . . .
>
> One gets tired of this sadness
> that sad separation brings
> because I cannot be with her . . .

V. Černý, a scholar of Old Czech love lyrics, finds striking parallels with the Minnesinger (troubadour) lyric, with the canzone, pastorale, love letter, romance, dancing song, and alba—taking leave of one's beloved at break of day, as in this lyric:

> 1. Od východu slunce větřík povévuje,
>   přěs hory dma horami se chvěje.
>   Lesní jek, zvuk, lom se tiší,
>   zvěř ustúpá, ptactvo křičí,
>   znamennajic, ukazujíc,
>   žet' noc odstupuje pryč.

> 2. Vysoko jest vzešla dennice jasná,
>   dalekot' jest v plano odešla,
>   kvapíc, pospíchajíc od hor.
>   Vše stvoření i lidský sbor
>   nespí a chtie vzhuoru vstáti
>   Čas námá, milá, rozžehnati.

(Translation:

> 1. A breeze is blowing from the sunrise,
>   blowing over the hills, rustling in the hills.
>   In the forest the sounds die down, the noises, the crackling,
>   the game slips away; the birds cry out,
>   telling, announcing
>   that the night is fading away.

> 2. The bright morning star had risen high,
>   it has sunk down into the emptiness in the distance,
>   rushing, hastening from the hills.
>   All creatures and the host of mankind
>   sleep no longer and are about to arise.
>   It is time for us to part, my dearest.)

V. Černý has sought to demonstrate a connection with the Western Minnesinger lyric and believes that there was possibly an influence from Southern Germany or Austria. Old Czech prose also took a step toward Western Europe. Of special interest are the theological works that Tomáš ze Štítný wrote for his children (see 3 above).

He began by translating theological works of the Church fathers, especially Bonaventura, and went ahead to write short treatises of his own and longer works in the form of sermons: *Books on the General Questions of Christianity, Sermons for Sundays and Holidays,* and *Books on Christian Instruction.* Almost all of his work is taken from the Latin Church fathers and medieval theologians. As was usual, these sources were fashioned into an organic whole.

Štítný's contribution to the language is of particular importance. He elevated Czech and made possible the theological, moral, and philosophical writing that was to ensue. There are also mystic tendencies in his work.

10. The East and South Slavs were confronted at the time with serious ideological problems, not only with developing a new literary style (see 2–3), but also with accepting the mystic teachings of Hesychasm, which had originated in Byzantium and which advocated a particular kind of asceticism in order to attain the upper reaches of mysticism: solitude, constant prayer, and a special posture, with head bowed and breath bated. The Greek literature of the Hesychasts, which reached new heights of philosophical speculation, was influential in the Balkans and in Russia.

The Orthodox Slavs were particularly interested in the Hesychasts' psychological descriptions of the prerequisites for mystical achievement. The Hesychast ideology was propounded in a number of works, and the writings of the Hesychast theoreticians Gregory the Sinaite and Gregory Palama, the Saints' Lives of them, and older works of the Church fathers were translated and eagerly received by Slavic ascetics.

The way had been paved by the peculiar Russian hermit movement, which had attracted many pious men to the solitude of the North. In the Balkans, the center of Slavic Hesychasm was a monastery founded by Gregory the Sinaite, a place that attracted many Bulgarian and Serbian monks. Among the Russians, Hesychasm was promoted at a monastery (now Zagorsk) founded by an outstanding representative of the hermit movement, Sergej of Radonež. The Kiev Crypt Monastery was also influenced by the Hesychasts of Mount Athos. The great achievements of Russian literature, the works of Epifanij the Wise, and of art, the icons of Andrej Rublev, are products of the Hesychast movement. The works of Balkan literature are weaker as literature although they contain in the saints' lives of the time more specific material from the teachings of the Hesychasts. An important Russian representative of Slavic Hesychast literature was Nil Sorskij, primarily a compiler, who was named after the Sora, the river on which he had made his hermitage. His *Predanie i ustav* (Tradition and Monastic Rules) gives a clear idea of mysticism and emphasizes the psychological tasks of the ascetic, who should not be too strictly regulated.

The writings of an opponent of this movement, Josif Volockij (of Volokolamsk), also took the form of a compilation and argued that monastery life should be strictly ascetic and that the Church should work closely with the state. He wrote at the same time as Nil Sorskij and gave Russian literature the direction that it followed in the sixteenth century. Josif Volockij amplified his views in his polemic against those heretics whom he called "Judaizers" (*židovstvujuščie*); the latter were quite numerous in Novgorod and Moscow in the late fifteenth century. Of the writings of the Judaizers, we are familiar with only the translations of scientific and pseudoscientific literature from the Hebrew (philosophical works of the Arabs and of Moses Maimonides and the pseudo-Aristotelian *Secreta secretorum*). The main stream of literary development in Russia followed the tradition of the Bulgarian school of Trnovo with its ornate style. Russia's best representative of this ornate literature was probably Epifanij the Wise. His saints' lives presented new ideas in poetic form, while the sermons and other works of Nil Sorskij dealt with theological questions. Unfortunately, we cannot be sure of the extent of their effect.

In the shorter vitae of North Russian hermits and in the important Life of Saint Sergij of Radonež there is an account of the mystic way, from the purification of the soul (katharsis) through enlightenment (photismos) to the mystic union with God (henosis). Significantly, tales of miracles and anthropomorphic visions have given way. In their place we find visions of light typical of the Hesychasts, who saw in the "divine light" a special substance. A doctrine of an "inner way" to perfection is offered in the place of superficial asceticism and set numbers of prayers.

The role of Christian doctrine and missionary work is emphasized. The great Life of Saint Stefan of Perm written by Epifanij the Wise makes use of older literature and stresses the significance of Slavic missionary work. In describing Stefan's work among the Finns (Permians, now Komi) the author reflects on Christianization.

The most characteristic features of the works of the Balkan Trnovo school and the Russian lives by Epifanij are found in the religious lyric and are anticipated by the prayers of Cyril of Turov (Russia, twelfth century). These features became more prominent through the use of new stylistic devices, especially neologisms and many synonyms. The inner life of man was still portrayed in traditional terms, though somewhat expanded by the Hesychasts. Their contribution consisted of compound words derived from the stem *svĕt* ("light"), the epithets *duxovnyj* and *duševnyj* ("spiritual"), and numerous new metaphors and discussions of the "inner man."

There are notable works in which we find a profoundly pessimistic condemnation of conditions in the world—the feeling that it is impossible to be just, that just men are banished or killed.

This is the theme of the Old Czech songs on banished truth and justice. To some extent these songs anticipate the Hussite pre-Reformation (see Chapter VI).

Of interest are the form and content of an old Croatian song of censure from the second half of the fourteenth century. Here are several stanzas:

1. The light is waning, the sun is going down,
   Truth is slipping away, love is growing cold, darkness is coming on.
   The devil is gathering his hosts.
   The day is coming when the Scriptures will be fulfilled.

6. . . . But no one thinks about it; everyone eats, drinks, and dances.
   If someone were to tell them, "You are doing wrong," they would do wrong to
   him.

10. Whoever would adhere to God's truth
    and follow his Son, Jesus,
    and lament his sins in humility and piety,
    such a man they persecute in their rage.

11. They say, "You are a hypocrite and a deceiver! . . .
    Take him to the Inquisitor to be questioned!

12. Holy Father, this man is a heretic!
    he goes about hungry, thirsty, naked, and barefoot and passes judgment on us.
    We beg of you that this hypocrite be burned!"

There are twelve syllables to a line in the original; the verse is syllabic, and all the lines in a stanza have the same rhyme. The theme is a familiar one, the persecution and execution of a just man (see, for instance, Plato, the *Republic*, II, 5, 362 A).

11. The Late Middle Ages provide a good example of the various, sometimes vague literary relations between the Slavic peoples.

The most prominent role in this relationship was played by Bulgarian literature, which has been discussed above and which influenced South Slav and Russian writers before the period of Turkish domination. Representatives of the Bulgarian Trnovo school wrote among their Serbo-Croatian neighbors and went also to Russia, to Moscow and Kiev. Noteworthy among the latter are the metropolitans and writers Kiprian (Moscow) and Grigorij Camblak (Kiev) and the successor to the outstanding stylist Epifanij, the Serb Paxomij Logofet. Newly translated works, such as the *Areopagitica* (probably translated in Serbia in the thirteenth century), also came from the South Slavs.

This literary relationship has been traditionally referred to as the "second South Slavic influence" on East Slavic literature, but lately an effort has been made (D. Lixačev) to discover the contribution of original Russian work and to call the period the "Russian pre-Renaissance" instead. Unfortunately, this "pre-Renaissance" was not followed by a "Renaissance," at least not in the field of literature.

At the same time, Czech, which was becoming increasingly important as a colloquial and literary language, was significantly influencing Polish. Various elements of the Polish lexicon, which are still partially preserved, attest to this close cultural relationship. The vocabulary of the time, of which many words are still used, contains a number of sound forms that are peculiar to Czech but not to Polish:

1. The syllables *-la, -ra* instead of *-lo, -ro*: *władác, własny, straža, brana* (-brama), the name Władysław.

2. The sound *h* instead of the Polish *g*: *hańba, hardy, hojny, hołota ohydny* (Old Czech *ohyzdný*), *błahy, hrabja.*

3. *u* instead of the old nasal, in modern Polish otherwise *ą* or *ę*: *lug, kusy, okrutny,* the name Wacław: *ą* instead of *ę.*

4. *i* instead of Polish *'u*: *litowác, litość.*

5. The lack of Polish palatalization: *obywatel, rzetelny, wesele, serce.*

From this time on Polish orthography came under the influence of Czech. It has remained so by and large, although the Czechs began to introduce a new orthography (probably suggested by Jan Huss) as early as the fifteenth century.

Charles IV, Emperor of the Holy Roman Empire, made his capital, Prague, a center of European life; and Croatian monks came and brought with them their Glagolitic alphabet. To the Catholic West Slavs, Latin was an essential part of their education and the basis of their religious and cultural lives (there were already universities in Prague and Cracow). Latin was a unifying bond among them no less strong than Church Slavonic among the Orthodox Slavs.

This period, the fiteenth century, could well be set apart from preceding periods. The new ideology seemed to be giving notice of a new age. And here the paths of the Slavic literatures separate for a time once again.

V

THE RUSSIAN LITERATURE OF THE MUSCOVITE PERIOD; SIXTEENTH AND SEVENTEENTH CENTURIES

1. The Russian literature of the sixteenth and first half of the seventeenth century is peculiar. The period amounts to a kind of literary autarchy, the almost complete isolation of the Russians from the literatures of the West and of the other Slavic peoples. (The literatures of other East Slavs were already going their own ways.)

This state of affairs followed a series of political and ideological conflicts. On the one hand, Moscow subdued other Russian principalities that had previously enjoyed independence, if only illusorily, and threw off the last vestiges of the Tartar yoke. On the other hand, the views of Josif Volockij, which supported and extoled the Muscovite state, prevailed over the "inner Christianity" of Nil Sorskij and his followers (see IV, 10). In the sixteenth century, Moscow conquered the two Tartar states Kazan and Astrakhan; the Tartar population was absorbed into the Muscovite state, and as a result there was a certain increase in the influence of Tartar culture.

The emergence of the Muscovite tsardom (previously it had called itself a "grand duchy") and the efforts at cultural autarchy were encouraged by the fact that after the conquest of Constantinople by the Turks, Moscow considered itself the *only* truly Christian Orthodox state. Roman Catholics as well as Lutheran and Calvinist Protestants seemed to be heretics or unbelievers to the Orthodox Muscovites, who were ignorant of the basic theological questions. The idea of Moscow as the third Rome is typical. This phrase, rather accidentally coined by an obscure monk, Filofej of Pskov, played a somewhat less important role than modern West European scholars have thought, although Ivan the Terrible made the concept his own and used it in diplomatic relations.[1] Even more appropriate than the idea of Moscow as the successor to Rome and Constantinople was the slogan, which now came into being *for the first time* and which had as little to do with reality as the other phrase, "holy Russia."

2. Some ties with the West were established, nevertheless. They had mainly to do with economic and technical problems, were reflected occasionally in the arts, and through diplomatic ties with the West (starting with Poland) led to the learning of Latin by the Russians. Ideological influences were slight. They were usually thought to be heresies and culpable deviations from established tradition.

Moscow's relations with Constantinople[2] diminished so far that they were practically limited to the requirements of the Church. When an educated monk, Maxim the Greek (Maksim Grek), was invited to Moscow as a translator, he proved to be a supporter of Nil Sorskij (IV, 10) and was consequently detained in Russia and spent years in prison. Maxim had studied in Italy, where he had met proponents of humanism, but his sympathies lay rather with the antihumanism of Savonarola.

3. Moscow went its own way. Its emergence seemed to require a literature that would reflect the grandeur and power of the state. The Metropolitan Makarij (1482–1563, from 1542 on, Metropolitan of Moscow) played an important part in this literary undertaking. He took the initiative in creating the *Čet'i-Minei* (*Reading Menaea*[3]); an enormous collection of all Old Russian literature. It included the saints' lives, extensive theological works (such as the *Klimax* of John Climacus or the *Areopagitica* of the Pseudo-Dionysius with a commentary by Maximus the Confessor), and secular works. It was often necessary to write new lives for those saints revered in Russia about whom no work had been written. More liberties were taken with history in the sizable *Stepennaja kniga*, where the genealogy of Russian grand dukes from Rurik to the tsars of Moscow was recounted and made to appear a legitimate succession. The *Stepennaja kniga*, a twelve-volume com-

1. Actually, Ivan IV never used the expression, "Moscow, the Third Rome," although he claimed to be the *only* orthodox Tsar (editor).

2. The last vestiges of the Byzantine Empire were conquered by the Turks in 1453 (editor).

3. Devotional, didactic, and literary texts arranged according to the calendar (editor).

pilation of world history, was written in this same encyclopedic spirit. The eleven volumes that have been preserved contain around eleven thousand miniatures, obviously influenced by West European art. New Russian chronicles, such as the Nikon Chronicle, are also a part of this literature and are written with boundless imagination.[4]

Other typical examples of this Muscovite literature are the *Stoglav*, which contains the decrees of the Church council of 1551 in one hundred chapters, and the *Domostroj*, which for no compelling reason is ascribed to the priest Sil'vester. It is characteristic of these and other works that they should have overlooked or condemned everything foreign and trusted entirely in the true Christianity of old Russian tradition, that is, that the authors of these works considered their views as "old Russian."

4. This extensive and ambitious literature could easily lead one to assume that there was domestic tranquillity in Moscow and that the political and social principles of the state were widely accepted if it were not for the presence of a quite different literature, a polemical literature that continued in an intense and acrid fashion the polemic between Nil Sorskij and his spiritual Christianity and Josif Volockij and his view of the politically involved Church (IV, 10). The main questions of the polemic were of a social and political nature: the right of monasteries to own estates with serfs, the various views on absolutism, especially the moral responsibility of the absolute ruler, justice as the underlying principle of the state, the obedience of subjects and their duty to bear patiently even injustice and severity from the government—the virtue of *dolgoterpenie* (long suffering). Members of the feudal opposition to the centralized power of the Tsars emerged as writers: Prince Andrej Kurbskij, who emigrated to the Polish-Lithuanian state and from there sent several letters to the Tsar; unsolicited advisers to the Tsar, such as Ivan Peresvetov, about whose personal life we know only that he was probably an immigrant from the West; clergymen, the followers of Nil Sorskij, such as Prince Vasian Patrikeev, who had become a monk, and the monk Maxim Grek, summoned from Mount Athos; the diplomat Fedor Karpov, who formulated his thoughts on a theoretical basis and knew and quoted classical authors; real or imagined heretics whose religious doubts were often due to Western influence. Tsar Ivan IV himself defended his principles in letters, especially in those to Prince Kurbskij.

4. Not quite; the Nikon Chronicle consisted primarily of the material from the annals and some devotional and literary texts (editor).

5. After the death of the son of Ivan IV, Tsar Fedor, in 1598 and the brief reign of the elected Tsar, Boris Godunov, there began an interregnum that lasted until the election of a new tsar from the house of Romanov in 1613. During the short reign of the False Demetrius and the military intervention by Poland (in which Ukrainian cossacks took part) and Sweden and as a result of the attempt to put a Pole on the throne of the tsar, some circles in Russian society acquired at least a vague idea of the Western habit of life and mind. The cultural influence was by and large weak, but interesting works on the interregnum and other events of the seventeenth-century attest to the influences. In literature one finds the first evidence of poetry, rhythmic language,[5] and rhyme.

Under the first two Romanovs, Michael (1613–1645) and Alexis (1645–1676), a number of attempts were made, mostly with the help of Ukrainian and Polish collaborators, to acquaint Russians with the literary works of the West in translation. Although many translations were made, few were printed, and manuscript copies were not widely circulated. It was only in the second half of the seventeenth century that Russian literature began really to take an interest in developments in Western Europe and in other Slavic literatures, that is, at the time of the literary baroque.

6. The style of the works of this period is not very even, and they cannot be said really to be examples of belles-lettres although there are pages of poetic and rhetorical merit. Style fluctuates between real rhetorical ability, as in the writing of A. Kurbskij, Fedor Karpov, and at times Tsar Ivan IV, and a heavily ornamental style that is primarily concerned with the manner of expression and neglects and obfuscates the subject matter, as in the chronicles, many parts of the Reading Menaea, and the saints' lives.

Colloquial Russian words and syntactical usage began gradually to appear more frequently in the literary language at this time, especially where they did not have to compete with traditional Church Slavonic usage. The number of Tartar borrowings increased after the conquest of Kazan and Astrakhan. Among the native Russian words that found their way into the literary language are *obrok* and *pobor*, among the Russian forms, *tvoevo* and *ničevo*, among the Tartar borrowings, *altyn*, *den'ga*, *jam*, *jamščik* (cf. Chapter I, 2).

The ornate style abounds in complicated, syntactical constructions

---

5. Rhythmic language may be found in the Russian writing of the twelfth century (editor).

and topoi (*loci communes*). Here are several examples of rhetorically effective style. Prince Kurbskij addresses Tsar Ivan the Terrible and asks,

Why have you, o Tsar . . . variously murdered the generals whom God has given you, spilled their victorious blood with royal arbitrariness in the temples of God, and stained the church steps with their blood? [Why] have you invented for those who wish you only well unspeakable tortures, persecutions, and ways of death by accusing them of treachery, sorcery, and other spurious offences and by attempting to transform light into darkness and call sweet things bitter? . . . Have you fallen into unprecedented heresy and do you no longer wish to appear before the incorruptible Judge . . . who is my Christ and who sits on the throne of the cherubim; at whose right are the Highest Powers—and He is the Judge between you and me. . . . My blood, which I have shed for you like water, calls out against you to my God.

From the Tsar's reply:

Know that whosoever sets himself against [temporal] authority sets himself against God as well, he is an apostate, and this is the worst of all sins. . . . And if you are just and pious, why were you not willing to accept suffering and death from me, the obstinate ruler? You have destroyed piety, Christian law, and faith for the sake of self-interest and the pleasures of this world. You are like the seed that fell on rock, grew, and, when the sun shone on it, fell, and bore no fruit.

Timofeev's account of the interregnum, written about 1619, begins with a description of the last battles with foreign troops in Russia:

We received the sudden and unspeakable grace of God and freed ourselves from slavery with the help of the few men who were left, who clothed themselves in threefold firmness of battle against Pharaoh; and the snakes who had nested in our country and who had hissed at us full of wrath were extirpated from all the places of our land at the sign of God and by God's merciful providence. . . . They were suddenly deracinated and cast out, and we were brought from death to life for the second time; and God commanded us to live again, and bade us clothe ourselves in our former splendor and beauty as in a robe, and prepare the possession of his servant, the great Sovereign Tsar and Grand Duke, Michael Feodorovich of all Russia, fulfilling the words of a psalm of David. . . .

This is typical of the endlessly long sentences favored by rhetorical writers of the period; everything concrete is made as general as possible and there is much use of anacoluthon.

7. Russian literature of the late Muscovite period (sixteenth and seventeenth centuries) undoubtedly produced a number of works of poetic and rhetorical perfection. Other works give significant indications of the ideological developments that to a large extent prepared the way for the "Europeanization" at the beginning of the eighteenth century

and for the distinct, but not very distinguished period of baroque literature. This was a literature that could never fully free itself from the "pathos of reality" and viewed the entire art of writing as a process of reporting and informing. The fragments of folklore that survive suggest that there was a broad gap between it and what was considered to be literature. The baroque was transmitted for the most part indirectly from West European sources. Ukrainians, White Russians, and Poles served as intermediaries (cf. Chapter VIII). It was not until the time of the epigones, in particular G. Deržavin, that the baroque achieved real poetic distinction in Russia, for the "Europeanization" of Peter the Great had bypassed the arts—out of indifference, lack of understanding, and perhaps caution.

Absolutism had been recognized as being ideologically wrong in the fifteenth and sixteenth centuries by Nil Sorskij, Maxim Grek, Fedor Karpov, and others.

Around 1540, Fedor Karpov gives his views, with many citations from classical authors, especially Aristotle, in a letter to the Metropolitan Daniil, who was one of the most radically faithful servants of Muscovite absolutism but apparently not faithful enough—he was eventually deposed and exiled. In Karpov's view, the state cannot be based on the principle of limitless patience (*dolgoterpenie*) on the part of its subjects. If subjects accept all actions by authorities without objection, there is no point in having princes and laws. Whoever has nothing, that is, no rights, has nothing to lose. "Patience without rights (justice) and without law destroys all the benefits of society"; it "promotes evil ways and creates men who because of their poverty are disobedient to the ruler." By "poverty" he probably means to suggest absence of rights as well. Karpov, an experienced diplomat, quotes Aristotle, Ovid, and Suetonius, but his warning was not heeded. Peresvetov was also ignored when about 1550 he wrote to the Tsar on the necessity for justice in the administration of the state. The results of the governmental practices of the time were disorder, the interregnum at the beginning of the seventeenth century, and the schism in the Church, *raskol*, at the end of the century.

6. Daniil was deposed and exiled, not by the Tsar, but by the boyars during the childhood of Ivan IV (editor).

VI

THE HUSSITE MOVEMENT

1. The transition of Czech literature from the Middle Ages to the Renaissance was interrupted by religious and social conflicts just as the beginnings of the Renaissance had reached Bohemia. The religious movement called Hussitism after its founder, John Huss, created a large and notable literature, which did not aspire to the status of belles-lettres but which took on literary and aesthetic values from necessities inherent in the use of language. Through their literature, the Hussites sought to forge a weapon for their religious and social-political battle; like every weapon, it was at first a work of craft and later a work of art.

2. The Hussite movement was essentially disunited. Huss, his predecessors, and followers were striving to restore the original condition of the Church, which was now corrupt. The central question with which the movement was concerned was the availability of Communion in both forms to all Christians, not merely to priests. This amounted to reintroducing an old rite, one which had not been abolished in the Western Church until the Middle Ages. Later attempts by the Russian Slavophiles to portray the Hussite movement as an effort to return to the bosom of the single "orthodox" Church were, of course, nothing but misinterpretations. One should not forget, however, that Hieronymus of Prague visited the East Slavic regions of the Polish-Lithuanian state (possibly even Pskov) and found there, in the customary Communion in both forms, some support for this demand by the Hussites. But the ideological ties with the Eastern Church were weak and were soon lost sight of in the face of contemporary problems of Western Church life and of the social and political needs of Bohemia.

Among the most important general motives behind the movement was the struggle against the secularization of the Church, to which the Renaissance contributed decisively. The consciousness of the Church had, of course, already been shaken by the double papacy, and it was against this background that the Czech song about "exiled truth" (that is, justice) had appeared.

The decline of the Western Church from its former power and the attempt to "improve" the condition of Church life led to new opinions about the relationship of the restored Church to the state. There were various shades of opinion, from the theocratic view of the primacy of Church over state to the somewhat anarchistic view that rejected the state as an essentially un-Christian organization of power. This aspect of Hussite ideology attracted those who were dissatisfied with social and political conditions—not just the nobility, but also the bourgeoisie and even the "common people."

The central theological problem of Hussitism was genetically connected with the theoretical views of John Wyclif, which were based on philosophical realism and had actually to lead to a revival of theories already shaken by the new philosophical currents of nominalism. Although Huss's teachings differ from Wyclif's in many respects, the content of his theological views, like that of Wyclif's, looks essentially to the past.

Hussitism was basically a contradiction. The hegemony of theological problems shows that this *new* direction had its roots in the *old* medieval tradition. The Hussites demanded for the Church the *restoration* of old rites, but their social program contained decided *innovations*. Combining theological doctrine with social, political, and national demands was actually an anachronism and was based on the medieval concept of the unity of culture within the religious sphere (R. Jakobson). The Hussite movement was directed *modo obliquo* against the incipient Renaissance. But a combination of new and old is not an unusual paradox in Church history, a kind of "pseudomorphosis." Radical movements leading to revolution may be hidden behind the mask of conservatism.

3. Hussitism signified for Czech literature a turning away from increasing secularization and a return to religious problems. But this religious exterior of Hussitism was constantly being broken through by the social and political motives of the "Hussite revolution," that is, the movement that soon made use not only of ideological weapons but of military weapons as well.

The literature of the movement was forced to assume two faces. Theoretical presentations were made appropriately in Latin, but works of propaganda and agitation were written in Czech to enlist support among the people. We are concerned with this Czech branch of Hussite literature. It created forms and stylistic devices essential to its tasks. Even the opponents of the Hussites were forced in their polemical literature to submit to the rules of the unwritten "poetics" of Hussite verse.

4. The most important writer of the period was Huss himself. Following the custom of the time, he set down his theological views in Latin. After 1410 his sermons were directed at a popular audience and were at first aphoristic and later systematically catechistic. He wrote polemics in the form of letters and sermons (mostly in Latin) against the conditions of Church and secular life. Besides the problem of Communion, Huss's polemics were primarily concerned with simony, the sale of sacred objects and of Church offices.

Huss opened new avenues for the literary language. His interest in Czech is attested by the treatise *Orthographia Bohemica*, which was written by him or someone close to him around 1406 and which set down the basic rules for the new, perfected Czech orthography. The *Orthographia Bohemica* became the principal basis for scholarly Slavic transliteration. Huss's Czech works represent a further step in dealing with scholarly questions in the vernacular (his predecessor was Thomas Štítný in the fourteenth century—see Chapter IV).

The Czech works of the early Hussites followed the same line of development. After Huss was burned, Jakubek (Jacobellus, died 1429) was for a time the central figure of the Hussite literary movement. Disputes between various branches led to a polemic literature within Hussitism. A representative of the moderates was Jan Rokycana (c. 1395–1471), who, like Jacobellus, was primarily a writer of sermons.

Many works of the time have been lost or destroyed, and many, like the sermons, were probably never preserved in writing.

5. The rhetorical style of the sermons had by necessity to be simple and make relatively little use of metaphor. The language was designed mainly to communicate the thought of the Hussites. The many quotations from the Bible and the pathetic passages introduce some elements of the "high," ornate style into the sermons. From Huss's *Statement of the Faith:*

It is good that a man should not take frivolous things to be true but that he know the truth of God and cling to it till death, for truth will free him in the end. . . . Therefore, faithful Christian, seek the truth, hear the truth, love the truth, hold to the truth, stand for the truth until death. . . . [Chapter VD].

Before his departure for Constance, where despite the emperor's letter of safe conduct he was condemned and burned by the Church council, Huss had a presentiment of his fate: "You may not see me again in Prague before my death. If it should please Almighty God to give me back to you, we shall be the happier to see each other, and even more so if we meet in the joy of heaven" (from a letter of October 1414[1]).

6. The many songs of the Hussites are surprisingly similar. Their composers, who were almost always anonymous, strove for exactness of expression rather than beauty. Their songs were primarily instruments of "Hussite missionary work," that is, of religious propaganda. Poetic ornamentation was used only when it served to make the thought more effective. Without passing negative judgment one can speak of a "decline" or more properly of a simplification of the formal aspect of the songs. Anti-Hussite poetry may be similarly characterized.

The intention to spread propaganda is often suggested in the song itself.

> Ke cti, k chvále napřed buoží
> a hřiechuom na otpuštění,
> zvláště svatokupeckých,
> netoliko usty mluvme,
> ale také zpievajme
> pro výstrahu jiných!
> Dietky, nejprvě počněte,
> svatokupectvie oznamte
> otcóm, matkám i kněžím (. . .)

> To the honor, to the praise of God above all else,
> and to the forgiveness of sins,
> especially the sin of simony,
> we should not only speak with our mouths,
> but let us also sing
> as a warning to others!
> Dear children, begin first,
> tell what simony is
> to fathers, mothers, priests . . .

Other songs begin: "Let us take note of this order, let us go straight to Communion. . . ." "What recently happened must be proclaimed. . . ." —and so on.

Since the Hussites were soon compelled to resort to military action,

---

1. From this point on, quotations will be taken largely from poetry, and from prose only when the passages are of particular stylistic significance.

one finds in many of their songs the conviction that true Christians are "soldiers of God." The polemic against the Hussites and their controversies among themselves were also expressed in verse.

The relatively large number of songs that have been preserved attests to their broad dissemination and to the resilience of the Hussite tradition in the face of the political victories of their opponents. Many songs were subsequently forgotten or saved only in copies abroad, for instance in Vienna. Large collections of texts have been preserved in a manuscript in Bautzen and in a Catholic vicarage in Bohemia (the Budyšínský rukopis and Jistebnický kancionál).

Especially important works in verse are the "Song of Truth = Justice" and the "Conversation of Man with Death."

7. The Bible played an important part in Hussitism. It is understandable that the second, third, and fourth versions were made on the basis of the pre-Hussite Czech translation of the Bible. These versions are preserved in many manuscripts. The last version was used as the basis for the printed "Kralitzer Bible" in the sixteenth century (see Chapter VII, 8). Besides the orthographic and lexical changes in the new versions, the morphological simplification introduced by Huss is particularly noteworthy (among other things the aorist and imperfect, which had died out in the vernacular, were dropped).

8. Of the writers in the mid-fifteenth century, Petr Chelčický in particular should be mentioned. His works were written in the thirties and forties and were partly published beginning in 1521. We know almost nothing of his life (in the opinion of F. M. Bartoš he was born around 1380). Besides several shorter treatises, he wrote a postil designed to be read and a work, *Net of Faith* (*Siet' viery*, published in 1521). Chelčický's writings are equally remarkable from the point of view of ideology and of style. Like Štítný, he was a self-educated layman. He was attracted by Huss's ideas and carried them to the point of denying not only the "evil world" but, operating from a Christian ascetic point of view, the very fundamentals of secular life: the state with its unChristian methods of rule, especially war, and even the Church in so far as it was a secular organization. His system of thought is an unusual example of consistent "Christian anarchism" (he was highly regarded by L. N. Tolstoj).

Chelčický's style is simple but not awkward. By and large, he wrote freely on the Gospels and, unlike Štítný, did not make use of models. His style is simple and transparent, although too broad and marked by anacolutha and syntactical mistakes. His works continued to be influential and after eighty or ninety years were printed repeatedly.

In his works there is a typical prolix, repetitious flow of thought. To explain the metaphor in the title *Net of Faith* (the Hussites confine themselves by and large to metaphors from the Scriptures) he requires several pages!

On the other hand he is capable of presenting thoughts briefly and succinctly. A short parallel to the *Net of Faith* is his brief treatise *On the Three Kinds of Men* (*O trojím lidu*). Although the style is somewhat primitive, there is a breadth of presentation, achieved by the propagandistic intent of the work, which is designed to be understood by the simple reader.

9. Huss's ideas were received by other Slavs, especially Catholics faced with the same problems as the Czechs. The most pronounced effects, though not lasting ones, were felt in Poland, where East Slavic subjects were influenced by Hussitism. When the radical Hussites were driven out of Czech territory, they found refuge, among other places, in Hungary. A certain Hussite influence on the Croats is also discernible.

It is quite possible that the essentially vague East Slavic movement of the Judaizers (Kiev, Novgorod, and Moscow), whose theological views we know by and large from the works of their bitter enemies, goes back to the influence of Hussitism. The views of the Judaizers are strongly reminiscent of those of the radical wing of the Hussites (V. Stroev, D. Čiževskij, R. Jakobson).

Questions of Church policy (the fight against simony) and of theological dogmatism (doubts about the rationally incomprehensible doctrine of the Trinity, the Incarnation of Christ, the rejection of the veneration of saints, and so on) may have been influenced by Hussitism. But the scholarly interests of the Judaizers do not reflect this influence. The problems surrounding their heresy should be investigated more thoroughly.

10. Although radical Hussitism was suppressed, representatives of the moderate wing (4 and Chapter VII, 8) maintained their position in Czech intellectual life in the sixteenth century and joined the new confessional organization the "Bohemian Brothers." The waning of the Hussites' revolutionary spirit also weakened their resistance to the secularized Renaissance. To a large extent, the sixteenth century witnessed among the Czechs the coexistence of two intellectual currents that had originally been opposed: the current that succeeded Hussitism and the current of the Renaissance, which was influenced by the West. The influence of Lutheranism also began to make itself felt, especially among the Slovaks.

VII

RENAISSANCE

Czechs

Scholarly literature—translations and compilations,
descriptions of travels
Daniel Adam Veleslavín (1545–1599)
Řehoř Hrubý z Jelení (died 1514)
Šimon Lomnický z Budce (1552–1622)
Jan Blahoslav (1523–1571)—late Hussite

Croats

Petar Hektorović (1487–1572, from Hvar): translations of Ovid,
fishing idyll, *Ribanje*
Marin Držić (1520–1567) playwright
Dinko Ranjina (1536–1607, Dubrovnik): lyrics
Dominko Zlatarić (1558–1609, Dubrovnik): translations
from Italian, lyrics

Poles

Marcin Bielski (1495–1575): prose writer, author of a world chronicle
Mikołaj Rej (1505–1569): moralistic and satirical verse
Jan Kochanowski (1530–1583): lyrics, translation of the Psalter,
Treny, epigrams (fraszki), etc.
Szymon Szymonowicz (1558–1629): Latin works, Polish idylls (sielanki)
Sebastian Klonowicz (1550–1602)—transition to the baroque
Piotr Skarga (1536–1612): saints' lives, sermons—
transition to the baroque

Eastern Slavs

Vernacular translations of the New Testament
Ivan Vyšenśkyj (died before 1625)—transition to the baroque

1. The Renaissance is traditionally taken to have been a "rebirth"
of the arts and learning after their "decline" in the Middle Ages. Even
if the Renaissance did see itself this way, we need not accept this interpretation in its entirety. It is true that the Renaissance did move closer
to ancient culture, even though the approach was narrow: Greek was
taught, and the style of the literary language of the time, Latin, was
considerably improved ("humanism").

But the Renaissance was not just a "rebirth" of the classical age; it
was a "rediscovery" of man and nature. It would be more appropriate to
speak of a "re-evaluation" of man, since man was also the center of attention in the Middle Ages: religious literature dealt predominantly with
the problems of men. But in the Middle Ages man was portrayed in his
relationship to God and was viewed as the "image and likeness of God."
The Renaissance, however, placed man in the framework of nature.
Whereas the Middle Ages required man to be contrite of heart and to
subordinate his will to the will of God, the Renaissance sought to free
man from these fetters and to give the will and arbitrariness of natural
man an unobstructed field in which to operate. This meant liberation
from the medieval consciousness of dependence on the Beyond.

The image of man was secularized. His will was directed at self-
assertion and was thought to require the greatest possible development
of his powers and human essence. The fully developed "superior man"
demanded a superior place for himself in nature and society and no
longer felt subject to authority or tradition. This new human ideal is
totally different from that of the Middle Ages.

The "rediscovery" of nature is also largely a matter of a change in
point of view. After much progress in the study of nature in the Middle
Ages, to which P. Duhem referred as early as 1915, the Renaissance
crossed the boundaries of basic method and opened the gates to natural
philosophical speculation, which was often misleading. Astrology,
alchemy, and magic assumed an important place in the Renaissance view
of the world.

This change in the view of man and nature brought with it a secularization of culture. Man and nature were taken from the sacred sphere and

no longer regarded from the religious point of view. Instead, one attempted to understand them on their own terms.

2. To the arts and literature the Renaissance was especially important since it meant the cultivation of style on the model of the Classics and of Latin. The new view of man and nature helped to establish new aesthetic principles. A new ideal of beauty came into being along with an understanding of beauty quite alien to the Middle Ages. Basic to the development of literature was the new manner of viewing history. The past was to be understood from the literary sources that it had left behind. One had to be able to read these sources, and the fundamentals of philology as the art of reading and criticizing texts were established. This new attitude toward literary texts gave rise to a poetry that required commentary and the attention of experts. Here the classics were instructive. The rhetorical "Ciceronian" style was especially preferred. Often the eloquence of language made the content, especially of ideological works, opaque, since "beauty" was preferred to exactness of expression.

The Renaissance, which so opposed traditional authority, fell into the hands of a new authority, that of the image that it had itself created of the classical age.

The "liberation" of man from narrow moral and religious precepts led to the discovery of new subject matter, in particular human drives and passions; even those of "the lower sort" were now portrayed, although perhaps with satirical intent. Here too the classics and their satires served as a model. In its attacks on tradition, Renaissance satire often went much further than classical. In the tradition of old bucolic poetry, but in new and special ways, Renaissance literature portrayed the "common folk" and made use of the vernacular and, to a limited extent, of folklore.

There were soon systematic presentations of poetic theory, the rules of which were taken to be authoritative. Aristotle, Horace, Cicero, and Quintilian were particularly esteemed as models. As in Renaissance prose, there is in the poetry of the period a tendency to formal complication. Difficult "figure poems" ("versus echoici," "versus cancrini"), like the emblematic poems in baroque poetry, were widely circulated. There is often euphony and play on words.

3. When the Renaissance reached the Slavs, it was nearing the end of its development. Among the Slavs it was often modified by Hussitism and the Reformation. Secular and reformatory currents flowed along side by side—at times attracting one another, at times repelling. But

individual poets frequently made their own decisions about the secular
Renaissance and Church reformation and set out to go their own way,
deviating considerably from the broad path of the Renaissance (we
cannot here treat these cases in detail).

4. The influence of the Renaissance on the Slavs, or at least on those
of the Slavs who were in close touch with West European culture in the
fifteenth and sixteenth centuries, began with their interest in Latin,
which in Western Europe had long been in use as a literary and official
language. Among the Slavs there were soon neo-Latin poets, who had
considerable influence on later vernacular poetry. Besides original
poetry in the vernacular, there were many translations of classical poets
and of recent Western Renaissance literature. Romance literature was
particularly important, first Italian and then, to some poets, French
poetry. The cultivated style of Erasmus, even in his nonpoetic works, was
influential. The universities in Prague and Cracow provided information
about the new intellectual life of the West. Real, direct influence by
West European Renaissance literature is to be found primarily on the
Czechs, Croats, and Poles. Many ideas of the Renaissance were conveyed to the East Slavs by the Poles (cf. 12).

5. The Czechs first came into contact with humanism in the fourteenth century. In the fifteenth century the Hussites turned their
attention to religious problems although they had many connections
with the humanists (e.g., Aeneas Sylvius Piccolomini). It was only after
political and Church affairs were stabilized around 1500 that Czech
Renaissance literature began to emerge and develop along the pattern of
the extensive Czech verse and prose of the Middle Ages. The dominant
interest was in ideological and scholarly themes. Studies abroad (in
Italy and to some extent in Germany), visits by foreign humanists in
Prague (for instance, by the German Konrad Celtes) and a lively
correspondence with West European Humanists (among others Erasmus)
were important stimulants to the Czechs. Soon many translations of
classic and contemporary literature were made and circulated, in print
and in manuscript. Besides Czech translations of Cicero, Lucian,
pseudo-Lucian works, Isocrates, and others, the more difficult Greek
works were translated into Latin in Bohemia. We have Czech translations of much Renaissance literature, and there is evidence that it was
read; among the authors translated were Petrarch, Boccacio, Pontano,
Aeneas Silvius, Lorenzo Valla, Marsilio Ficino, particularly Erasmus,
and many minor writers of the Renaissance. The introductions and

epilogues to these translations reflect the desire for cultural and political change that was expected of the Renaissance.

In his introduction to his translation of Erasmus, Gregor Hrubý z Jelení pointedly recommends a reconciliation of the classics with Christianity in order to oppose obsolete Aristotelianism:

In an orderly fashion and so far as it is suitable everyone who is able to should study the secular authors if he wishes to understand these good men correctly and completely. . . . They occupied themselves altogether with classical learning, with poets, orators, and historians, and especially with the teachings of Plato. . . . But our teachers have discarded Plato and have read and followed only Aristotle although Plato is in many respects closer to Christian truth.

To learn the art of politics and even of war he recommends reading Cicero.

Besides the Czech neo-Latin writers, who were also respected abroad, mention should be made of such Czech humanists as Viktorin Kornel ze Všehrd, Gregor Hrubý z Jelení, who has already been mentioned, and the author of an extensive Czech chronicle, Václav Hájek z Libočan. Many translators, compilers, and authors of original prose works played a significant part in developing Czech prose style.

Of great importance for the development of literature was the art of printing, which was well advanced, not only among spokesmen for the Renaissance, but among the Hussites as well.

Especially noteworthy is Daniel Adam Veleslavín (1545–1599), who was not only a publisher but also the author of several works, mostly compilatory, to which he made additions of his own, partly in verse.

The translated works were of various kinds, some of them by the Church fathers. Among the original works were legal and historical writings, and accounts of travels were widely circulated. In comparison with the Middle Ages, the sphere of poetry had become considerably smaller. The spiritual song remained alive but went back to the old tradition. Works in the new style included moralistic, didactic books of advice on everyday life, which were in part satirical. It was not until later that Šimon Lomnický z Budče appeared. He was protected by the powerful Rosenberg family; in his later poems one finds elements of Baroque style. The son of the Hussite king, George of Podebrady, Hynek (Ignatius), wrote purely secular poems, such as "May Dream" ("Majový sen"), in which rather daring erotic scenes are presented, scenes that had previously been possible only in the songs of wandering medieval scholars.

Tu poče mi se ve snách zdáti (...)
Ó má najmilejší, krásná paní,
já sem zapálil v tvém milování,
že hořiem právě jako v peci!
Prosím tvé milosti, rač se svléci
a lehnúti ke mně sem!
Pustím tě pryč přede dnem,
a ještě dobře před svítaním...etc.

Then I began to dream . . .
O, my dearest, lovely lady,
I am all aflame from your love,
I feel as though I were burning in an oven!
I beg your mercy that you
should take off your clothes and lie down with me!
I will let you go before day,
before the first light of morning . . .

The *Krátké naučení každému Hospodaři mlademu* (*Brief Instruction for Every Young Master of a House*) begins with the assertion that all men strive for happiness. After giving advice on managing one's affairs, the poet passes on to questions of education:

Moudrost jest poklad velebný,
a ode wšech chvalitebný...
Protož hospodaři mladý,
užij také této rady:
Nech Chytrosti, hled' Moudrosti,
pros za ní Boží milosti!

Wisdom is a great treasure
and praiseworthy above all treasures . . .
Therefore, O young master of the house
make use also of this advice:
set cunning aside, strive for wisdom,
pray God's grace for it!

One should send one's son to school:

Svěř ho Mistru učenému,
pobožnému a pilnému,
kterýž by ho pěkně učil (...)
a nejprvě čísti, psáti,
potom grammatyki znáti,
i také dialektyki,
retoriki i musyki,
toho sedmera vmění
nad něž v světě žádné není...

> Entrust him to a well-educated teacher,
> to a pious and zealous one
> who would like to teach him well
> to know first reading and writing,
> then grammar
> and also dialectic,
> rhetoric and music;
> these seven arts,
> there is none nobler in the world.

> ...nemám Pana žádného,
> ani nestojím o něho.
> Málo i na Regenty dbám,
> neb jsem jásobě volen sám (...)
> ja jsem svobodným Měštianem...

> I have no master over me
> and pay no heed to any.
> Nor do I pay much attention to the regents
> for I am free . . .
> I am a free citizen . . .

For the goal of human striving is freedom.

6. The Dalmatian coast of what is now Yugoslavia was to a large extent culturally, economically, and politically dependent on Venice, and Italian, or a dialect of it, was used along with Latin in commerce. The rich Dalmatian city republics were early drawn into the sphere of influence of Italian humanistic culture. Many young Dalmatians studied at the university of Padua, and Dalmatia had close economic ties with Italian cities. The first Dalmatian poets wrote in Italian and Latin. They submerged themselves entirely in Italian life and only occasionally remembered their Dalmatian home. Marko Marulić's Latin epic, *Davidias,* and his spiritual works, which were also printed in the West, fall intellectually within the boundaries of Late Medieval Latin literature, as do the works of Aelius Cervinus, who mentions Slavs in his Latin poems. Marulić also wrote an epic in Croatian, *Judita,* in which one finds features of Renaissance poetics (P. Skok). But it was not until the sixteenth century that important Croatian works were written, by two poets from the island of Hvar, Hannibal Lucić and Petar Hektorović. Besides translations from Ovid Lucić wrote lyrical poems and a verse drama, *The Slave Woman (Robinja)*; and Hektorović wrote the eclogue *Fishing and Fishermen's Talk (Ribanje i ribarsko prigovaranje),* in which scenes of local life and nature are to be found along with many scenes from classical and Italian idylls.

Hektorović sees the common people as companions of the fishermen.

> Dokle užinaju, pojdoh posiditi
> pri moru na kraju, te se stah čuditi,
> da su ljudu mnozi viditi priprosti,
> zlorušni, ubozi, a imaju dosti.
> Jer s takimi ljudu budu pribivati
> razum, pravi sudi, i njih odivati.
> Kripost s njimi zato otajno pribiva
> kakono i zlato ko zemlja pokriva (...)

He thinks at once of classic examples:

> Čul si Diojena, ki blaga ne imiše,
> bačva nezadnjena kojemu stan biše,
> ter mu zavijaše Alezander cesar,
> jer u njem vijaše kriposti velik dar (...)

> While they were having lunch, I went to sit down a little while
> at the edge of the sea, and I was amazed
> at how many people, simple to look at,
> with shabby clothes, poor, still have enough.
> For among such people it is usual
> for reason and good judgment to dwell and to adorn them.
> Virtue therefore dwells secretly among them
> like gold that is covered by the earth . . .

> You have heard of Diogenes who had no property
> and who lived in a bottomless barrel
> but who was envied by King Alexander
> since he saw in him a great gift of virtue . . .

Peter Zoranić's idyll, *The Mountains* (*Planine*, 1569), is on the threshold of baroque poetry. Zoranić's love poems are reminiscent of folk songs. Poets from Zadar and Dubrovnik, Baraković, D. Držić, and D. Zlatarić, and other poets, who are sometimes anonymous—one finds anonymous lyrics in the late sixteenth-century collection ascribed to Dinko Ranjina—combine folklore and patriotic motifs with elements of Renaissance poetics and are the direct forerunners of baroque poetry. Here is an abridged example of a love poem from the Ranjina collection:

> O zvizde ljuvene,
> gdi ljubav drži sve strile ognijene,
> njiste li vi oni
> tatovi skroveni,
> ki srce ukrasti hotjeste jur meni?
> (...) pak srce vraťte mi, ko ukrast nebogu
> htiste mi, bez njega er živit nemogu.

O stars of love, where love keeps all its fiery arrows, are you not the stealthy thieves who intended to steal my heart? . . . then give me back my heart, you who would steal from a poor man like me, for I cannot live without it.

The images of the poem can hardly be traced back to folklore, and the many plays on words are just as much a part of *art* poetry:

> Oj, vilo, koj služu vernije neg sužan,
> (...) vaj, nestričan i tužan,
> zač gore dvaš goru neg gora, ka gori
> u moru, ku plavi, ke plovu, sve mori.

O fairy, whom I serve more truly than a slave . . . how unhappy and sad for I burn twice as badly as the wood that floats in the sea, tormenting all who sail there.

Significantly, all Dalmatian poets of the time had Italian names as well as Slavic. And besides poets who wrote in Slavic there were always those Croatian poets who wrote in neo-Latin.[1]

7. Polish humanism originated as a result of the influence of the Italian Renaissance and developed under French and German influence. The university of Padua again played an important part along with other schools, some of them German. No less important was the effect of humanists who came to Poland: Philipp Kallimach (Buonacorsi, in Poland from 1470, died there in 1496), Konrad Celtes (in Poland in the 1480s and 1490s), Heinrich Bebel (in Poland from 1492 to 1495), and others. New intellectual currents came with them to the university at Cracow, and their adherents were the first important representatives of Polish humanism, or neo-Latin poetry, and of scholarly literature (see below, 9). At first medieval Latin works were also translated. But by the second third of the sixteenth century there had appeared an original vernacular literature of considerable poetic quality.

Mikołaj Rej from Nagłović, a well-read member of the bourgeoisie who had been influenced by Protestantism, was a satirist of the predominantly bourgeois life of his time and often assumed the moralistic tone of a preacher of the Gospel. This first use of Polish in such extensive works was a remarkable step forward for the new vernacular literatures. At the same time, another writer, Marcin Bielski, appeared on the scene. He is the author of the extensive *World Chronicle* (*Kronika wszystkiego*

1. Marin Držić should be mentioned here. Držić was an extremely talented Dalmatian playwright who not only followed Italian models but also created several original characters and introduced into his medium some new and interesting devices (editor).

świata), satirical-moralistic prose works, and a play in verse. Bielski also reflects the influence of Western Renaissance literature, Erasmus, and Czech poetry as well as Polish Protestantism.

The art of a younger representative of Polish Renaissance poetry, Jan Kochanowski, is on a quite different level. Few works by his Slavic contemporaries still seem to us as fresh and full-blooded. His almost seven years of travel abroad, in particular his studies at the university of Padua, brought him into contact with the Renaissance and with classical learning. A trip to France acquainted him with French Renaissance literature. At home in the 1560s he published Latin and Polish verse. The variety of his genres is astonishing. He wrote epigrams (Fraszki), a genre that particularly flourished in Poland, satirical-didactic poems (Satyr), a didactic-political play, songs, lyrical poems, a verse translation of the Psalter, and finally, a year before his death (1584), elegies (Threny)— lamentations on the death of his young daughter, Ursula. His language is vivid, lucid, and beautiful and was certainly close to the hearts and minds of his contemporaries. Although one is first struck by the technical virtuosity of his works, one is also impressed by his politically tendentious thoughts, by his more or less keen humor, and, in the *Threny*, above all by the language of the human heart. These qualities are not impaired by the somewhat cold and formal perfection of expression, schooled as it was on Petrarch and Ronsard.

These first steps in Polish literature stimulated contemporaries of the great poet to write in prose and verse, in Latin and Polish, seriously and humorously. In many of the younger contemporaries of Kochanowski, such as Sęp-Szarzyński, Klonowicz, Sz. Szymonowic, one can detect features of baroque style (see Chapter VIII). These features can also be found in works by Kochanowski (W. Weintraub).

Kochanowski's songs are often reminiscent of Horace, as, for example, the imitation of Horace, *Carmen I, 9.*

> Patrzaj, jako śnieg po górach się bieli,
> wiatry z północy wstają,
> jeziora się ścinają,
> żorawie, czując zimę, przecz lecieli...

> See, how white the snow shines on the hills
> and winds rise up from midnight;
> the lakes freeze over,
> the cranes, sensing winter, have flown away.

And another scene:

> O piękna nocy nad zwyczaj tych czasów,
> patrz na nas jasno wpośrzód tych tu lasów,
> gdzie jako pszczoły, wkoło swego pana
> straż dzierżem niecąc ognie aż do rana...

> O night, lovelier than usual at this time,
> look down brightly on us in the midst of these woods,
> where like bees around our master
> we keep watch, fanning the fire till morning . . .

Or the symbol of the poet:

> Kto mi dał skrzydła, kto mię odział pióry
> i tak wysoko postawił, że z góry
> wszystek świat widzę, a sam, jako trzeba
> tykam się nieba?

> Who gave me wings, who, a suit of feathers
> and placed me so high that from these heights
> I behold the entire world and when need be
> touch heaven?

Or these lines from *Thren VIII:*

> Wielkieś mi uczyniła pustki w domu moim,
> moja droga Orszuło, tym zniknieniem swoim!
> Pełno, nas, a jakoby nikogo ne było:
> jedną maluczką duszą tak wiele ubyło.
> Tyś za wszytki mówiła, za wszytki śpiewała

> Teraz wszytko umilkło, szczere pustki w domu,
> nie masz zabawki, nie masz rośmiać się nikomu.
> Z każdego kąta żałość człowieka ujmuje,
> a serce swej pociechy darmo upatruje.

> You have brought great emptiness to my house,
> my dear Ursula, by your disappearing!
> There are many of us, but it is as though no one were here:
> so much is lost by one little soul.
> You spoke for us all, sang for us all. . . .
> Now everything is silent; there is utter loneliness in the house,
> no diversion, no cause to laugh.
> From every corner one is seized by sadness,
> and the heart looks in vain for solace.

Characteristically, there are constant references to the classics in the

Threny: Heraclitus, Simonides, Proserpina (= Persephone), Niobe, Sappho, Charon, Brutus, Orpheus, Pluto. Mythological allusions are juxtaposed with the Christian God (Bóg, Pan). One can see how many elements of Renaissance poetics were felt to be needed in even a personal lyric elegy!

The most significant Polish preacher of the sixteenth century, Piotr Skarga, who died in 1612, completed the transition to Baroque style in his sermons, not all of which have been printed.

8. Bilingualism is an almost general characteristic of Slavic Renaissance literature (Slavic, Latin, Italian). Besides secular poetry, there is also religious verse, often reformatory. As a result of the interest in the Slavs shown by the Wittenbergers, especially Melanchthon, the Slavs were rather close to the Reformation.

Among the Czechs this is reflected mainly by Hussite literature of different casts and later by Lutheran literature; in Poland the Calvinists and the theologically and socially radical Socinianists—anti-Trinitarianists, or Unitarians, also called "Arians" in Poland—played an important part. The style of writing of these groups was not always on a level with that of secular Renaissance literature, although their ties with it were often close. They were more serious and less interested in poetic embellishment. But this literature also contributed significantly to the development of the language.

Of particular interest among the Czechs is the versatile leader of the moderate Hussites, Jan Blahoslav, who wrote musicological, homiletic, and grammatical works in addition to his religious writings and was instrumental in the newly revised translation of the Bible (the "Kralická Bible," 1579 ff.). In his introduction to the art of preaching, Blahoslav took a somewhat sceptical view of Renaissance stylistics with its wealth of ornamentation, and in this respect he continues the Hussite tradition. Among the Poles, Stanisław Orzechowski (Orechovius or Orichovius) is a representative religious writer of the time. He called himself "gente Ruthenus, natione Polonus" and received an education in Rome and Wittenberg that was not altogether suitable for his Catholic religiosity. Wujek's Catholic edition of the Bible (completed in 1599) and the attempts by Protestant writers to render the Scriptures, especially the New Testament, into simple vernacular were also important contributions. The Slovenian Lutheran Primus Trubar undertook a number of printings in Germany for Slovenes and Croats. The Croat Antun Dalmatin published the Croatian Bible in Germany in 1584. His Slovenian namesake, Juraj Dalmatin, published the Holy Scriptures in Slovenian beginning in 1576; the work was completed in 1584. These publications were of significance in the development of the South Slavic languages, especially Slovenian.

9. The Renaissance prompted scholarly undertakings among the Slavs and contributed to the development of the vernacular in secular and Church literature. Even stronger was the effect of the reform movement, which sought to spread God's word to all people in their own language. This gave rise to the grammatical and lexical works of the Czechs. Besides Blahoslav (see 9) one should mention M. Benešovský's Czech grammar, 1577, the Latin grammar of the Slovak V. B. z Nudožer, the dictionaries of T. Rešel and Daniel Adam z Veleslavín, 1598, and a related work, Jakub Srnec's collection of proverbs.

Historical works told the West about the Slavs.

Theological works by Slavic adherents of the reform movement, especially by the radical Socianists, were highly regarded abroad—among others by Spinoza, Locke, Milton, Newton, Hugo Grotius (see also VIII, 1).

The Croatian Flacius Illyricus (Vlačić) made a place for himself in the history of the German Reformation, disturbing his contemporaries with his radical theological views. The Pole Andrzej Frycz Modrzewski (Modrevius) was the author of an important book on public law, *De republica emendanda* (Basil, 1554, an abridged German edition in 1557).

10. It has recently been pointed out that Hungary, especially the court of King Matthias Corvinus, was a gathering place at which humanists from the various Slavic peoples, Croats, Poles, Czechs, and Slovaks, collaborated and created a considerable tradition of Latin and Hungarian Renaissance literature. As a result of a common Latin literary language and of the travels of Slavic humanists to other Slavic countries the various Slavic literatures were also in close touch with each other (I. Goleniščev-Kutuzov).

11. The development of vernacular literature served to perfect orthography (Hussite orthography among the Czechs, see Chapter VI, 4) and create an acceptable literary vocabulary, which included many words required to express the new concepts and secular and erotic ideas.

12. Among the East Slavs, the Renaissance was of secondary importance, but here too one could collect extensive materials on the influence that it had.

The Renaissance was conveyed to the East Slavs mainly by the Poles, who passed on their culture easily to their subjects the White Russians and the Ukrainians. This influence was not widely felt, however, until after the spread of baroque culture. The effect on Great Russia or Muscovy came later and was less pronounced. White Russians and Ukrainians passed on the Polish influence to Russia.

The White Russian and Ukrainian nobility and bourgeoisie had been exposed to Polish culture in the Polish-Lithuanian state. Everyone in these circles whom we know well, who had studied abroad, and who wrote in Latin came under the influence of Polish culture. Good examples are Orechovius or Szymonovicz (see above), who in his idylls written in Polish and Latin also pictures Ukrainian peasant life.

The influence on the White Russians seems to go back further. After studying in Cracow and Padua, Franzisk Skorina set up printing presses in Prague in 1517 and later in Vilnius and printed a Bible translated into a White-Russian version of Church Slavonic. When this undertaking proved unsuccessful, Skorina emigrated to Prague. In the 1560s the White Russian Protestant (Calvinist, later Socianist) Simon Budnyj began to publish Slavic works, among them the Catechism. But after about ten years he began writing exclusively in Polish.[2] From a manuscript which has since disappeared and from which Bodjanśkyj published several religious songs translated from German we know that poetry was already being written by the White Russians.

Somewhat later, the new literature appeared in the Ukraine, first of all a redaction of the Holy Scriptures made in the second half of the sixteenth century, with emphasis on the Gospels and a strong use of the vernacular. In various cities "civic schools" were founded and later an "academy" in Ostrog. The complete edition of the Bible published in Ostrog in 1581 restored the Church Slavonic tradition of Biblical language. In the 1590s an interesting polemic literature was written in defense of Greek Orthodoxy and in opposition to Catholics and Socianists. Scarcely any features of the new ideology are to be found here, and few of the new rhetorical style. In the works of the most significant Ukrainian polemicist of the time, Ivan Vyšenśkyj, who died before 1625,[3] one finds the first signs of baroque style. It was at this time that the first printed grammar of Church Slavonic appeared (Meletij Smotryćkyj, 1619), along with a brief Church Slavonic dictionary (Zizanij, 1596). A larger dictionary by P. Berynda followed in 1627.[4]

2. Polish historians usually claim that Simon Budnyj was a Pole from Masovia (editor).

3. Ivan Vyšenskyj energetically fought the Roman Catholic efforts to convert Western Russian peoples to the Roman faith and defended Orthodox Russian (as he called himself) tradition (editor).

4. A very large role in the revival of literature in the Western Russian lands,

There is evidence that the classical authors were read in these circles, and we have quotations from Renaissance literature—among others from Petrarch, Boccaccio, Aeneas Silvius, L. Valla, Machiavelli, Pico de la Mirandola, Cusanus, Cardanus, and Erasmus. Quotations can, of course, be secondhand. It is not until the baroque that we can demonstrate a serious interest in Renaissance literature from descriptions of private libraries.

Scarcely anything was known of Renaissance literature in Russia until the seventeenth century. The Greek monk Maxim Grek, who worked as a translator in Moscow in the sixteenth century, had studied in Italy but later took a negative view of the Renaissance. His acquaintances learned something about the Renaissance, from him or from Polish sources. In a letter written before 1560 the diplomat Fedor Karpov quoted Aristotle, Ovid, and Sallust. The Russian prince Andrej Kurbskij, who had fled to Poland, translated Cicero into Slavic there and read Erasmus—but he had probably not been familiar with them before going to Poland. The Russians learned something more about the Renaissance in the seventeenth century. There is no persuasive evidence that they had previously known very much about it at all (M. Alekseev, I. Goleniščev-Kutuzov).

13. The Renaissance did not reach the Slavs until the last phase of its development. As has been emphasized, it was often modified by reform movements and often repressed. Much of what the Renaissance sought to do was never fulfilled. Enthusiasm was replaced by cold rhetoric, the universal, versatile man proved all too often to be a self-centered adventurer who strove only for power. The freedom that had been longed for turned out to be caprice, and to a large extent the knowledge of nature proved to be illusory. The satirical literature of the Renaissance was more influential with the Slavs than works of literary beauty. The baroque, which had already appeared in the West, now reached the Slavic countries and conquered them with little resistance.

Belorussia and the Ukraine, was played by Great Russian emigres, Prince Andrej Kurbskij, abbott Artemij, printers Ivan Iedorov, and others who escaped from Muscovy during the reign of Ivan IV (editor).

VIII

BAROQUE

Croatians (Dalmatians)

I. Gundulić (1588–1638): The epic *Osman*
J. Palmotić (1606–1657): plays
J. Bunić-Vučićević (1594–1658): lyrics, the epic *Magdalene Repentant*
Ignjat Djordjić (1675–1737)

Poles

M. Sęp-Szarzyński (about 1550–1581)
Krzysztof Opaliński (about 1610–1656): satires
Andrzej Morsztyn (1608–1693)
K. Sarbiewski (1595–1640): Latin poetry
Wespasian Kochowski (1633–1700)
Wacław Potocki (1635–1696)
Samuel Twardowski (1660)

Czechs

Jan Amos Komenský (Comenius) (1592–1670)
Bedřich Bridel (1619–1680)
Adam Michna z Otradovic (1600–1676)
de Waldt (beginning of the eighteenth century)

88

Slovaks

J. Tranovský (1591–1637): Latin odes, Lutheran song book
Matthias Bél (1684–1749)
H. Gavlovič (1712–1787)

Ukrainians

Antonij Radyvylovśkyj (1688): sermons
Saint Dmitrij of Rostov (Tuptalo 1671–1709):
saints' lives, sermons, poetry
Ivan Velyčkovśky (1727)
Hryhorij Skovoroda (1722–1794): philosophical dialogues, lyrics

Great Russians

Simeon Polockij (1629–1680) (of White Russian origin)
V. K. Trediakovskij (1703–1769)
Antiox Kantemir (1709–1744)
M. V. Lomonosov (1711–1765)
G. R. Deržavin (1743–1816) (belated echo of the baroque)

1. Slavic baroque literature has for some time attracted the attention of Slavists. As early as 1893, E. Porębowicz published a work on Jan Andrzej Morsztyn (1613–1693) as a Polish poet of the baroque and demonstrated the influence of Italian baroque poetry on Morsztyn. Research on the period was advanced when in 1930 J. Vašica called attention to the significant but previously neglected Czech baroque poet B. Bridel (1619–1680) and published a series of articles on other Czech poets of the baroque. Besides articles by other scholars (Z. Kalista, V. Bitnar) on Czech baroque poetry, works soon appeared on Ukrainian (D. Čiževskij) and Russian (I. Eremin, Čiževskij) literature of the baroque. Croatian literature has also been dealt with, but not yet adequately.

In treating Slavic literatures of the seventeenth century (from about 1590 to 1740), it was formerly the custom to leave out of account their stylistic unity and to consider them the product of pure arbitrariness and an "unhealthy" striving for originality at any price. Since the content of works was judged and appraised from the ideological point of view that was then "modern" (1850–1910), the works were found alienated from life and the masses and thought to be belated epigones of medieva scholasticism. In an age in which philosophical positivism and literary realism predominated (even without the influence of Benedetto Croce, who condemned Italian baroque literature) it was inevitable that this entire era should be rejected. The period was regarded as a decline from the preceding Renaissance or an aberration on the way to the subsequent classicism.

More recently the term "baroque" has been used pejoratively, and an unproductive polemic discussion has developed around the existence of Slavic baroque poetry (although the existence of baroque style in Slavic music and plastic arts has been recognized). Baroque literature has been taken to be the "literature of the Counter Reformation," although one can trace the same stylistic developments among Protestants—among the Poles, for instance, the Anti-Trinitarians (Unitarians) or Socianists, among the Czechs, J. A. Comenius—and in the Greek Orthodox Church. Sometimes baroque poets, those in Russia for example, have been regarded as random, individual cases.

2. Like Renaissance literature, baroque literature was originally influenced by the West. As it happened, the various Slavic literatures were particularly close at the time of the baroque.

The earliest impulses radiated from Italy to the people most closely connected with Italy, either culturally (Italian universities were cultural centers) or economically and politically: the Croats, the Poles, and the Czechs. Traces of baroque style appear rather early among these peoples, in the last third of the sixteenth century. Later, influences from France, Spain, and Germany were also felt. Mainly as a result of Polish influence, Ukrainian and White Russian literature were won over to the baroque, and all three literatures decisively influenced Great Russian literature from the middle of the seventeenth century on.

One must remember that baroque literature did not develop without peripeteia in the Slavic lands: among the Czechs and Poles there was religious and political discord; in Russia, an essential reform of the literary language in connection with "Europeanization," which resulted in a break in the baroque literary tradition;[1] among the Ukrainians and White Russians, a political decline.

1. It was the rift between the followers of the old Muscovite literary and intellectual tradition—the so-called old believers (e.g., Avvakum and Denisovs)—and the main or official literary school of modernizing the Russian state (Polockij, Lomonosov, etc.) (editor).

The connection between Slavic baroque poetry and West European can be shown in the following diagram:

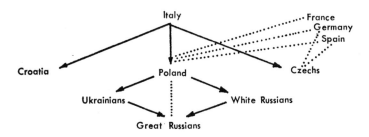

Secondary effects on the lesser Slavic literatures cannot be dealt with here.

3. Among the Croatians, elements of baroque style can be detected in a poet of the sixteenth century, D. Zlatarić (1558–1609). The seventeenth century is the golden age of Croatian (Dalmatian) literature: besides the great epic poet I. Gundulić (1588–1638), whose incomplete epic *Osman* is one of the most important Slavic epics, there was the playwright I. Palmotić (1606–1657) and the lyric poet I. Bunić-Vučićević (1594–1658). Their works are closely connected with Italian literature—the literary center of the time, the aristocratic republic Dubrovnik (Ragusa), maintained close cultural ties with Italy.

Although Dalmatian writers came from the upper class of their republic, in Polish literature all educated classes and all creeds were represented. Traces of baroque style can be found in the work of M. Sęp-Szarzyński (1550–1584), who died early and who was a young contemporary of the great Renaissance poet Jan Kochanowski (see Chapter VII). These features appear more clearly in S. Klonowicz (1545–1607), whose work is satirical and didactic, and in the Polish idylls of Sz. Szymonowicz (1558–1629), who wrote mainly in Latin. Typical of Polish baroque are Jan Andrzej Morsztyn (1613–1693, other members of his family also wrote baroque poetry), who was the greatest master of poetic form and on whom the influence of Marini was considerable; the author of epigrams and odes W. Kochowski (1633–1700); and the extremely productive Waclaw Potocki (1625–1696), who wrote unevenly but at times excellently in several veins. Among numerous other writers one should mention Samuel Twardowski (1600–1660), St. H. Lubomirski (1636–1702), who also dealt with questions of poetic theory, the satirist K. Opaliński (about 1600–1656), and, with certain reservations, the preacher Piotr Skarga (1536–1612).

Among the Czechs there were baroque motifs by the end of the six-teenth century. But the first representative works of the baroque are the early, moralistic-satirical works of Jan Amos Comenius (also called Komenský, 1592–1670), especially the famous *Labyrinth of the World and Paradise of the Heart* (1617). Among religious lyricists Bedřich Bridel (1619–1680) and Adam Michna z Otradovic (1600–1676), who was also a composer, are especially deserving of mention. Among the many preachers who sometimes published only a few, artistically out-standing sermons one should mention Fabian Veselý (1648–1729) and A. F. de Waldt (1683–1752), both of them remembered for their large collections of sermons. The Protestant Slovak J. Tranovský (Latin Tranoscius, 1591–1637) wrote Church songs that are still in use and poetry and songs in Latin.

Ukrainian baroque literature is even more religious than Czech. Among the many preachers, some of them talented, we shall mention only Dmitrij of Rostov (surname Tuptalo, 1671–1709), a preacher, poet, and hagiographer, who, like many Ukrainians, wrote in Moscow and in Russian. Some of the many chroniclers may also be included among the secular poets; among them is the epigrammatist and "master of the small form," the priest Ivan Velyčkovśkyj (died around 1724), an imitator of the neo-Latin epigrammatist Ovenus. A late representative of Baroque mysticism, H. S. Skovoroda (1722–1794), is also important. In the lan-guage of most of these writers Church Slavonic elements are still quite usual.

Polish-Ukrainian baroque literature was taken to Great Russia by the White Russian priest Simeon Polockij (1629–1680), who had been educated at the Kievan Academy and had gone to Moscow to preach and teach. His pupils were not as important as writers who came after the modernization of Russia by Peter I and after the secularization of the language. Among these later writers are the satirist Prince Antiox Kantemir (of Rumanian descent, 1709–1744) and the scholars V. K. Trediakovskij (1703–1769) and M. V. Lomonosov (1711–1765). Tredia-kovskij and Lomonosov freed Russian versification from the rules of Polish syllabic verse and laid the foundation for syllabic-accentual verse. The most important Russian poet of the late eighteenth century, G. R. Deržavin (1743–1816), still reflects the tradition of the baroque.

4. One should mention that this period was a time of many anonymous works among all the Slavs. These works include plays, some of them intended for school theaters, and occasional poems, often quite inter-esting.

During the baroque, an unprecedented number of scholarly works, most of them in Latin, appeared among the Slavs. These works were of quite different kinds, from theological text books and treatises written by Polish anti-Trinitarians (Socianists) and the Greek Orthodox Urkainian Bishop Feofan Prokopovyč (who wrote in Russian) to the scientific, physical, and astronomical writings of M. V. Lomonosov, who also dealt with Russian grammar and rhetoric. Piotr Skarga and Saint Dmitrij carried on hagiographical research and presented their findings in Slavic art prose. Mention should be made of the Church Slavonic grammar that was written by the White Russian Meletij Smotrickij (1577–1633) and was influential in the Balkans. The Catholic Croat J. Križanić (1618–1683) left behind "Slavophile" political writings and valuable scholarship on intonation or musical stress in Serbo-Croatian. The lexical contributions of this period are also important, especially the works on language teaching by J. A. Comenius, who was a significant pedagogic theoretician, theologian, and philosopher (D. Mahnke). The Czech author of several historical and hagiographical works, B. Balbín (1621–1688), also wrote a Latin "defense" of the Czech language. There were similar works among the Czechs and Poles. Historians with political and national tendencies in their chronicle writing were to be found among various Slavic peoples. The Slovak Matthias Bél (1684–1749) collected and partly published topographical and historical material on Hungary, including the Slavic regions. In the eighteenth century the Croat R. Bošković (1711–1787) published important physical and astronomical works. Unfortunately we still know little about lecture notes preserved in manuscript form and written by Slavs or on Slavic themes, such as poetics.

There is a rather large group of Slavic poets who wrote primarily or exclusively in Latin. Comenius, for example, wrote Latin plays for school theatres; and many of his Latin works, such as *Angelus pacis* (1669) and *Unum Necessarium* (not published until 1681), are poetically significant. Important writers among the neo-Latinists were the Czech playwright K. Kolčava (1656–1717) and in particular the Polish lyricist K. Sarbiewski (Sarbevius, 1595–1640), whose odes were read along with the *Carmina* of Horace in eighteenth-century schools. Latin works by Slavic writers were often published in Western Europe.

5. One has to admit at the outset that it is difficult to characterize baroque literature, for reasons that we shall presently discuss.

It is perhaps easiest for one to understand the essence of this style when one bears in mind that the baroque was to some extent an attempt to return to the Middle Ages but that it wished to preserve many of the achievements of the Renaissance, and among Protestants, those of the Reformation. As a result, various elements of Late Medieval and Renaissance style are mixed in the baroque. This characterization is of course not exhaustive, but it accounts for the essential features of the baroque.

In what respect was there a return to the Middle Ages or an attempt to return? One finds a resumption of Late Medieval tendencies, for example, in questions of artistic theory. Instead of the harmonious transparency of the Renaissance there is complex multiplicity, best typified by Late Gothic. Instead of the simplicity of the Renaissance there is in the baroque a complexity that causes every simple line to be adorned with countless diverting and decorative figures. Perhaps most important, instead of the anthropocentrism of the Renaissance the baroque places God at the center of the universe; this return to theocentrism reminds us very much of the Middle Ages. Instead of the worldly character of a largely "secularized" culture, culture again takes on a religious cast. Instead of man liberated from all bonds, sometimes only supposedly, man recognizes social and religious norms. All of this means that the role of the Church and state has become more prominent.

At the same time, the baroque assumes in many ways the legacy of the Renaissance. The "rebirth" of the classics continues, although the baroque interprets them differently and attempts to reconcile them with Christianity.

Consequently we find names of classical heroes and gods in literature, and even in religious writings. Classical mythology with its traditional mixture of Greek and Roman elements was a source of images and symbols for writers. The fusion of the Christian with the classical is sometimes grotesque: the Virgin Mary is Diana; Neptune's trident is interpreted as a symbol for the Christian cross; poets call on both saints and muses.

The baroque is also concerned with nature—the greatest discoveries of modern science, from Galileo and Kepler to Harvey and Linné, were made during the baroque! Nature, however, is thought to be only the path to God; whoever remains within nature has lost his way.

Encyclopedic undertakings that also treat the natural sciences are characteristic of Slavic thinkers and theologians (the Protestant Comenius and the Catholic Bošković).

The Renaissance ideal of the "noble" man has not disappeared, but the noble man no longer wears the mask of a condottiere; rather he is trained to serve God or to look to the future life.

Comenius asks that "all mankind be made as much as possible to re-
semble the image of God in which it is created, that is, truly sensible
and wise, truly active and zealous, truly constant and honorable, truly
pious and holy and thereby happy and blissful—here and in eternity
[*sic!*]." (*Pampaedia I, 8*).

What is especially typical of baroque culture and what lends it its
individual character is "dynamism." In the plastic arts this means the
preference of the "dynamic" curve to the straight lines and semicircle
of the Renaissance and to the acute angle and parallel lines of Gothic
style. In life and in literature one finds a longing for change; at the risk
of catastrophic consequences one loves tragic tension, bold combinations, and adventures.

The nomadic life of many baroque writers did not necessarily reflect
their wishes. Comenius wandered through Europe as a student and
later as an exile; he accepted invitations to England, Sweden, and Hungary. Polish anti-Trinitarians went abroad as refugees. Križanić went
to Moscow with utopian intentions, was exiled to Siberia, and was not
able to return home for many years. There were also men who volun-
tarily left home forever, such as A. Morsztyn who died as "Comte de
Chateauvillain" in France. By the seventeenth century, study abroad
had already become a tradition with the Slavs.

In nature too one found change, tension, and motion. The baroque
did not shy away from a decisive "naturalism": one dared to portray
nature with its hard, strict, dark, and often unaesthetic features. Along
with descriptions of intensive, sanguine, colorful life (the erotic quality
of baroque literature is often pervasive), frightening and terrifying pictures of death are a specific theme.

A series of poems by A. Morsztyn is entitled *Swińska plebanija* (*The
Swinish Pastorate*), and this is not the worst example. After his religious
conversion, W. Potocki removed a number of obscene epigrams from
his *Ogród fraszek* (*Garden of Epigrams*). The authors of popular comic
poems were evidently of the opinion that "naturalia non sunt turpia."
Toward the end of the century a wave of "anti-Petrarchism" prompted
writers to limit eroticism to matters of sex.

Poems and prose works on the "four ultimate things of man" were
popular—on death, doomsday, heaven, and hell. Examples are a Czech
book (Olomouc, 1626); a Ukrainian *Book of Death* (1622); and a Ukrainian poem in the *Precious Pearl* by Kirill Trankvillion Stravrovećkyj
(1646). Various "death dances" and horrible war scenes are customary
in historical writing and chronicles of the time.

The baroque did not think it the task of art to awaken a calm esthetic or religious sensation, but to stir, to excite, to shock. The principal stylistic features of baroque art and literature are closely connected with this aim of disquieting, thus the desire for intensity, exaggeration, hyperbole, the predilection for paradox and oxymoron, the tendency to "oddness," to the grotesque, to tension and antithesis and to large forms, to the comprehensive and universal.

All the oppositions between heaven and earth in Bridel's important work *Co Bůh? člověk? (What is God? What is Man?)* are, of course, based on antitheses, just as in the religious works of Gundulić, Bunić, and others. Gundulić's epic *Osman* begins;

> Sve što više stereš krila,
> sve ćeš paka niže pasti! (I, 3 f.),

> The higher you spread your wings,
> the farther you will fall . . .

and:

> tko bi gori, cto je doli,
> a kto doli, gori ostaje (I, 15 f.),

> Whoever was high is now low,
> whoever was low is elevated to the heights . . .

Paradox and oxymoron are popular. A series of poems is reminiscent of "falsehood fairy tales"; others present "menus" made up of inedible and nonmaterial objects. A. Morsztyn sings the praises of ugly women. The themes of poems are often grotesque: beauty patches, tobacco (A. Morsztyn), epigrams on noses (W. Kochowski), on various kinds of death, on cats, on all sorts of trades (the Ukrainian monk Klementij), on the dogs of beloved ladies. Even in religious poetry we find the boldest reversals of metaphors and topoi (the "locus horribilis" in saints' lives is the reversal of the traditional "locus amoenus"). Other grotesqueries are various "concetti" (see below) and frequent ambiguous riddles, of which A. Morsztyn is the master.

Among the longer works are epic (there are several Croatian epics on Biblical themes) and didactic poems. Besides those works of Bridel already mentioned there is his *Meditations*, in which a familiar metaphor, the world as a book, is developed in all its details. Epigrams, written mostly in long cycles, are also important, especially those of W. Potocki, who composed hundreds, and W. Kochowski. In Ukrainian literature the cycles are usually short and are called "wreathes."

6. Heavy ornamentation and a variety of ornamental devices are

typical of baroque literature. Among the most important devices are the euphonic: besides anaphora and epiphora (the "echo poems"—*carmina echoica*—are a variation of the latter) there are various other kinds of sound harmony in poetry and in art prose.

Probably inspired by the *Musurgia* of Athanasius Kirchner, the Czech poet J. Kořínek composed his *Nightingale Sonnets* of semantically unconnected sounds in imitation of the nightingale's song. Alliteration, repetition of individual word stems or syllables, and euphonic word play are customary in Slavic baroque poetry. This repetition of words, which is generally avoided in poetry, occurs especially often in epigrams. W. Kochowski and I. Velyčkovśkyj translated an epigram by Ovenus based on word repetition and both increased the number of repeated words. Kochowski:

> *Nago się* wszyscy *na świat ten* mizerny *rodzim,*
> z tego *świata* strojniejszy w koszuli odchodzim.
> Więcej wracamy matce neżeli nam dala,
> ktora *nago na ten świat rodzić się* kazała.

[We have italicized the repeated words.]
> We are all born naked into this world of suffering,
> we leave the world better clothed, in a shroud.
> We give Mother [Nature] more back than she gave us,
> [she] who sent us naked into the world.

Another artistic device is rhythm, which gives rise to a complicated stanza that is at times partly destroyed and partly emphasized by enjambment. Unusual, surprising rhymes are used, and the euphony is often heightened by internal rhyme. These stylistic effects are not used modestly but boldly.

One frequently encounters selected rhymes with unusual endings. In A. Morsztyn, for example, there are twelve words that end in "-odze" in twenty-one lines. In a 304-line poem by Zbigniew Morsztyn on the siege of Cracow there are eighty-eight rhymes in "-aku". Here are some examples of compound rhymes in W. Potocki: *Marija, i ja; ja cie, bracie; po tem, złotem; co ma, lakoma;* and in Velyčkovśkyj: *tátja, na tja; na to, zlato,* etc. Clever use is also made of identical rhymes. Poems are written to "bouts rimés"—rhyming words or syllables to which verses are to be written. Internal rhymes are used, for instance, in the "versus leonini": *Čysta ptycja, / holubycja / svojstvo to imiet', / že de misto / jijz ne čysto, / tamo ne počiet'.* (The pure bird, the dove, has the peculiarity of not resting in a place that seems to it unclean.) (Ukrainian, anonymous, seventeenth century).

The metaphysics of baroque literature is conspicuous and often strange. The meaning of a metaphor is frequently changed to the opposite meaning; an image that is usually positive is given a pejorative interpretation, and so forth. Commonplaces are partly or wholly transformed. Metaphors, hyperboles, and other stylistic devices often appear in long series; and the usual enumerations or "catalogues" are favored. Baroque catalogues are distinguished from those of the Renaissance primarily by their variegation and disconnectedness—here too one attempts to surprise and produce grotesque effects. Even in religious poetry one resorts to bold paradox.

In A. Michna a Otradovic's poem "The Spiritual Hunt" the object of the hunt is the heart of the Mother of God! Skovoroda uses an emetic as a metaphor for Communion: it is supposed to cleanse the soul. In the *Meditations* of Bridel, already mentioned, the basic metaphor—the world as a book—is broken down into a number of partial metaphors. In a long poem by A. Morsztyn more than a hundred drinks, from wine to dirty water, are cleverly characterized in epigrams.

It is apparent from our discussion that the long, epic form and the short, epigrammatic form were both known to baroque poetry. Playful forms of various kinds were also widely disseminated, from the euphonic works already mentioned to poems intended more for the eye, like the figure poems (in the form of an egg, cup, cross, even the Russian-Orthodox cross with eight ends, the crescent of the moon); the "chronological poems," in which especially emphasized letters form a date; the "versus cancrini," the lines of which can be read word for word or letter for letter from right to left or from left to right, at times reversing the sense; the alphabet poems, the stanzas of which and sometimes the words of which (as in Velyčkovśkyj) begin with letters in the order of the alphabet. Acrostics too can be made out only with the eye, not the ear. Letters arranged in a pattern discernible to the eye spell out various words and sentences in some poems. Poetry of this kind was taken seriously and seems to have pleased both the poet and the reader. Even the peculiar macaronic poems, written in various languages mixed together, were popular.

Here are the opening lines of a "versus cancrinus" by A. Morsztyn to a lady:

> Cnota cię rządzi, nie pragniesz pieniędzy,
> złota dosyć masz, nie boisz się nędzy...

You are guided by virtue; you are not greedy for gold, you have enough gold; you have no fear of want . . .

The poem has just the opposite meaning if one reads it from right to left. And it still sounds like a poem!

Macaronic poems mixed Latin and Polish in Poland, Croatian and Italian among the Croats. We also find mixtures of Slavic languages, such as Polish and Ukrainian and other, random idioms: there is a poem written in 1642 that contains Polish, Ukrainian, Lithuanian, Greek, Latin, and German words along with words from an unfamiliar language (Gypsy dialect or rogue's language).

We run across dialects, children's language, and argot of various kinds:

In "Flis" ("Raft") by Klonowicz, words from the raftsmen's idiom are used; in Kořínek's portrayal of Kuttenberg and in Roździeński's "Officina ferraria" (1612), one finds the argot of Czech and Polish miners.

Among the choice forms of poems are sonnets, octaves, "versus rapportati" (the last line repeats the content of the poem), and "versus reticulati," in which the meaning becomes apparent only after one has read the individual words in horizontal rows.

Here is an example of "versus rapportati" by Bunić:

> Bio je videti, kada se raskrili
> i hoce letjeti lijepi *kuf* pribili;
> bio se može rijet' nad stvari se ine,
> ke zdrži ovi svijet, čisti *snijeg* planine;
> bijelo je i svijeće od *lira* gledati,
> kada go prolić veselo razvrati:
> i *mlijeko* je, bijelo, koje je prižela
>
> iz stada premila pastierka vesela;
> bijela je i *zora*, kad zrakom navijesti,
> da nam će doskora veseo dan dovesti.
> Nathodi daleko bjeloća me vile
> *kufa, snijeg, lijer, mlijeko,* zrak *zore* primile.

The splendid white swan is white when he spreads his wings and prepares to fly; the fresh snow in the mountains is whiter, one might say, than all the other things of this world; the blossom of the lily is white to look upon when the spring gladly opens it; white too is the milk that the lovely, gay shepherdess brings fresh from the herd; white too is the morning star when it announces that it will soon lead on the cheerful day: but the white of my fairy exceeds all of these by far: the swan, the snow, the lily, the milk, and the morning star.

The last lines of a "versus reticulatus" by A. Morsztyn, run:

> ...oczy, usta, piersi
> rozum, zmysł i wolą

> blaskiem, farbą i kształtem
> ćmią, wiążą, niewolą.

Your eyes, mouth, bosom darken, bind, enslave understanding, senses, and will by brilliance, color, and form.

Finally, conceits, or extended metaphors, were borrowed from the West, were used as a basis for poems, sermons, or tales, and played an important part in the composition of Slavic baroque works. An example is the portrayal of love, secular or religious, as a torment, a sickness, or a paradoxical combination of frost and glowing fire (the heat of summer or hell fire) or of life and death. In A. Morsztyn we find,

Do trupa

> Leżysz zabity, i jam też zabity,
> Ty—strzałą śmierci, ja—strzałą miłości,
> Ty krwie, ja w sobie nie mam rumianości,
> Ty jawne świece, ja mam płomień skryty.
>
> Tyś na twarz suknem żałobnym nakryty,
> Jam zawarł zymsły w okropnej ciemności,
> Ty masz związane ręce, ja wolności
> Zbywszy mam rozum łańcuchem powity.
>
> Ty jednak milczysz, a mój język kwili,
> Ty nic nie czujesz, ja cierpię ból srodze,
> Ty jak lód, a jam w piekielnej śrzeżodze,
>
> Ty się rozsypiesz prochem w małej chwili,
> Ja się nie mogę, stawszy się żywiołem
> Wiecznym mych ogniów, rozsypać popiołem.

To a Corpse.

You lie slain, I am slain too, you, with the arrow of death, I, with the arrow of love. You have no more blood, and I, no more color. You have visible candles [around you], I have hidden fire.

Your face is covered with a black cloth, I have closed my senses in the awful darkness. Your hands are bound, but since I lost my freedom, my reason has been fettered with a chain.

But you are silent, and my tongue complains. You feel nothing, and I am suffering a dreadful torment. You are like ice, and I am in hellish fire.

You will soon decay to dust. I cannot disintegrate to ashes since I have become the eternal element of my flames.

In a sonnet, "On the Cross on the Breast of a Lady," Morsztyn combines two conceits with religious and erotic implications. Both of the conceits are imitations of G. Marini.

7. If one considers the content of a number of these works, one is struck mainly by the willingness to renounce beauty. It is perhaps to be expected of such cruel and tragic times that images of suffering and death should play an important part. The ugliness of the grotesque is only the beginning. Historical scenes and saints' lives offer many opportunities for portraying cruelty. The idea of eternal change and the transience of everything on earth leads to treatments of the tragic fall of the high and mighty, of the ruin of the beautiful and good and is therefore connected with profound, ideological subjects. On the other hand, it is important for our understanding of baroque literature to keep in mind that the high and beautiful were believed to be concealed behind the low and common and that the immortal was thought to be concealed beyond the mortal.

The basis of baroque symbolism is such that the deeper meaning of symbols can easily be interpreted. Lucidity, however, is not always the aim; sometimes a quality of darkness and ambiguity is conveyed, and the reader has the illusion of seeing to infinity. Great value is placed on peculiar, original symbols as elements of metaphysics. In the emblematic books, which were particularly numerous and popular during the baroque, there are whole collections of these symbols.

8. The peculiarity of baroque literature is of course not confined to the formal aspects just discussed. In intellectual history the content of an era is usually not limited to a single current but is expressed by various currents that diverge in part and in part converge around two opposite poles, two centers of gravity in the intellectual universe. In the baroque era, one of these poles was God and the other was nature. Consequently, the natural sciences and mathematics flourished, since the basis for studying nature in the baroque was number, measure, and weight—incidentally, this thesis was advanced by the *Liber sapientiae* and could therefore be adopted by theologians. During the baroque the Slavs achieved little of real significance in the sciences but did at least begin to show a productive interest and to make scientific collections that led to several lesser discoveries. The first scientists and mathematicians among the Slavs were largely clergymen!

The baroque was the time of great theological systems and of religious wars that eventually involved the Slavs. It was also a period of mysticism, the influence of which on the Slavs can be seen in various writers (Bridel, Comenius, Skovoroda).

Few men of the baroque really were to become explorer's of the world's secrets or to take refuge in isolation with God. Most of them plunged into the eddies of religious and social strife in order to realize their plans and ambitions. Baroque man crossed oceans to seek out new lands that offered an opportunity for political activity and for the religious conversion of the natives. (Czech clergymen took part in missionary work in the Far East and West.) Baroque man was also busy in his study making plans for "improving human conditions" (*Emendatio rerum humanarum* by J. A. Comenius) and drawing up proposals for political, Church, scientific, educational, and even linguistic (lingua universalis) reforms.

Among the Slavs there were plans for "eternal peace" (Comenius) and a search for religious tolerance by the "Fratres Poloni," that is, the anti-Trinitarians who waged their literary battle at home and in exile in all of Europe and whose works were published in a handsome collection by Hugo Grotius. There were also ecumenical attempts and plans for organizing scholarly work in colleges (or academies, according to Comenius in *Via lucis*, which was written in 1640 but was not published until 1668). The reform in methods of teaching (on the one hand, Jesuit schools, on the other hand, Comenius's pedagogy) was the most far-reaching of the time.

Along with these positive plans there was sharp satirical criticism of contemporary conditions, of intolerance in religion, of the oppression and exploitation of the peasants, and of the privileges of the nobility.

In the sermons of Piotr Skarga and the satires of P. Opaliński one finds broad criticism of contemporary conditions in Poland. The works of the anti-Trinitarians were directed mainly at religious intolerance and social injustice. Comenius criticizes the "world" in general in several of his works. A passage from the *Labyrinth* will serve to illustrate his method of making material strange:

The Accomplishments of the Nobility (*Labyrinth 21,4*). . . . their principal pursuits (on the basis of the freedom granted to this class, as they said) consisted in bestriding the pavement, letting their legs dangle from horses, hunting rabbits and wolves, requiring compulsory service of the peasants, confining them in the tower and releasing them at will, carousing at a long table heavily laden with dishes, and spreading their feet as far as possible, bowing and scraping and licking women's hands, whiling away the time at checkers and dice, chattering shamelessly over lewd and obscene matters, and the like. They said that they had in writing that everything they did was to be looked on as refined and noble. . . .

9. As with other periods, the weakening of the baroque, the immanent

threats to it, and finally its passing away were all closely connected with specific features of the period.

First of all, there was the overestimation of external features, of the decorative side of art and life, not of the superficial, but of aspects of culture that have a strong effect on men. Deeper, internal questions often gave way to the dynamic and the impressive without the artist's having been deliberately negligent. It is dangerous to try to heighten everything that is tense, contradictory, impressive, wondrous, or peculiar. Baroque artists and poets were misled into playing an artistic game and lost themselves in the labyrinth-like ornamentation of this game, overestimating the value of originality as such.

In various branches of literature, such as the sermon, which was still an important genre among the Slavs, there was a pronounced development of the rhetorical, declamatory, and even theatrical style. Of course, baroque literature was intended for the people of the time, and writers sought to reach not only the upper but also the "lower" strata of society. This was the first real approach to "popular" taste. Baroque literature, like baroque art in general, was well received by the "common people" and left many traces that still persist in folklore and in folk art.

10. Among some Slavic peoples the baroque played a special role by bringing forth a new flowering of literature, art, and culture. Flourishing times like this, or the periods of romanticism and realism later, are more than a historical phenomenon. They give rise to a strong and lasting tradition, contribute appreciably to the national character, and leave indelible marks on a people. The constructive elements of the baroque were long influential among some Slavic peoples, and the effect was later enhanced by romanticism (see chapter XI), in many respects related to the baroque. To a large extent the baroque became the "historical fate" of some Slavic peoples.

Baroque culture was conditioned socially as well as intellectually, more so than many other cultural periods. Baroque culture is unthinkable without its centers, the places where it was fostered. It was closely connected with the courts of princes and noblemen, with Church centers, with institutions of higher learning, which were mainly clerical, and occasionally with small circles of intellectually interested people, usually noblemen. The preponderance of this or that group determined the nature of the baroque among the various Slavic peoples. Baroque culture persisted in some of these centers long after the end of the baroque period as such. Often baroque literature sank to the lowest strata of society and was maintained there, as in connection with religious events (songs for processions, pilgrimages, and the like). Many important baroque writers continued to be thought great and impressive, if not wholly understandable, in a world almost entirely alien to them.

Among the features of baroque literature common to many Slavic peoples is its universality. Works were adapted from previous literary periods and often recast in a new style. The baroque was also frequently successful with adaptations in the plastic arts.

11. Many difficult and often neglected problems stand in the way of research into Slavic baroque literature. Among them is a consideration of Latin works written by Slavic authors; quite different classics were influential in the baroque than in the Renaissance. The tragedies of Seneca for example, were especially popular, and in philosophy Plato gave way to Aristotle.

Although renewed interest in Church Slavic among Greek Orthodox Slavs could not repress the vernacular, every writer had to decide linguistic norms for himself. There arose a mixture of languages, which may have struck many people as delightful at the time, as in macaronic verse, but which was later regarded as linguistic decay. As a consequence, many works that were considered brilliant in the baroque period were later forgotten. Not even strong elements of the vernacular could redeem these works in the eyes of classicists or romanticists.

IX

CLASSICISM

Poles

A. Naruszewicz (1733–1796)
Saint Trembecki (1735–1812)
I. Krasicki (1735–1801)
F. Karpiński (1741–1808)
F. D. Kniaźnin (1750–1793)
J. U. Niemcewicz (1757–1841)

Russians

A. P. Sumarokov (1718–1777)
M. M. Xeraskov (1733–1807)
G. R. Deržavin (1743–1816)
I. I. Dmitriev (1760–1837)
N. M. Karamzin (1766–1826)
I. A. Krylov (1768–1844)
V. L. Puškin (1770–1830)

Czechs

Beginnings of the new lyric poetry
Š. Hněvkovský (1770–1847): burlesque poetry

Slovaks

Augustin Doležal (1737–1802)
Ján Hollý (1785–1849)

Ukrainians

I. Kotljarevśkyj (1769–1838)
P. Hulak-Artemovśkyj (1790–1865)
H. Kvtika-Osnov'janenko (1778–1843)

Serbs

Dositej Obradović (1742–1811)

Croats

A. Kačić-Miošić (1704–1760)
M. A. Reljković (1732–1798)

Bulgarians

Paisij Xirendarskij (1722–1798 [?])

1. The last stages of the baroque in the Slavic countries were complicated and were determined in part by immanent literary causes and in part by the political and sociological development of the Slavs. Protest against the "bombastic," artificial style of the baroque, in many cases directed at a particular genre, such as the sermon, satiety with an over-rich style, the weariness of Baroque writers at being expected always to provide newer and bolder effects—these were the inherent causes that moved writers and readers to long for a new style. On the other hand, there had been great social and political changes in the Slavic lands. After the troubled seventeenth century, only the two major Slavic states, Russia and Poland (besides Ragusa), remained independent and were able to develop brilliant court cultures. The other Slavs, such as the Czechs and Ukrainians, lost the modest political and cultural independence that they had previously had. The Enlightenment of the eighteenth century was not conducive to national ambitions. One preferred to turn to the great nations and cultures, to go to the brilliant centers of en-

lightened absolutism, to neglect one's own national culture, and to let the next generation forget its own native language and to grow up in a foreign culture, although this might be a related culture as in the case of Russia and the Ukraine. The splendor of the court cultures contrasted sharply to the provincial, epigonic cultures of the smaller, politically dependent Slavic peoples.

2. The literatures of these provincial cultures pursued the baroque tradition. It was the clerical writers who clung to the baroque most tenaciously. As late as the early nineteenth century, clerical writers still preached and wrote in the familiar old baroque style. Later there was an affinity between the baroque and incipient romanticism, which went back in part to the mystic currents of the eighteenth century.

The religious literature of the baroque continued to hold sway over the broad masses of people, and various poems of the baroque have become folk songs. The religious life of the people, the processions, pilgrimages, and Church festivals, remained under the spell of baroque songs, which in a sense became spiritual folk songs, at least in the Catholic countries, among the Czechs, Poles, and Croats. Among the Protestant Czechs and Slovaks, baroque spiritual songs became church hymns. Greek Orthodox Slavs had no place in their church for the new religious songs and preserved spiritual poetry of the baroque as a part of their folklore.

Baroque syllabic poetry was often the source of East Slavic "spiritual songs" (*stixi duxovnye*, V. Adrianova) sung by beggars and by wandering singers to the accompaniment of a barrel organ.

3. Courtly literature did not at once develop a new classicist style. Rather this style appeared in the West in opposition to the baroque and was nourished in part by residual memories of the Renaissance. Wherever the Renaissance had accomplished little or nothing, classicist poetics had to start from the beginning; and even then there were echoes of the baroque, in religious and gallant poetry and often in solemn odes with their grotesque hyperbole, which provoked only ironic smiles from the classicists. An offshoot of the baroque, the rococo, reflected the baroque in some of its developments.

We will not be able to deal with the controversial question of the decidedly baroque features among some French poets who are usually considered to be classicists and who strongly influenced the Slavs. By and large the Slavs had only a vague idea of French classicism.

4. For reasons that we have touched on, classicist literature is fully represented among only two Slavic peoples, the Poles and the Russians.

The Polish state slowly declined and was divided among its three neighboring states late in the eighteenth century. But Polish ties with the West and the great literary tradition of the Renaissance and the baroque still brought forth writers and works of quality. Among the writers, A. Naruszewicz, Saint Trembecki, and the enlightened bishop I. Krasicki are especially worthy of note. Lighter lyrics, anacreontics (F. Karpinski), and fiction developed and were followed in the nineteenth century by the works of epigones, some of whom, such as Niemcewicz with his balladic *Historical Songs*, struck a new note. Classicism eventually did battle with romanticism but had no hope of success.

Odes to nature (sun, clouds, rivers) by Naruszewicz are typical of the times, serious and heavy. Krasicki is lighter and more lucid. In his epics *Myszeida* and *Monachomachja* he satirizes the life of a monk. His short fables or "apologies" illustrate his gift for pointed expression.

Pan i Pies

Pies szczekał na złodzieja, całą noc się trudził:
obili go nazajutrz, że Pana obudził.
Spał smaczno drugiej nocy, złodzieja ne czekał;
ten dom okradł: psa obili za to, że nie szczekał.

Master and Dog

A dog barked at the thief; he kept it up all night: in the morning he was beaten because he had waked up his master. The next night he slept soundly and did not lie in wait for the thief. The thief robbed the house: the dog was beaten for not barking.

The Ukrainian adaptation of this fable was made by Hulak-Artemovśkyj and runs to more than a hundred lines!

The poems of Trembecki are distinguished by their clear language. Here is a landscape:

W końcu szerokich równin, gdzie się woda sączy,
która z odleglych wiader Wisła z Narwą łączy,
jest miejsce, któremu się uśmeicha fortuna.
Owieczki tam wydają najdobniejsze runa,
bydło przynosi z pola pełnejsze wymiona,
ziemia z wysoką lichwą powraca nasiona,
pszczoła obficiej robi miód droższy niż złoto,
pasma rolnicze ciagnąć nie śpieszy się Kloto,
a kmiotek często indziej smutny i ponury,
tu wszytkie wesełością przechodzi Mazury („Polanka")

At the edge of the broad plain where water flows, connecting the Vistula with the Narew from distant sources, there is a place that fortune smiles upon. There the sheep give the best wool, cows bring from the field the fullest udders, the earth returns the sowing with high interest, the bee makes honey more plentifully, and the honey is more expensive than gold; Kloto does not hurry to plow the furrow; and the peasant who in other places is sad and dispirited, exceeds here the bounds of gladness.

An example of Anacreontic verse is this song by Karpinski:

Przypomnienie dawnej miłości

Potok płynie doliną,
nad potokiem jawory,
tam ja z tobą, Justyno,
słodkie pędził wieczory...

Dziś, kiedy nas w swym gniewie
los rozdzielił opaczny,
znaki nasze na drzewie
popsuł pasterz niebaczny,

I ślady się zmazały!
Las zarasta krzewiną;
potok, drzewa zostały,
ciebie nie masz, Justyno!

A stream runs through the valley; over the stream there are maples; Justina, I have spent sweet evenings with you there.

Now that a hostile fate has angrily parted us, our carving on the tree has been marred by a careless shepherd.

The traces have vanished too! The forest is grown over with brush. The stream and the trees remain. You are not there, Justina!

5. Russian classicism was of considerably lower quality. Although Polish classicism worked out a detailed system of poetics, Russian classicist poets, such as the Russian baroque poets of the eighteenth century—Kantemir, Trediakovskij, Lomonosov—developed an inconsistent eclecticism—from want of literary education and of tradition. Classicists had some success in combatting the bombastic style of baroque poets; and after about 1765 there were the noteworthy, if still rather pale classicists A. Sumarokov and M. Xeraskov and comedy playwrights, especially Fonvizin. Significantly, the greatest Russian poet of the eighteenth century, Gavriil R. Deržavin, was stylistically indebted to the late baroque (D. Čiževskij, C. Backvis). The same may be said of the author of elegant and nimble Anacreontic poems A. A. Rževskij, who flared up like a meteor in Russian literature at the beginning of the 1760s.

Russian classicists continued the tradition of the solemn ode, with which all tsars and generals of the time were hailed. Xeraskov is the author of two major epics, *Vladimir* (the Christianization of Russia) and *Rossiada* (the conquest of the Kazan Tatar state by Ivan IV). Attempts at epics by other poets are not important. A. Sumarokov wrote tragedies, as did V. Ozerov, who took liberties with the rules of poetics as early as the beginning of the nineteenth century.

"Orthodox" Russian classicism—Sumarokov and Xeraskov—is pale in comparison with the baroque poetry of Lomonosov. Toward the end of the classicist period V. L. Puškin set forth an attractive program for classicist poetry:

> Кто мыслит правильно, кто мыслит благородно,
> тот изъясняется приятно и свободно (...)
> Поэма громкая, в которой плана нет,
> не песнопение, но сущий только бред (...)
> Творенье без идей мою волнует кровь.
> Слов много затвердить не есть еще ученье,
> нам нужны не слова, нам нужно просвещенье!

Whoever thinks properly and nobly expresses himself pleasantly and naturally (. . .) A resounding poem that has no plan is not a song but pure delirium (. . .) A work that does not have ideas disturbs me. To have learned many words is not necessarily knowledge. We need not words but enlightenment.

Russian classicists were not able to adapt to their own purposes the lighter language that was "pleasant and free." The heavy lexical tradition of Church Slavonic was not easily cast off. Few poets succeeded in overcoming the monotony of classicist style; those who did succeed, in particular, the brilliant G. R. Deržavin, reverted to elements of baroque poetry. In an ode to Count Zubov (1797) Deržavin portrays the Caucasus, a motif that was to become popular among the romantics:

> О юный вождь!—сверша походы,
> прошел ты с воинством Кавказ,
> зрел ужасы, красы природы:
> как с ребр там страшных гор лиясь
> ревут в мрак бездн сердиты реки;.
> как с чел их с грохотом снега
> падут, лежавши целы веки;
> как серны, вниз склоня рога,
> зрят в мгле спокойно под собою
> рожденье молний и громов (...)
>
> Ты видел,—как во тьме секутся
> с громами громы в облаках,
> как бездны пламень извергают,

как в тучах роет огнь бразды,
как в воздухе пары сгорают,
как светят свеч в лесах ряды,
Ты видел,—как в степи средь зною
огромных змей стога кипят
как блещут пестрой чешуею
и льют, шипя, друг в друга яд (...)

O, youthful commander! On your campaigns you and your armies have marched through the Caucasus and seen the horrors and beauties of nature: angry streams plunging and roaring from the ledges of dreadful mountains into the darkness of the abyss, snows that had lain for centuries crashing down from the peaks, chamois, their horns raised upward, watching in the mist below them the birth of lightning and thunder. . . .

You have seen—bolts of lightning battle one another in the dark, abysses cast out flames, fire dig furrows in the clouds, vapors burn in the air, candles shine in rows in the forests [*ignis fatuus*]. You have seen whole ricks of enormous snakes teem in the intense heat of the steppe, their brightly colored scales shining, and hiss and pour poison into one another.

These views of nature are in part (snakes, volcanoes) inventions on the part of the poet. Elsewhere, Deržavin decorates his scenes with incomparably rich coloring. He also wrote baroque figure poems, a fondness shared by the Anacreontic poet A. Rževskij.

6. The classicist period was not ideologically unified. One often hears of the "Enlightenment of the eighteenth century." This Enlightenment was, of course, less pronounced in Germany than in France. In Poland and Russia there were a few unimportant followers of the French Enlightenment (of Voltaire and the Encyclopedists). Otherwise, the Slavic Enlightenment was a vague reflection of Western models. It was only in political writing, and there only late, that consistent adherents appeared, such as the Russian opponent of absolutism and serfdom A. N. Radiščev. In Poland there were even adherents of the moderate Enlightenment among the clerics of the Piarist order! One of them was the previously mentioned I. Krasicki, Bishop of Ermeland (Warmia).

The rather weak Enlightenment was opposed by religious and mystic currents, the Russian adherents of which gathered around the publisher and freemason N. Novikov and created an extensive literature.

Polish classicists also created a religious poetry (Konstancja Benisławka), as did the Russian—Deržavin's ode "God" became famous, and one finds religious motifs in Xeraskov. There are anonymous translations of epigrams from Angelus Silesius, many of them excellently rendered.

7. Much more important than the "Enlightenment" was the current

usually called "sensibility," or "sentimentalism," that appeared toward
the end of the century. Sensibility had been affected by various currents
from the West, among them the bourgeois novel, Rousseau's cult of
feeling, and "Sturm und Drang," which was not entirely understood or
especially influential, although its spokesman, Jacob Lenz, came from
Moscow and Klinger had taught at a millitary school in Russia. A form
of late classicism, sensibility radically reformed the linguistic usages
of eighteenth-century Russian classicism. Differentiated, "sublime"
language was replaced by the uniform language of "good society,"
which was already in use colloquially and in letters. This linguistic reform was primarily the work of N. M. Karamzin, who was joined by
several other writers, in particular I. Dmitriev and V. L. Puškin. It was
only now that the simplicity and transparency demanded by classicism
were really realized.

Karamzin simplified prose style considerably and, under Western
influence, adopted certain features of the sensibility style: "I come to
this spot often . . . I come here on gloomy fall days to mourn together
with nature. The wind howls dreadfully in the walls of the deserted
monastery, around the graves grown over with tall grass, and in the
dark halls between the cells. Resting there on the ruins of tombstones, I
hear the dark moan of the times that the abyss of the past has devoured,
causing my heart to tremble and shiver. . . ." This is the beginning of a
novella by Karamzin.

Emotional language is even stronger in the verse of Karamzin and his
followers. Karamzin characterizes his own work: "Poetry is a flower
garden of the sensitive heart." Even older poets turned to this "poetry of
night and graves." Kapnist (1757–1823) wrote,

> Уже со тьмою нощи
> простерлась тишина.
> Выходит из-за рощи
> печальная (!) луна.
> Я лиру томно строю
> петь скорбь объявшу дух—
> приди грустить со мною,
> луна, печальных друг!

A silence has spread with the darkness of night. The sad moon rises behind the
grove. Languidly, I tune the lyre to sing of the sadness that has seized the spirit—
come and mourn with me, O moon, friend of those who are sad!

The older generation of classicists (A. Šiškov, senior) sought to oppose
Karamzin's linguistic reforms but could not defeat them. The last sig-

nificant epigone of classicism, I. A. Krylov, was exclusively a fabulist toward the end of his life (died in 1843) and as such made an important contribution to the literary use of the vernacular (which was permitted in this genre by classicist poetics).

In Polish literature the development of classicism required no revolution like Karamzin's. The literary language was not burdened by any stylistic and lexical tradition as was that of Church Slavonic.

8. The poetics of classicism was based on the tradition of ancient poetics that had been renewed by the Renaissance. The designation "pseudoclassicism," often used in Russian and Polish literary history, should be rejected because of its pejorative sound: the Slavic classicists attempted seriously and sincerely to follow the classical literary ideal as they understood it. They do not deserve this derogatory name, which also creates the illusion that along with "pseudo" classicism there was some kind of "genuine" classicism. The poetics of Aristotle (in many respects misunderstood), Horace, and Quintilian was occasionally reinforced by the poetics of the Renaissance and even the baroque—baroque poetics was based on ancient models—but was mainly supplemented by the doctrines of Boileau.

There was a general tendency to retain traditional poetic genres, the names of which often appeared as the subtitles of works: "ode," "elegy," and less frequent genres, such as short fables ("apologues"). Harmonious beauty was a basic aim and required that all parts form a harmonious whole (*concilitas*).

Every genre was to be kept pure, and there were precise rules for each of them; the rules for "serious" genres were especially strict, in particular for plays. The principal matters to be kept in mind for the tragedy were the selection of serious or "sublime" themes and persons—princes and heroes—and the preservation of the three unities of action, time, and place—one day for the development and resolution of the action. Comic scenes were to be avoided. The feelings and confessions of heroes were best expressed in conversation with intimate friends. As a result, when the "coarse, rough" plays of Shakespeare were reworked, the cast was doubled—in *Hamlet*, for instance, the queen was given a woman friend to whom she could pour out her heart. Poetic norms depended mainly on their "naturalness" or fidelity to nature.

The rules for the middle (narrative prose, idyll, lyric, parlor song, satire, and epistle) and lower genres (comedy and fable) were considerably more flexible, and both talented writers and amateurs crossed the narrow boundaries of genres and rules of style.

Literature was supposed to be pleasant but primarily useful. It was believed that one made literature pleasant by adhering to poetic norms and useful by having a moral effect on the reader, that is, by being didactic. Didacticism was achieved in various ways: by interspersing didactic observations, by introducing virtuous characters to make didactic speeches ("raisonneurs" in plays), by assigning rewards for virtue and punishment for vice. In some genres it was left to the reader to draw his own moralistic conclusions from a work. One peculiar didactic form was the "utopian portrayal" of ideal men and conditions. The awakening of sympathy and other "good feelings" was also considered beneficial.

9. Polish and Russian classicist literature were "complete" literatures in that all or most literary genres were represented. Although the other Slavic literatures continued, their audience, their opportunities for publishing, and the number and at times the talent of their writers were very limited (see above, 1–2). These peoples had "incomplete" literatures, literatures in which only certain genres were represented and which can be thought of only as supplements to the foreign literatures that mainly satisfied the needs of the reading public. The main foreign literatures were Russian and Polish for Ukrainians and White Russians; German for Czechs, Slovaks, and Slovenes; and Hungarian and Czech for Slovaks and some Croats. Slavs with "incomplete" literatures frequently wrote in these foreign languages or, on scientific or religious subjects, in Latin and Church Slavonic. Attempts were made, with inadequate means, to create new literary languages for the smaller Slavic peoples. The efforts to introduce a restored form of Church Slavonic into the Carpathian Ukraine was totally unsuccessful. Both Serbs and Croats tried to develop "modern" literary languages. Although both languages were strengthened, the literature continued to be predominantly religious.

The "incomplete" literatures consisted almost exclusively of genres in which classicism allowed the use of the vernacular. Among these genres were the art song written in imitation of the folk song, the idyll, and humorous works, including travesty, which was permitted even by Boileau. The "complete" literatures also produced works for which Pope's *Rape of the Lock* might have served as a model. Either they used sublime epic forms to present low or comic subjects, as Boileau and Pope had done, or they made use of well-known epic subjects—the *Aeneid* and the *Rape of Persephone* were familiar and popular—to present a low or comic circle of contemporary people. These travesties were written mostly in vulgar language, perhaps with a use of dialect, for example, Blumauer's *Aeneis*. The aim of these works was to provide light entertainment, although at times they were inclined to be didactic.

Even venerable Czech literature produced works of this kind. Lyric poems—religious, popular, secular, even Anacreontic—were nourished by the baroque tradition and could not advance beyond mediocrity. More important are S. Hněvkovský's naive, didactic works or his travesty *Děvin*, an epic on the legendary Old Czech maiden's castle (1805).

Hněvkovský himself characterizes his work as a mixture of styles. He says that he wrote on "the battle of the maidens partly in a serious heroic style, partly in a humorous, and partly in a romantic one . . . all three kinds mixed together." By "romantic" style he means that he has included love scenes.

Travesty made its way into Ukrainian literature more easily since the literary language was based on Church Slavonic, with admixtures from Great Russian and Ukrainian, and not yet on the vernacular. The leading Slavic master of travesty was perhaps the Ukrainian Ivan Kotljarevśkyj. His *Aeneid* (1798 ff.) was superior to its Russian (Osipov) and German (Blumauer) models in facility of verse, in the grotesque disguise of Aeneas and his Trojans as Ukrainian cossacks, and in the expression, even in this form, of moral and national motifs. Kotljarevśkyj also wrote light musical plays and travesties on odes. It was not until much later that the White Russians followed his lead. In 1834, during the romantic period, an excellent classicist writer, H. Kvitka-Osnov'janenko, began writing Ukrainian novellas in addition to novellas in Russian.

The attitude of classicism to the folk song and the common people was expressed in both sentimental drawing room songs and travesties. A contemporary of the more moderate Kotljarevśkyj, Professor Hulak-Artemovśkyj, wrote travesties on the odes of Horace. In a travesty of the ode to Delius we find this description of the peasant's life:

> Чи коротаєш вік в журбі
> чи то за поставцем горілки (...)
> Чи п'яний під тином хропеш,
> чи до господи лізеш рачки,
> чи жінку макогоном б'єш,
> чи сам товчешся на кулачки (...)

Whether you spend your life in sorrow or in front of a shelf of liquor bottles . . . whether you snore drunkenly under a fence or crawl home on all fours, whether you beat your wife with a rolling pin or get into a brawl with someone. . . .

No translation can render the vulgarity of this language. The Slovak idylls of J. Hollý (see below) are, of course, different, but one wonders whether they reflect the peasant's life more truthfully.

The Croat M. A. Relković wrote a humorous, satirical epic, *Satyr or the Wild Man* (1762), and fables, published posthumously in 1804. Among the most serious works of the incomplete literatures are those of the Serb Dositej Obradović, who studied in Halle and Leipzig and published an autobiography, *Commonsense Advice* (*Sověti zdravago razuma*, 1784), and fables (1788), and the idylls of Ján Hollý, which were not published until the nineteenth century and were followed in the 1830s by his unimportant classicist epics.

10. The language of classicism was not always clear, transparent, and simple, as in Krasicki and Trembecki. It was also characterized by new usages: neologisms required by cultural change and compound words foreign to the Slavic languages.

We find among writers of the different Slavic peoples:

in Naruszewicz: nieprzeskoczne, gorolotny, wszystkożywny, złotomowny struny, gwiazdołowne skiełka, wodokowy styczeń, etc.

in Krasicki: głębokomyslny, swiętowymowne milczenie, złotostemolny pieniądz, grzecznopoczciwy, grecznomodny, etc.

in Karpiński: wielofarbne pleci, róznowzory, żółtopióry rosnoszybne okna, prędkowierna wieś, wielkorody dub, wielkomyślna muza, etc.

in the works of the Slovak writer Hollý: lubozvučný, bujnotravný, lubohlasit, lubohvizdat, strašneznácí, dobreskušený, belorunný, ploskonosý, samorastlý, jasnomodrý, štvorohranatý, etc.

In Russian poetry compound words are traditional, but Deržavin's descriptions of colors are original:

sizojantarnyj, zlatobagrjanyj, temnogoluboj, srebrorozovyj, etc.

As we have mentioned, language was made lighter, especially by the later classicists.

Occasionally Karamzin "Russified" or otherwise simplified foreign words that he had originally used in his account of his travels. Niemcewicz wrote in a much fresher language than his predecessors, the classicists of the sixties and seventies, but one finds in him early signs of romanticism.

The incomplete literatures are important. They strike one as being ruins (even Czech literature) from which literary languages will develop or through which they will survive and which will serve to awaken the national consciousness. The Ukrainian literary language was advanced considerably, for example, by Ukrainian travesty literature, written in genuine vernacular.

11. Classicist poetics was much less of a restraint on the free development of literary creativity than is often thought. It was for other reasons that classicism began to give way. The gradual intrusion of feelings into the inner life—promoted in literature by various currents from the West, from the bourgeois novel to Rousseauism—opened the eyes of writers and readers to a certain "dryness" in classicist literature, to the possibility of freer forms, and to the fact that the Enlightenment could not satisfy the needs of the heart, that the battle of classicism against "prejudices" destroyed the bases of religious and aesthetic sensitivity. National consciousness was awakened and strengthened during the wars of liberation, and the French Revolution lost the appeal that it had once had. All of this served to pave the way for the new romantic school.

X

ROMANTICISM

Poles

K. Brodziński (1791–1835)
A. Mickiewicz (1798–1855)
J. Słowacki (1809–1849)
Z. Krasiński (1812–1859)
C. Norwid (1821–1883)
S. Goszczyński (1801–1876) and other representatives
of the "Ukrainian School"

Russians

V. A. Žukovskij (1783–1852)
P. Vjazemskij (1792–1878)
A. A. Bestužev-Marlinskij (1797–1837)
A. S. Puškin (1799–1837)
M. Ju. Lermontov (1814–1841)
F. I. Tjutčev (1803–1873)
N. V. Gogol' (1809–1852)
V. F. Odoevskij (1803–1869)

Czechs

K. H. Mácha (1810–1836)
K. J. Erben (1811–1870)
Božena Němcová (1820–1862)

Slovaks

L'. Štúr (1815–1856)
Janko Král' (1822–1876)
A. Sládkovič (1820–1872)
J. Kalinčiak (1822–1871)

Croats

L. Gaj (1809–1872)
P. Preradović (1818–1872)
I. Mažuranić (1814–1890)

Serbs

P. P. Njegoš (1813–1851)
I. Jovanović-Zmaj (1833–1904)

Slovenes

F. Prešeren (1800–1849)

Ukrainians

T. Ševčenko (1814–1861)
P. Kuliš (1819–1897)

Sorbs

J. A. Smoleŕ (1816–1884)

---

1. Literary romanticism, a movement that led an almost unprecedented, victorious advance throughout European literature in the first
half of the nineteenth century, had a particular significance for Slavic
literature in that it was associated with the national awakening of the
Slavic peoples. In the case of the Czechs and Bulgarians, romanticism
meant a national "rebirth." In other cases it meant the first awakening
of national awareness or the appearance of a long-forgotten conception
of cultural self reliance and individuality. It was precisely in the most
important Slavic literatures, Russian and Polish, where romanticism
guided contemplation of national historical fate and destiny to a con-

cern with the philosophy of history and to its native development in the specific form of Slavophilism, often designated as "Panslavism" in the West, or of "Messianism" in Poland.

It would be entirely erroneous, however, in spite of the fact that it is sometimes done, to limit the romantic movement among the Slavs to these political motives. For literature, too, stimulated by the appearance of several important, sometimes brilliant writers, assumed a new stylistic expression.

The fundamentals of romantic literature are not always readily apparent in Slavic literary theory (see 12). The effect of Western European theoretical writings, for example, the works of Schlegel, is weaker than that of the literary models, and particularly strong influences emanated from the poets who belonged to the second wave of Western European romanticism, particularly from Byron. Among the Slavs, specific ideological fundamentals of the romantic Weltanschauung were contrary to their relatively unclear poetic theory. Romanticism, in contradistinction to classicism, belonged to a trend that demanded a certain ideological attitude from its adherents, one that may clearly be seen in Slavic romantic literature. Consequently, it will be necessary to devote more space in this chapter than in any other to an analysis of ideology.

2. Romantic literature to be sure is stylistically multifarious, even variegated. This is associated with originality's being seen as a positive aesthetic value (as it was in baroque poetry). In the West the romantic movement was prepared for by various forms of preromanticism that spontaneously gave expression to a dissatisfaction with the form and ideology of classical poetry. Ossianism, the poetry of night and the grave, the "bourgeois novel," "Rousseauianism" with its cult of feeling, various mystical currents, "Sturm und Drang," and the ideas of Herder met with but slight response in Slavic literature. It is true that they did lead to the development of some trends, such as Russian "sentimentality," Karamzin's so-called "sentimentalism" (see Chapter IX). These responses were not, however, cognizant of the fact that this was a question of fundamental literary change, even one of revolution.

3. Strength and efficacious initiative for the adoption of the new ideology came from the opposition that, in the Slavic countries also, was directed against only one side of classicism, against rationalism and its specific form the Enlightenment. It was only with individual poets that dissatisfaction with the too narrow and obdurate demands of classical poetics, in particular with the classical theory of genres, arose. Characteristically, it was in the work of those poets who had still maintained

certain elements of the baroque during the classical period where the first premonition of romanticism appeared, for example, G. R. Deržavin in Russia.

It was not possible, however, for the Slavs to revert to baroque literature, as baroque had done with the literature of the Late Middle Ages. There was an unbridgeable barrier between the literature of the baroque period and that of the newly emerging romanticism: on the one hand the language of baroque poetry, and in part its poetics, was entirely antiquated; on the other hand, many of the baroque poets were still to too great an extent under the influence of ecclesiastical ideology. In any case the Slavic romanticists seldom referred back to the baroque sources, they created their romantic ideology with the help of the newer philosophy.

4. The romantic ideology stands in opposition to the Enlightenment because the romantics did not recognize reason as the fundamental power of the human soul, neither in the realm of knowledge nor as the guiding force of human will, and above all they conceded to the rational elements of spiritual existence no pre-eminence over feeling. "Cold reason" was but the "cadaver of feeling." Reality was to be grasped and comprehended by our intellect as a living whole. Feeling and will are cognitive powers having equal rights with intellect.

> Нет веры к вымыслам чудесным,
> рассудок всё опустошил
> и, покорив законам тесным
> и воздух, и моря, и сушу,
> как пленников их обнажил,
> ту жизнь до дна он иссушил,
> что в дерево вливала душу,
> давала тело бестелесным...

> There is no longer belief in miraculous fictions,
> reason has desolated all
> and, having to narrow boundaries subjected
> the air, the seas, the land,
> it has denuded them as prisoners,
> has dried up to the core that life
> that instilled a soul into the trees
> and that lent body to the disembodied.
>   [Tjutčev]

The poet calls the perceptions that were destroyed by reason *"belief in miraculous fictions,"* but he sees in this expression no repudiation of their worth. The original cognitive power was not "discursive," but "intuitive." And poetry, which builds upon intuition, is a source of cognition equal to science.

In addition, there are sources of cognition that lie outside of any "normal" psychic life and, consequently, madness is often able to penetrate more deeply than reason, reach spheres that are otherwise closed to mental comprehension.

An apology for madness is found, not only in the title of a novel by the Russian Romantic, N. Polevoj, *Blaženstvo bezumija* (*The Blessedness of Madness*), but also in various works of Puškin. The true personality of the card player reveals itself in madness (*The Queen of Spades*); the petty bureaucrat Evgenij who has gone mad perceives the essence of the eternal struggle between the individual and the reason of state, embodied in the figure of Peter the Great (*The Bronze Horseman*), etc.

The Romantics go even further. The programmatic poem of the young Adam Mickievicz, *Romantyczność* (*Romanticism*), is actually a glorification of madness. A girl imagines she is speaking with her dead lover; the crowd believes that she really sees him, only the enlightened scholar can not grasp that which is inaccessible to his eyes and prescription glasses. "Have heart and see into the heart!" the poet calls out to the reader.

We find something similar in Puškin's poem with the misleading title, *God, grant that I go not mad (Ne daj mne, Bog, sojti s uma)*. The poet says he dreads it, however, "not because I value my reason so highly that I would not be glad to part from it" but rather only because the mad are treated so horribly. If the mad poet could remain free then madness would guide him to a strange union with nature:

> ...как бы резво я пустился в тёмный лес!
> Я пел бы в пламенном бреду,
> я забывался бы в чаду нестройных, чудных грез.
>
> И я б заслушивался волн,
> и я глядел бы, счастья полн, в пустые небеса.
> И силен, волен был бы я,
> как вихорь, роющий поля, ломающий леса...

As though rollicking I would run into the dark forest!
I would sing in flaming delirium,
I would forget myself in the intoxication of incoherent, wonderful dreams.
And I would hark unto the waves
and I would look, full of happiness, into the empty heavens.
And I would be strong and free,
as the whirlwind that tears up the fields, that splits the forests . . .

We encounter a further defense of madness in the conversations of the participants in V. F. Odoevskij's *Russian Nights*. His main thoughts are, 1. there are no clear borders between the mentally healthy and ill; 2. the thought process of the mad is reminiscent of poetic inspiration; 3. the same holds true for the thought processes of discoverers and inventors—both are fully possessed by one idea, both find relationships between heterogenous objects that, for the "healthy" mind, are alien one to another.

They have, as it were, the capability of detaching parts from objects that are closely associated for normal people and combining them in an unknown symbol.

One considers the ideas of the mad to be absurd. But no healthy person is capable of uniting so many fundamentally different ideas. There is no great person who, at the genesis of his new discovery, was not considered mad. A person is called insane when one sees that he finds relationships between objects that seem impossible to us. But is not every invention, every new thought, an engendering of relationships between objects that are unnoticed by others or even incomprehensible to them? On this level is not the inspired state of the poet or the inventor closer to what is called madness? In a word, what is often called insanity is the state of ecstasy . . . the highest level of intellectual human instinct. . . . [*Russian Nights*, 1844, "2nd Night."]

Other romantic poets express their aversion somewhat more modestly by opposing the "heart" as seat or symbol of emotional life to reason. We encounter the "heart" right up into the later years of the Ukrainian P. Kuliš who sees the highest worth of national and individual life in the "heart." This concern may also be seen in the work of the Croat, P. Preradović, as for example in his sonnet *Pamet i srdce*, in which he has Heart address Reason:

> Tvoju visost Bog ti blagoslovi
> al nediraj u pravo ničije,
> iz mog žara ti si svjetlo božje!

> You thank God for your importance
> but touch the rights of no one:
> from my glow are you the light of God!

To expressions of the rejection of the "rational" may be added the poet's "self-styling" as an illogically acting person who is completely alien to the rationally organized world.

In the stories contained in *Russian Nights* we see the great artists Piranesi, J. S. Bach, and Beethoven as geniuses who stand beyond the "normal" human condition.

5. The distance between the normal person and the madman or genius is so great that it is possible to speak of an entire scale of intermediate states existing between the two. And consequently, for the romantic, every person is capable of attaining depths and heights that lie beyond "neutral" existence. This is made possible because the human soul stands on the boundary of two worlds:

> О вещая душа моя,
> о сердце полное тревоги,
> о как ты бьешься на пороге
> как бы двойного бытия!

> O my prophetic soul,
> o heart full of unrest,
> o how you beat as though on the threshold
> of a twofold existence.

> [Tjutčev]

Next to conscious psychic life there is the "unconscious" that, for the romantics, was not necessarily the "subconscious." The forces of the unconscious can break into the normal psychic life from below or even from above and disturb its motion. We meet this conception of "romantic psychology" in Novalis, G. H. von Schubert, and C. G. Carus; Odoevskij considers Schelling to be the founder of the new psychology, the "Columbus of the soul."

These forces were designated "The Night Side of the Soul." Poetic inspiration and mysterious presentiments, dreams, visions, and ecstasies, magnetism, hallucinations, somnambulism, epilepsy, and even the "artificial paradises" of narcotics belonged to the Night Side, in short, every not quite every-day, "abnormal" lapse of the psychic life.

It is indicative that the "dream" was called the "representative" of the Night Side of the Soul. Hence Tjutčev wrote:

> Как океан объемлет шар земной,
> земная жизнь кругом объята снами;
> настанет ночь—и звучными волнами
> стихия бьет о берег свой.

> То глас её, он нудит нас и просит...
> Уж в пристани волшебный ожил чёлн;
> прилив растет и быстро нас уносит
> в неизмеримость тёмных волн (...)

> As the ocean embraces the earthly sphere,
> so is the earthly life embraced by dreams;

Night falls and with resounding waves
the elements beat on its shore.
That is its voice, it lures us and pleads . . .
Already the magic bark in the harbor has come to life;
the flood swells and carries us quickly away
into the immensity of the dark waves . . .

Puškin in his childhood poems used the Russian word *son*, at the same time meaning "sleep" and "dream," in the meaning of illusion (*son pustoj*—"the empty dream"). Later he utilized the word for all manifestations of the Night Side of the Soul: *tvorčeskie sny* = creative dreams, *sny poezii svjatoj* = dreams of holy poesie, *poetičeskij son* = poetic dream. Further, the heroes of his novel appeared to him, *v nejasnom sne* (in an unclear dream vision); *byvalo milye predmety mne snilis'* = the dear objects (women) would appear to me in a "dream." *V sladostnyj bezgrešnyj son dušeju pogruzilsya on* = he submerged with his soul into an innocent sweet dream.

The word *son* ("dream," in this broad sense) is also replaced by semantically related words: *mečta* (dreaming), *zabven'e* (forgetting one's self), *prizraki* (visions), and even *bred* (delirium; compare with the "mania" in Plato's *Ion*)—*poezii svjaščennyj bred*—the holy delirium of poetry. The word is used by other Russian poets in the same meaning.

The belief in clairvoyant dreams is also reflected in the role that the dreams play in plot development.

In Puškin we find many clairvoyant dreams. The narrator Grinev sees his future in a symbolic dream after his first encounter with Pugačev, the future rebel (*The Captain's Daughter*). The future False Demitrius was supposed to have seen his fate in a dream (only in outline). Dreams also play a role in the *Queen of Spades* and *The Snowstorm*. Dreams are often significant in Gogol's stories as well.

What is important is that "Night" is construed as the depth of Being and frequently forms the essential background of the action.

The number of "nocturnal poems" is quite large. In addition to Tjutčev, his contemporary S. Ševyrev belongs to the romantic poets decidedly of the Night. Numerous poets (Czech and German) wrote nocturnal poems in Czech poetry, for example K. H. Mácha and his imitator, V. B. Nebeský.

As well as V. Žukovskij, in his ballads, the Czech (Mácha) and Polish (Mickievicz, Słowacki, Goszczyński) poets had a particular preference for nocturnal plots. By the same token, however, nocturnal scenes appear particularly often in the Ukrainian stories of the young

Gogol' and in Puškin's work. Sometimes this is only the aftereffect
of "Ossianism."

6. The Night Side of Nature corresponds to the Night Side of Life.
Nature is only one additional world, but there was also an inclination to
conceive the diversity of the spheres of being. There are, perhaps, even
several worlds. Just as man is not a machine, that is, he comprises not
only a physical but also an intellectual whole that can not be explained
by individual experiences—outer influences or inner—or associations;
so too nature is in no way a conglomerate of atoms. Nature is a living
entity, even if one at times painfully senses the crevice that yawns between it and man. The Being of Nature is a symbol of human existence.

Favored nature symbols, in addition to the "Night," that both represent the existence of man as well as personify nature are the sea (symbol
of spiritual unrest, movement, dynamism), the waterfall (typical in the
romantic literature of Russia, the country in which there are but few
waterfalls), the wind, etc.

The conception of a living nature is, of course, represented in romantic
scholarship as well as in literature. The romantic poets often discuss
the philosophy of nature.

Thus, Tjutčev writes,

> Не то, что мните вы, природа:
> не слепок, не бездушный лик, —
> в ней есть душа, в ней есть свобода,
> в ней есть любовь, в ней есть язык...
> (...) Вы зрите лист и цвет на древе:
> иль их садовник приклеил?
> Иль зреет плод в родимом чреве
> игрою внешних, чуждых сил?

> Nature is not what you think it is:
> no sculpture, no souless countenance,—
> it has a soul, it has freedom,
> it has love, it has speech . . .
> You see leaf and bloom on a tree:
> or has the gardener pasted them on?
> Or does the fruit ripen in the womb
> by the play of external, alien forces?

The Czech poet F. L. Čelakovský represents in his poetry the fundamental motifs of Schelling's philosophy of nature. Prince V. F. Odoevskij and his romantic friends became enthusiastic about the philosophy
of nature of Schelling and Oken. The crevice between human being and
nature, however, was also perceived.

> Поочередно всех своих детей,
> свершающих свой подвиг бесполезный,
> она равно приветствует своей
> всепоглощающей и миротворной бездной

In turn she greets all her children,
who perform her useless deeds,
equally with her all-absorbing and peace-making abyss.

[Tjutčev]

Nature is "element," "abyss" (Russian, *bezdna*). There lives a chaos in nature that is related to and answers the chaos of the human soul.

7. Modern man would also be able to speak with nature. The voice of nature ("wordless speech"—*reč bezglagol'naja* —Boratynskij) is, however, only comprehensible to man's "heart." In prehistoric times man was related to nature differently; they spoke with each other in "unearthly languages" (*jazykami nezemnymi*, Tjutčev).

This original unity of man and nature is now destroyed. Earlier,

> Dzisiejsze dziwy dziwami nie były:
> grały widomie niewidomie siły,
> i pilnowały człowieka, jak dziecka.
> W powietrzu, w drzewach, w kamieniu, pod wodą,
> krewne spółczucie ludzi znajdowali;
> bo nie gardzili na-ow-czas przyrodą;
> bo ją, jak matkę, znali i kochali...
>
>   (Goszczyński)

> Пока человек естества не пытал
> горнилом, весами и мерой,
> по детски вещаньям природы внимал,
> ловил её знаменья с верой,
> покуда природу любил он, она
> любовью ему отвечала:
> о нем дружелюбной заботы полна,
> язык для него обретала (...)
> Но чувство презрев, он доверил уму,
> вдался в суету изысканий
> и сердце природы закрылось ему,
> и нет на земле прорицаний.
>
>   (Boratynskij)

What today is a miracle was earlier no miracle:
the invisible powers played visibly
and cared for man as for a child.
In the air, in the trees, in the rocks, under the water
man found a kinsmanlike compassion,

for at that time they did not disdain nature,
but rather knew and loved it, as a mother.

As long as man did not test nature
by yard, scale, and measure,
but as a child harked to her voice,
with faith grasped at her omens,
as long as he loved Nature, she
answered him with love:
full of friendly care over him,
she acquired language for him . . .
But despising feeling, he trusted reason,
gave himself up to the vanity of investigation
and Nature's heart was closed for him,
and there are no longer any prophecies on earth.

While Tjutčev characterizes the natural scientists as "slaves of educated vanity" and considers them "deaf and dumb," Odoevskij believes
that the original relationship between man and nature can be recreated;
one must merely "elevate reason to instinct," concede place to the
"instinctual forces" (*instinktual'nye sily*). Since the forces of instinct
live on in poetry, science should become poetic.

The Slavic romantics' pursuit of folklore grew out of an interest in
prehistory and its residue in superstition and in the "predjudices" that
were especially hated by the Enlightenment. The first good collections
of fairy tales, songs, proverbs, and numerous discoveries belong to the
achievements of Slavic romantic scholarship. Even some, not numerous,
forgeries hardly lessen this achievement. Prehistory, to whose evidence
modern folklore as well was naively attributed, however, is not enough.
Although as good as nothing was known of proto-Slavic mythology,
it and prehistory appear in various forms in literature.

Later the accomplished fairy tale collector and epigone of romanticism,
A. Afanas'ev, attempted to reconstruct Slavic mythology on the foundation of folklore (*Poetic Views of the Slavs on Nature*, 1865 ff.).

In literature the Czech, J. Linda, utilized his phantasmic conception
of Slavic mythology in a novel (*Dawn over Pagandom*, 1818). J. Słowacki
treated prehistory in an impressive but phantasmic work, *Lila Weneda*.

The scholarly achievements of the romantics in history were much
greater. It is important to note that the romantics abandoned entirely
the contemptuous treatment of past epochs that was spread during the
Enlightenment. For the romantics, every epoch had its inner meaning
and value and a definite significance as a link in the development of a

nation or of all mankind. Here lay the roots of the serious historicism that passed beyond the narrowness of romanticism.

Above all, "people" no longer now appeared to be a coincidental heap of humanity. The romantics conceived of the "people" as a collective personality and a community of fate. Language was understood as an expression of the national character or the "national spirit." The conception of Slavic unity and of the unified character of the Slavic nations (see the views of the first romantic Slavists, the idealized depictions of the peace-loving, humanity-loving, prehistoric Slavic peoples) remained for the present uncontested. Allegiance to various political and cultural circles stood in the way of modern Slavic unity. The problem of the individual languages of the "minor" Slavic nations led to tensions between Czechs and Slovaks, between Ukrainians and Great Russians. Consequently, the awakening of the Slavs encouraged the collapse of their unity at the same time, that is, their separation into individual national groups.

8. The questions of romantic poetics found but occasional statement in theoretical writings among the Slavs (see 12). The new literature desired to free itself from the limitations of classicism, above all, from the theory of genres. As a consequence, even the names of the genres disappeared in the titles of works. The designation "elegy" was able to preserve itself for some time. The ballad appeared as a new genre the value of which was seen in the possibility of manufacturing national and popular materials. The mostly short, lyrical poem was widely spread. The large epic works often offered mixtures of various genres. A particularly new type was the so-called "Byronic epic."

The most significant verse epics of Slavic romantic literature belonged to the "Byronic" or free-epic genre, for example, *Evgenij Onegin, A Novel in Verse* (the proclamation of the new form, for the novel traditionally belonged to the prose genres) by A. Puškin and *Pan Tadeusz* by Mickiewicz, as well as smaller epics, *Konrad Wallenrod* by Mickiewicz, several of Puskin's epics, *Beniowski* by J. Słowacki, numerous of Lermontov's epics, above all the most mature, *Mcyri*, and the incomplete *Demon*. Just as "Byronic" are the numerous epics of Ševčenko, Kuliš, and Janko Král'.

The Byronic epics carry distinctive features of free form. The stories were often fragmentarily presented and contained numerous digressions of a lyric and reflective character, while even long philosophical reflections were not rare. Apostrophizings to the readers, the characters, the work itself, and the rhetorical questions of the author to himself ("abdubitatio") were many. Allusions to, or even the concrete treatment of topical, current questions, or of the personal problems of the poet were just as permissible, as was everything that contradicted the classical tradition. Typical too was the bold mixture of serious and humorous elements; ironically expressed serious thoughts are on the whole characteristic of romantic literature. There were, of course, epics of more traditional construction: to these certainly belongs the important philosophical epic of the Montenegrin Count and Bishop Petar Njegoš, *Luča mikrokozma* (*The Ray of the Microcosm*), which was tied to the older European philosophy.

Drama is only partly constructed in the manner of the Shakespearian style (Puškin's *Boris Godunov*). The dramas often were not divided into acts; *Boris Godunov* consists of thirty smaller and larger scenes. The introduction of many secondary characters, among which are those from the "lower levels of society," the change of the location of the action, and the lengthening of the plot time, in contrast to the unity of place and time in Classic drama, and above all the mixing of serious and comic scenes, again signify essential deviations from classical poetics.

Puškin also wrote "small tragedies," another new form. The dramas of Słowacki and the comedies of the Russians (A. Griboedov) and Poles (A. Fredro), who in some degree follow the classical tradition, deserve special note.

A new genre that renewed the tradition of the Middle Ages and baroque period was that of the mystery play. Hardly meant for staging, its dramatic form was suited for the proclamation and discussion of theological and philosophical ideas. As well as people, the mystery plays presented supernatural beings, angels, devils, and personified representatives of the ideas.

Mysteries were written by the most important Slavic writers of the time. Perhaps the most gradiose plan was for Mickiewicz's *Dziady* (*The Death Feast*) which, typical for romanticism, remained a huge fragment. Beginning with a treatment of the problems of individual life, the poet's train of though intensifies itself to the point of historical-philosophical meditations concerning the Polish present. Z. Krasiński's important dramas *Irydion* and the *Godless Comedy* (*Nieboska Komedia*) are concerned with the philosophy of history with a strong streak of topicality, not general, but which overshadowed their ideological content—the Polish revolt of 1831, the *Vormärz* and Revolution of 1848.

The *Drama Sveta* (*Drama of World History*), until recently only known as a fragment, by the Slovak author Janko Král', was supposed to have presented historical-philosophical pictures that were just as grandiose. In contrast, the Slovak, Andrej Sládkovič, treated philosophical problems in his *Sôvety v rodine Dušanovej*, in which the characters are personified concepts of Hegelian philosophy. Just as philosophical are the *Intermezzo* in K. H. Mácha's *Máj* and the dark *Protichůdci (Antipodes)* of his imitator, Nebeský. Questions of Ukrainian national destiny appear in the foreground in T. Ševčenko's work, *Velykyj L'och—The Large Grave*, as well as in part in Mickeiwicz's *Dziady*. Puškin planned a large work, *Faust*, of which only fragments were completed, the weak *Scenes from Faust, Scenes in Hell*, and probably too the so-called *Scenes from Knightly Times*.

As already mentioned, another new form was the ballad, a narrative poem in strophic form with a strongly lyrical and dramatic strain. One can hardly fit the diversity of these ballads into one defined form. Historical and numinous—fantastic—materials are prevalent. Elements of Ossianism still often play a definite role. The ballad frequently permits the plot to disintegrate into individual scenes, the connections between which are produced by the reader's fantasy.

In Russia it was Žukovskij who more than anyone else translated Schiller and Uhland and who himself wrote original ballads. He was one of the best Slavic translators of those we know today. Original ballads were often associated with the "Celtic" tradition of Ossianism. P. Katenin who stood on the threshold of classicism and romanticism advocated the "nationalizing" of ballads. He brought his language close to that of the people and transferred his plots over to the simple Russian milieu. Many of Puškin's ballads for example, *Ženix—The Fiance*, *Utoplenik—The Drowned One*, also belong to this type of "nationalized" ballad. In Polish literature the most prominent were the excellent "numinous" ballads of Mickiewicz. It was perhaps in the ballads of the Czech, Erben that the zenith of Slavic ballad writing was attained, in his collection *Kytice—The Ostrich*, through the utilization of popular fairy tale motifs. Prešeren, Ševčenko, and Janko Král' wrote numerous ballads, although those of the latter two frequently have the scope of small epics.

A special role in the history of the Slavic ballad was played by *Lenore* by the German poet Bürger, which entered into all Slavic literatures either in translations or in connection with the related motifs of Slavic fairy tales, for example, Erben's *Svatební Košile—The Wedding Nightgown*, Katenin's *Ol'ga*, Mickiewicz's *Ucieczka—Flight*, the Ukrainian *Marusja* by Borovykovśkyj, the Russian *Svetlana* by Žukovskij, and others.

Historical ballads frequently had strongly national tones corresponding to the "Slavophile" spirit.

Imitators of folk songs were just as numerous as in German romanticism. Many of these imitations have become real folk songs.

Here are but some examples: *The Red Sarafan* is a song by N. Cyganov (1791–1851), *The Evening Bells* (*Večernij zvon*) is a translation by I. I. Kozlov (1779–1840) of a song by the English poet Thomas Moore (*Those Evening Bells*), *Trojka* (*Vot mčitsja trojka*) is a poem by F. Glinka (1786–1889). The best known song, *Stenka Razin* (*Iz-za ostrova* . . .) originated as late as the last third of the nineteenth century.

Numerous Ukrainian "folk songs" in quite the same manner originated in the romantic and post-romantic period. Such poets as T. Ševčenko and Janko Král' were best able to reproduce the tone of the folk song.

The "literary" fairy tales (*Kunstmärchen*) formed a genre just as venerated as the imitative folk song. In form they approach either the ballad or the Byronic epic.

Russian fairy tales in verse were written by Žukovskij and Puškin; partly, however, they are paraphrases of foreign originals. Žukovskij's *Puss-in-Boots* is a rendering of the French fairy tale by Perrault; Puškin's *Car Dodon* is a story from *Alhambra* by Washington Irving; *The Fairy Tale of the Fisherman and the Little Fish* is a paraphrase of Grimm's Low German fairy tale *Vom Fischer und syner Fru*, which the poet read in a French translation. Słowacki's drama *Balladyna* had its origin in a fairy tale. "Miniature poems" were a further "speciality" of romantic poetry.

Many of Tjutčev's best poems belong to this genre. Čelakovský wrote hundreds of from two- to six-line epigrams; Mickiewicz wrote a series of ingenious two liners that are in part translations of epigrams from the *Cherubinischer Wandersmann* of Angelus Silesius and in part reproduced thoughts of the German writers Jacob Boehme, Baader, or Mickiewicz himself. As an example, we may take a nature poem by Tjutčev:

> Песок сыпучий по колени . . .
> Мы едем—поздно—меркнет день,
> и сосен—по дороге—тени
> уже в одну слилися тень.
> Черней и чаще бор глубокий—
> какие грустные места!
> Ночь хмурая, как зверь стоокий
> глядит из каждого куста!

Knee-deep quicksand . . .

> We are riding—it is late—the day wanes,
> and the shadows of the pines along the way
> have already merged into one shadow.
> The deep pine forest grows blacker and thicker—
> how sad are these places!
> The gloomy night peers as a hundred-eyed animal
> from every bush!)

The last lines are reminiscent of Goethe's *Willkommen und Abschied* (*Welcome and Departure*) "... where darkness from the bushes with a hundred black eyes peered." The depicted landscape is probably not Russian but Bavarian!

Fragments were often published by authors. The fragment was a form that was prized by the romantics just as ruins and torsos. Short stories did not originate in American literature but previously in European. Many of Puškin's and Gogol''s novellas would be "short stories" in the present sense.

In prose, the content of the historical novels was new: the portrayals of distant times were founded upon the assumption that every historical epoch was *fraught with meaning*. The meaning of past epochs was shown not only in the fates of "great men," but also in the fates of the unknown representatives of those epochs. Walter Scott's influence was quite strong. It was difficult for the majority of Slavs, above all for the Russians, to portray their past which was so little known to them. As a consequence there were many distorted pictures of the Slavic Middle Ages. The historical adventure novel and penny-dreadful shocker attained no particular poetic heights.

Good examples of short novels that were rich in content were offered by Puškin (*The Captain's Daughter*) and Gogol' (*Taras Bulba*). The Pole, M. Czajkowski, wrote voluminous and "exciting" novels. Also of note is the Ukrainian P. Kuliš's *Čorna Rada* (a general popular meeting, gathering). The tradition of the romantic historical novel was active long after the romantic era.

9. The themes of romantic poetry and prose, some of which have already been mentioned (night, madness), must be noted: these themes are new in part, and several disappear later with the exit of romanticism.

People who are outside of everyday life (artists, geniuses), outside of society (robbers, criminals, hermits, wanderers), or guests from other worlds (good and evil spirits), and representatives of the simple people are typical figures in romantic literature.

Never were so many stories and novels written about artists, for example, Gogol''s *Portrait* and *Nevskij Prospect*, or, above all, never were so many poems dedicated to the artist, that is, the poet.

Degenerate inclinations and "solitary people" (the despised and persecuted poet-prophet), the person who was "thrust" into the world, the one who seeks his father in vain (Mácha), the criminal (the patricide in *Máj* by Mácha), and the "demonic" person (Wacław in the work of the same name by Słowacki, Arbenin in Lermontov's *Maskarad*) were all portrayed.

The Polish mystic poets see whole hordes of good and evil spirits about every human, and Satanic temptation or the struggle with the devil are the themes of numerous Polish mysteries and dramas: in Mickiewicz's *Dziady*, in the *Godless Comedy* of Z. Krasiński (Masynissa), in various dramas by Słowacki, especially *Samuel Zborowski*, and in Gogol''s short stories, the devil is always at work, while the hero must even struggle against the antichrist (*Portrait*). Lermontov made a demon the hero of an unfinished epic.[1]

Passion—regardless of whether good or evil—now became justified in romanticism in contrast to the centuries-long tradition that stemmed from the Stoics. Passion is a sign of sincerity of experience, freedom from convention, and the mark of a strong personality.

Among the passions love plays a prominent role in romantic literature. It is far from the conventional play to which it was degraded in the eighteenth century. True love seizes the entire person, penetrates into the depth of his soul; eroticism is related to religion. Eroticism is on the one hand a purifying force of its own; on the other hand, unfulfilled love can mean death.

The love sonnets of Prešeren or Mickiewicz bear witness to the new conception of love. That love is a human's fate is proved by Puškin in his tale *Metel'*—*Snowstorm* and in the unfinished *Egyptian Nights*. Gogol' speaks of death from love (*Nevskij Prospect*). The *Fragment (Ułamek) of an Old Slavic Manuscript* by Z. Krasiński offers a metaphysical theory of love.

Youth is an important theme of romantic literature because the "Romantics are always young," that is, they perceive themselves as "young" with all the advantages and disadvantages, virtues and shortcomings of this period of life.

---

1. Here is meant Lermontov's *Demon*. Lermontov wrote some eight versions of this poem, some of which remained unfinished, some produced to satisfy the requirements of censorship. *Demon* was published only after Lermontov's death, and it is thus hard to determine which version should be considered the definitive text (editor).

The images of living nature (see above, 6), of nations fighting for freedom, as, for example, Philhellenism, and consequently, the freedom of their own nations, that is, all Slavs except the Russians, the only Slavic nation to be free in the romantic era, are the themes of the national and "Slavophile" literatures. Serbocroatian literature is dominated by such motifs, and Polish literature contains the image of a suffering, crucified people that is to bring to humanity new ethic and religious values (see below, 12 c).

Religious motifs often associated with the conception of religion as one area of the emotions occur in isolated cases.

Religious motifs are especially strong with the Polish romantics (see below). In Russian literature they are somewhat represented by Tjutčev and the Slavophiles (Khomjakov) and in the half-forgotten late works of F. Glinka.

Mickiewicz's biblically stylized *Books of the Pilgrimage of the Polish People* are ideologically messianic and found imitators in the writings of the Slovak L'. Štúr (*Starý a nový věk Slováků*) as well as in the Ukrainian *Books of the Genius of the Ukrainian People*, probably written by the historian N. Kostomarov.

Exoticism, leading away from everyday life, offers a special thematic area. Exoticism was found in the near Orient, in the Gypsies living among the Slavs, and frequently in the Ukraine.

The Ukraine was felt to be an "exotic" land and therefore appeared in Russian and Polish literature. The Russian poet Ryleev had already written about the freedom efforts of the Ukrainians and was followed by Puškin. But it was Gogol' (as with some lesser poets of his environment) who raised the Ukraine to a Slavic "Ausonia." This trend was much stronger in Poland where Bohdan Zaleski, Goszczyński, and Malczewski were characterized as representatives of the "Ukrainian School."

Some Polish poets even wrote in Ukrainian (Tymko Padura became especially famous). The Orient was also significantly represented in Polish literature.

The certain onesidedness to the, in itself, diversity of romantic literary themes created even among the romantics a pleasure in self-parody. That much more comprehensible were the sharp attacks of the non-romantic contemporaries, especially the classicists.

The Russian journals spoke of the Russian romantics as people who believe that without "violence, dirt, blood, revolting scenes, scaffolds, and hangmen's assistants there can be no art." (*Severnaja Pčela*, 1834.) One was able to read similar statements in the Polish journals. The romantic writers "desecrate nature with a brush dipped in filth," they write in a style that is "empty, but full of noise, sparks, and soot, as in a smithy [*Balamut*, 1834]."

The classicist Kajetan Koźmian depicted the romantics' ideal in a satirical epistle directed at F. Morawski:

> Nie ucz się, lecz pisz jak chcesz! (...)
> ...— stargajmy przepisy (...)
> Usiądzmy z lutnią w ręku między wiejskie prządki
> i własnym ich językiem nowe tworąc wzory,
> śpiewajmy: wiedźmy, strachy, strzygi i upiory (...)
> Przedmiot gminny dostarczy rymów do osnowy.
> Cóż stąd że nieco trąci—ale narodowy...
> Sam przeto przedmiot gminny godzien wieszczów śpiewu,
> niech więc nasze pasterki paszą trzodę z chlewu,
> niech im pijany Maciek przygrywa na dudzie,
> po co smakiem salonów psuć prosty smak w ludzie? (...)
> W naturze wszystko piękne, godne oka, ucha,
> równie piękny koń dzielny, jak błotna ropucha (...)
> Witaj, wieku szczęśliwy do pychy powodem,
> ty nam obraz natury zdołasz wydać szczery,
> idź do jaskini łotrów, tam twe bohatery,
> spiesz wystawiać na scenie rosnące nadzieje:
> wspaniale rozbójniki, szlachetne złodzieje (...)
> Przed takimi cudami, któż by się nie korzył?
> Lecz nie Bóg, ale diabeł takich wieszczów stworzył!...

Don't learn, rather write as you desire . . . Let us rip up the rules [of poetics] . . . Let us sit ourselves down, lute in hand, among the village spinners, and, in their own language, creating new standards, let us sing the praises of witches, horrors, sorcerers, and ghosts . . . These base themes provide enough rhymes as a foundation. What difference does it make that they stink a bit? After all they're national! The base object is worthy of the poets' song. Let the shepherdesses drive herds out of the sty, let the drunken Maciek play his reed-pipe for them. For what reason should one spoil the simple taste of the people with the taste of the salons . . . Everything is beautiful in nature and worthy of being seen and heard, the good horse just as beautiful as the swamp toad . . . Greetings happy age that has grounds for being proud, you will be capable of giving us nature's true picture; hasten upon the stage to present our growing hopes: the magnificent robbers, the noble criminals . . . Who could not succumb to such wonders? However, not God, but Satan has created such poets!

10. The romantics attributed an extraordinary significance to language. The renovation of the language was necessary in most of the Slavic literatures, for classicism had frequently served itself of an archaic language, and in those literatures in which travesties played a special role the vocabulary was essentially limited (see Chapter IX, 8). In some Slavic nations the new or renovated literary language originated first in

the romantic period, as was the case with the Ukrainians, Slovaks, Slovens, and Sorbs. The conception of literature's elevated function and the leading role of the poet, absolutely free in his creativity, led to the idea that the poet also had the right, and even the duty, of working creatively in the use of language.

The words of J. Jungmann, the reviver of the Czech language are typical: "The poet should create a new, special language for himself, thereby lending his work the necessary artistic feature without which literature will never raise itself above the sphere of everyday language and never become a beautiful work."

By the utilization of elements from language levels that had, until then, been neglected, as well as through borrowings from foreign languages (see below), and by various means of lingual creativity an enrichment of the language soon occurred: in addition to neologisms there were new meanings applied to words already being used.

All these ways led to the origin of a language that was strongly resisted by the classicists wherever they were strong enough.

More than anywhere else, it is among the Poles and Russians, who possessed literatures with "standardized" vocabularies, that we encounter a lexical expansion by means of borrowing words from various lingual spheres that were considered "not literally capable." In Russian, the classicist Dmitriev attempted to influence Puškin through Karamzin so that the young poet would desist in using "vulgarisms." He considered "vulgarisms" to be words from the colloquial language of the time, as, for example, *na cypočkâx ču!* Words such as *udavit'*, *ščekotat'*, *činut'*, *rukavica*, were frowned upon.

Gogol', who had already used numerous real vulgarisms since 1831, was censured for the unaesthetic "dirt" of his language.

Mickiewicz's *Crimean Sonnets* aroused the indignation of the Polish classicists for the many Orientalisms that "spoiled" the language and made it "impure."

Puškin introduced numerous French, English, and other foreign words into the language of his *Novel in Verse, Evgenij Onegin*, with the clear intention of "scandalizing" the reader. He emphasized the effect of these borrowings by having them appear as rhyme words (see especially Chapter I where, in addition to words in Latin orthography, such as Madame, Monsieur, l'Abbé, dandy, vale, roastbeef, entrechat, beefsteak, far niente, there appear "prosaisms" as for example, *pedant*, *anekdot*, *ekonom*, *bolivar*, *bul'var*, *breget*, *kulisy*, *lornet*, *loži*, *lakei*, *fonari*, *kabinet*, *frant*, *karety*, *profili*, *kamin*, *splin*). Puškin justified this usage:

Но панталоны, фрак, жилет,
всех этих слов на русском нет...

But long pants, frock, vest,
All these words do not exist in Russian.

In addition many prosaic names of foreign authors—not only poets, such as Say and Bentham—are to be found, and then there are real "vulgarisms" and St. Petersburg colloquialisms as well.

Prince V. F. Odoevskij even introduced words from the thieves' cant into literature.

The situation was similar with the Polish writers. Mickiewicz's "Orientalisms," the use of which, however, was frequently occasioned by his themes, awakened the classicists' indignation. The Turko-Tartar words in his early ballad, *Renegat*, had most likely been known to many people since the seventh century, for example, aga, basza, cybuch, dywan, effendy, harem, turban, padiszach, nevertheless, K. Koźmain was able to write, "That may all be Crimean, Turkish, and Tartar, but it is not Polish. We have to travel to Stambul in order to learn Mickiewicz's language." Mickiewicz came from the Polish–White Russian lingual area and as a consequence many "provincialisms" or East Slavic words, as in the ballad *Romantyczność* (see above) duby (Polish, dęby), smalone (Polish, smolone), or declensional forms (mnie, ciebie where mi, cię are to be expected) are met in his work.

Juliusz Słowacki, who spent a part of his youth in Ukranian Kremenec, uses many words in Ukrainian phonetic form, or in a form near to it, as buriany, hospodyn, ihumen, mołodyca, podorožna, pohaniec, rozhovor, światka; in other cases he uses numerous Russianisms: cwiet (Polish, kwiat), ikona, kazna, kaznaczej, korabl, turma żerkało, żałoba (in the meaning of accusation), or words that may be both Russian or Ukrainian: chwost, czerń, porosza, wołokyta, and so forth.

There were also efforts toward lexical enrichment in progress in the Polish student circles, the so-called "filarety" and "filomaty," of the twenties. As well as numerous archaisms we encounter several dialectisms, East Slavicisms, and attempts to form neologisms. Mickiewicz is surely indebted for much to these efforts.

The language of the Czech romantic authors is distinguished by a lingual norm that was not yet sufficiently secured. Therefore one finds numerous, purely orthographic digressions from the earlier—those of Jungmann—and later norms in the work of Mácha. Dialectisms and words from the popular language are found in the work of Božena

Němcová. Later her well-known Slovakisms, the result of her stay in Slovakia, slip into her work.

It is hardly possible to speak of "departures" from nonexisting norms in the other Slavic literatures, South Slavic specifically, that had to form first their literary languages. There is rather a competition of vocabulary and morphological forms of various regions, that is, of various dialects.

Much more important was the creation of neologisms that, as always, were used by particularly talented creators of words.

Among the Russians E. Boratynskij and N. Jazykov, both of whom stood close to Puškin, and later the epigone, V. Benediktov, belonged to this class.

The creation of a philosophic terminology seemed important. The new Russian words were often intentionally or accidentally, conditional upon the word-building possibilities of Russian, reused loan words that had already been known in the oldest times, or word formations from philosophic-theological literature (Hexameron, Pēgē gnōseōs, etc; see Chapters II and III).

The case was different in Polish where the new terms were simply borrowed or had to be newly created: see, for example, the philosophical words no longer used such as chowanna (pedagogy), myśliny or umnictwo (philosophy), umnictwo piękne (aesthetics).

There is a modern study that presents a compilation of neologisms in the works of the Polish romantics and shows that of about 800 such words the lion's share belongs to Słowacki (ca. 250); several originated with Krasiński (more than forty) and Mickiewicz (only twenty-two).

Czech romanticism was able to build upon the creations of the preromantics, for example, the work of A. Marek and, above all, J. Jungmann, particularly his translations. The creations of M. Z. Polák, who was already on the verge of romanticism, such as the neologism rich, *Vznešenost přírody, Nature's Sublimity*, 1819, left behind little trace in the vocabulary of the later literary language. Mácha belongs to the Romantic word creators: numerous peculiar composita, among others names of colors, new formations of abstracts, and translated borrowings mostly belong to the ad hoc neologisms, created in a specific context, that often maintain the pronounced character of his individual style. Most of them today no longer belong to the fixed stock of the Czech literary language; their fate is almost exclusively bound to the popularity of *his* verses.

The problems of language were quite intricate. A group of Yugoslavian poets and scholars (L. Gaj, Stanko Vraz, and others) made an attempt to create a common literary language for Serbocroatians and Slovenians, the so-called "Illyrism". Without success! In contrast, L'. Štúr and his friends created a Slovak literary language based upon the central Slovak dialect (Liptov). S. B. Hroboň and M. Hodža distinguished themselves as masters of Slovakian neologisms; their innovations are mostly forgotten since they became known only later.

11. Problems of style to which the new vocabulary was supposed to be useful were, of course, very important. Overloading with poetic decoration was not demanded, however, it was permitted and valued.

The following features were the most important:

a. "Free form." It was at times intentionally placed before the eyes of the reader through the publishing of "fragments" and, in such narrative works as ballads, short stories, and "Byronic epics", by leaving the important facts of the plot in the dark.

Puškin numbered the individual stanzas in *Evgenij Onegin* and provided numbers for the "omitted" stanzas as well. Gogol' published a story, *Ivan Fedorovič Špon'ka*, as a fragment; from the manuscripts we see that the author also planned the story as a fragment from the very beginning. "Free form" is associated with the romantic conception of the poet as a creator bound by no laws or rules.

b. "Paradoxical plots" (*sujets*) that frequently turn the traditional schemes around are part of the composition of romantic works. That virtue does not conquer vice is a further deviation from classical tradition. The hero's tragic demise, too, is almost a norm in romantic epics.

Puškin's *Evgenij Onegin* also has such a paradoxical plot. It does not deal with one happy love but two unhappy ones, and in addition to the classical "I love you!" there is an "I do not love you," a second time the overcoming of love. The daughter of the *Stationmaster* in Puškin's story, as obvious from the ending, has in no way perished, as her father thought and as the film makers assume.

All of Lermontov's and Ševčenko's narrative poems are good examples of tragic epics; the customary ballad ending (see Mickiewicz or Erben) is the tragic demise of the heroes.

c. "Romantic irony" that is supposed to suggest to the reader the awareness that all in life is transitory in the face of the eternal and absolute appears in serious works as well as in "light genres."

For this reason the latest investigators have been able to characterize *Evgenij Onegin* as a "humoristic epic" (A. Isačenko) and *Pan Tadeusz* also as humoristic or as an "anti-prophetic epic" (Weintraub).

d. In particular, vagueness, the darkness of individual passages was the intention of romantic authors: the reality of which the poets speak is simply puzzling and mysterious.

Nebeský's *Protichůdci* (*The Antipodes*) is one of the vaguest works of the Romantics; all attempts at interpretation have, thus far, been unconvincing. Also in this class is Słowacki's *Król-Duch*. The poems of the language innovators as, for example, those of the Slovak S. B. Hroboň, offer purely lingual obstacles to comprehension.

Almost as popular as in the baroque were antitheses and ambivalent statements, blows against logic and consistent "normal human reason."

e. The fact that events lie in a double causality is connected with the vagueness of presentation. The events are related to each other as manifestations of this world and are woven into the deeper contexts of another world or worlds.

f. Everything in the world has a symbolic significance. Almost every romantic poet, however, had his own symbolism that was often conjured up by a single reoccuring word, a "keyword," or by an image.

g. Often the vagueness is connected with the poet's seeing his work as the expression of his personality, and he communicates comprehensible facts and ideas by means of all sorts of allusions to personal experiences meant only for "the in-crowd"—friends, the like-minded, protectors of the mysteries, etc. This freedom of personal expression too belongs to the romantic idea of "free form." There was much—owing to the censorship of the times—that the poets were able to convey to the reader only by allusion.

h. "Eloquent silence," a counterpart to speech, paradoxically enigmatic and profound at the same time, belongs to the most extreme level of vagueness. Indeed, language was considered truly incapable of expressing the most significant, the most elevated. Even symbols frequently could not suffice.

i. A special feature was the gradual infiltration of folkloristic elements into the language and style of the literary works. It is sufficient here merely to recall the extensive use of the *epitheta ornantia* of folk literature, not only in song and fairy tale, but in works of other genres as well. The creation of epithets suggestive of the "decorative epithets" of popular literature was also characteristic.

In Puškin's *Pesn' o Veščem Olege*, in addition to the authentic popular *sinee more* there occur such newly created epithets as *obmančivyj val* and *lukavyj kinžal* (blue sea, deceptive wave, insidious dagger, etc.).

One further finds the use of personified epithets that are related to nature—for the romantics, "living"—and to objects of *nature morte* as well.

For example, in Puškin's *Evgenij Onegin* there is a *lornet* (lorgnette) that is now "searching" (*razyskatel'nyj*), now "jealous" (*revnivyj*), now "disappointed" (*razočarovannyj*). One can hardly enumerate all the various types of epithets.

k. Quite characteristic was the great number of euphonic harmonies in the verse (and also in the prose) of some poets which was partly associated with the folkloristic tradition and also with the demand for "musicality" of language. Euphony did *not always* let itself be united with precision and clarity of expression.

The harmoniously rich works of Janko Král' and Ševčenko best bear witness to a blending of euphony with folk literature; Mácha is also a romantic representative of euphonic literature. The following poem by Ševčenko provides an example (the sound repetition and sound complexes are shown next to the text):

У неділю вранці рано	н-л-ран-ран-о
поле крилося туманом;	пол-лос-ту-ман-ом
у тумані на мотилі	ту-ман-н-мо-лі
як тополя похилилась	то-пол-по-ли-лась
молодиця молодая.	мол-од-мол-од
Щось до лона пригортає	ось-до-лон-ор
і з туманом розмовляє:	тум-ан-ом-ро-мо-л
«Ой, тумане, тумане!	тум-ан-е-тум-ан-е
Мій латаний талане!	ла-та-ни-та-ла-не
Чому мене не сховаєщ	ом-у-ме-не-не
отут черед лану?»	о-ту-ла-ну

On an early Sunday morning the field decked itself in fog; in the fog, on a grave mound, a young woman bowed herself as a poplar. She presses something to her breast and speaks with the fog: "O fog, fog! O my disrupted fate! Why do you not bury me here, in the middle of the field?"

12. We may enumerate only briefly the elements of the romantic ideology here.

a. Freedom aspirations—be they political or only related to spheres of intellectual culture or the life of individuals—are presumably common to all romantics. Consequently, the division of the romantics into "revolutionary" and "reactionary" groups, as frequently nowadays happens, is hardly justified. Quite often, especially in the case of those influenced by Byron, it is difficult to differentiate *for whom* and *which* freedom was meant—possibly only for the chosen, the "higher beings," the Titans. "Romantic restlessness" is perhaps the best designation to encompass all the various freedom aspirations of this side of the romantic ideology. The designation "Prometheism" (V. Černý) fits the work of some romantics quite well.

The "modesty" of many writers may be explained by the fact that in several nations they came predominantly from clerical families, as for example, the west Ukrainian ("Ruthenian") writers and the Slovak romantics who frequently rejected Byron.

b. The conception of a *living* nature that was seen as innerly related to man, particularly to the poet, was a general one, for it is literature that stands closest to nature's creative powers too. Nevertheless nature is also a force hostile and destructive toward humans.

c. Mystical tendencies were quite strong among some romantics, and it should not be forgotten that important Polish authors (above all Mickiewicz) were under the insurmountable influence of the—even today—enigmatic mystic, A. Towiański. Other, older mystical currents were also at work. Particularly important were the after effects of the eighteenth-century mysticism of Svendenborg and Saint-Martin. If mystical aspirations were typical only for isolated romantics, as for a time for V. Odoevskij in Russia, we nevertheless encounter an interest in mysticism among almost all romantic writers. There were also attempts to develop independent mystical systems of cognition which, however, remained only fragmentary for the most part, see especially the ideas of J. Słowacki or S. B. Hroboň.

d. For a long time Slavophilism was not peculiar to all romantics. The first Slavophiles, especially J. Kollár and J. Šafařík,[2] were actually quite modest ideologues of Slavic cultural unity, especially the representatives of the western and southern Slavic nations who saw in this unity support of the cultural and, partially, political development of their own nations. Among other things, their idealized conception of the character of the Slavs was peculiar to them.

The second group—the Russian Slavophiles—had, with few exceptions, no particularly clear conception of the other Slavic nations; their ideology was too strongly tied up with Greek Orthodoxy. They endeavored to work out essential differences between the Slavic and Occidental world. Before 1855 they had hardly any connection with official Russian political circles.

The third group was composed of the so-called Polish "Messianists,"

2. Jan Kollár (1793–1852), writer of a Panslavic poem *Daughter of the Glory*, was a Slovak poet; Pavel Josef Šafřík (1795–1861) was an outstanding Czech philologist and archaeologist, one of the founders of Slavic linguistics (editor).

including some philosophers as well as the romantic poets (the word
"Messianism" itself probably originated with Hoene-Wroński who was
no Messianist in the Slavophile sense), who had the tragic fate of the
Polish people in view and compared the fate of Poland with Christ's road
to Calvary.

Kollár's early hope of realizing Slavic "reciprocity" in the cultural
field was typical for the first group.

The Russian Slavophiles had broad sociopolitical ideals. K. Aksakov
wrote,

> A person within the community, just as a nation, has before him either the new
> way of *inner* justice (*pravda*), of conscience, of freedom, or the way of *outer* jus-
> tice, of law, of serfdom. The first way is the way of society, or better, of the
> *community* (*zemskij put'*), the second is the way of the *State*. . . . The essential
> difference between the Slavic and Occidental world lies in the conception of State.
> In the Occident the state is a fundamental principle, an *ideal* of nations. In the
> Slavic world the state is only the indispensible *outer* being, a *means* that is requi-
> site because of the imperfection of the human race.

The opinion of the Messianists for whom the national state was indeed
an ideal is quite different. "Suffering is the law and at the same time the
greatness of the world" (Z. Krasiński); the death and resurrection of the
Polish people are "its Christian mission," self-sacrifice is the basis of
Polish history (Mickiewicz).

The foundations of the Slavophile philosophy of history can be traced
back from Herder to Hegel.

e. In no other period of literary development has there been so much
written—including artistic writings—about the poet and his calling. The
poet is a teacher, leader, prophet, king, even a God, or at the least a
demonic demi-Godlike being. Consequently no human scale of standards
may be applied to him. Among the Slavs, whom the doctrine of genius
passed over without any strong effects, this high evaluation of the poet
appears as particularly surprising. The poet, however, was thought to be
alone and was mocked, persecuted, and destroyed by the people or
"mob." Poetry is the poet's creation but it is not accidental, it is not
merely invented, but "discovered," located in the concealed strains of
his being, and its effects are eternal.

Or, as frequently among the southern Slavs, only the effects of the
poet on the individual—the softening of suffering, catharsis according
to Prešeren, Jovanović-Zmaj, and others—or strains that would awaken
the nation were expected (Peradović and the Ukrainians). In some cases

the poet only continued the tradition of the old folk singers (see the Ukrainian romantics, or Vuk Karadžić).[3]

The theoretical views of the Slavic romantics were often dependent and inconsistent.

It is only with the Poles that we really find significant writings on romanticism. We can trace these theoretically important statements, with their sources in West European philosophy, from K. Brodziński (1818) until M. Mochnacki (around 1830) and Edward Dembrowski (1843). In contrast, the Russian theoretical writings are of little importance. The Russian romantics were frequently satisfied with but a sharp rejection of classical poetics.

13. Romanticism did not suddenly cease to exist; there were "mature forms" of romantic literature. First there is the "Biedermeier," a movement of little significance literarily among the Slavs, that presents romantic motifs in a diminished form. The fantastic is often replaced by paradoxes which are frequently external, the bold inspirations by erudition or by a zeal for compilation, pathos by reflection. Probably the most important factor was the grooming of external form.

There are only writers of secondary importance in East Slavic literature to list as representatives of Biedermeier. Perhaps the most important is the Russian poetess Karolina Pavlova. Tjutčev came close to Biedermeier in his later years. Among the Western Slavs, the most important representative of this form of late romanticism is Cyprian Norwid, one of the greatest and most enigmatic of Polish poets. In spite of all the originality which makes it difficult to place him within the framework of a particular movement, his religiosity and the reflective character of his poems, which sometimes *sui generis* grow into treatises, link him to Biedermeier. He pits the cult of work against the impetuosity of romanticism.

14. A more significant role along the way to realism was played by an important movement in Russian literature represented in the forties by the most talented writers of the younger generation, the so-called "natural school" (*Natural'naja skola*). Of course, even earlier than this, in addition to the works that depicted the higher world or the struggle of the two worlds, romanticism had included works that devoted their attention to the "lower" everyday world in order to intensify or awaken

3. Vuk Karadžić reformed Serbian and Croatian orthography and created the modern Serbo-Croatian literary tongue, switching from Church Slavonic traditional patterns to Serbo-Croatian spoken dialect (editor).

a longing for the other better worlds by means of their repulsive images painted in exaggerated, dark colors. To this class belong some late stories of E. T. A. Hoffmann, the early novels of Dickens and Balzac, the works of Jules Janins (which are almost beyond the limits of romanticism), and others.

The main stylistic characteristics of the "natural school" are, in the first instance, the depreciation or "abasing" of the themes and the plot heroes, the intentional emphasizing of the "dirty" sides of reality, and the treatment of the "physiology" of everyday life, that is, the almost automatic actions of individuals, such as eating, smoking, blowing one's nose, and the masses—the conventional actions of the average man. The landscapes and images of the cities bear the same gloomy features, for example, rain, dust, dirt, gray, unclean houses, and apartments, etc.

The language of the heroes, who also belong to the "lower" elements of the population, who are uneducated and exploited—the petty bureaucrat, artisan, peasant—is awkward, while the language of the fictitious narrator to whom the author entrusts the task of reporting is often just as awkward and "prosaic."

This can all easily be turned to the grotesque and become purely plotless reporting, the "social" coloring of which is self evident (the so-called "physiological sketch," Russian, *očerk*).

Mácha's novel *Marinka* is one of the rare earlier examples of this genre. Gogol' with his story *The Overcoat* and the "epic" (Russian, *poema*) *Dead Souls* is considered the founder of the "school" in Russian literature. He had, however, already published models of this style. Between 1842 and 1855 he was followed by the most important Russian realistic writers, Dostoevskij, Gončarov, Turgenev, Grigorovič; the Ukrainians Grebenka (Hrebinka); Ševčenko, in his stories written in Russian; Kuliš, who again later struck romantic tones; and numerous other writers. The inclination to lack of theme was characteristic.

The same authors rejected the "natural school's" stylistic forms at their transition to realism.

15. But romanticism was drawing to a close. More than with any other literary movement, the immanent inner weaknesses of romanticism played a contributing role. The generation of the end of the forties became cognizant of romanticism's "weaknesses." The romantics valued dreams and fantasies, nourished great plans and projects that, however, were never carried out—and that were, moreover, practically impossible to carry out. The overestimation of intentions and the neglect of their realization meant flight from life into a sphere out of which there fre-

quently led no way back to reality. In particular the nurturing of feeling and experience meant the neglect of accomplishment. Many romantics were excluded from public life after about 1845.[4] In addition to the exiled as Dostoevskij or Ševčenko, numerous writers, including important ones, ceased to be heard for decades or forever, as Janko Kráľ. "Detail work" seemed to them to be in vain and meaningless, and nevertheless their own aims were unattainable.

In spite of this, for a long time some achievements of romantic philosophy remained viable in the so-called realism. It was the elements of historicism, not to mention its scholarly achievements (many important Slavic historians and Slavists were romantics), that most of all opened the eyes of the Slavic nations to their own history on the one hand and to their national identity on the other. The high evaluation of folklore was also maintained. The romantic tradition has been effective right up into the present, particularly in historical works, such as novels and dramas.

The emotions were another area upon which the romantic philosophy had an influence even after the collapse of romanticism. The high evaluation of the human personality, the serious conception of love, the renewal of a feeling for nature, and to a certain degree the insight into the "depths of the soul" remained effective even in the psychology of later generations.

Some elements of the romantic style of life with its antibourgeois features also remained preserved, among other things "Bohemianism". Thus the rebirth of romanticism in a new form at the end of the nineteenth century was able to continue a tradition that, in some respects, was still a living one.

16. The romantic epoch was a period of closer relations between the Slavic literatures. During that time emanations from Russian romanticism began to spread, primarily among the Ukrainian, Slovakian, and Czech literatures. The development of these literatures was conditioned by Russia's far-reaching influence, even though Russian literature was only known among the Czechs and in the west Ukraine (Galicia) from occasional and not always adequate translations. The ideas of the Russian Slavophiles were also influential.

Significantly, the opinions about Russia of the radical Czech poet and politician Karel Havlíček-Borovský, who spent time in Russia and became acquainted with many groups including Slavophiles, are

4. In Poland, since 1830, the year of the unsuccessful insurrection against Russia; among the Austrian Slavs, since the Revolution of 1848 (editor).

strangely negative and pessimistic (see his *Obrazy z Rusi—Images from Russia*).

The influences of Polish literature were no less broad. The Czech political and literary movement in *Vormärz* and 1848 made use of Polish stimuli that, in their turn, go back to the Polish uprising of 1831.

In Russia as well an attempt was made—above all by the Slavophiles—to become acquainted with the Czech national movement, Slavicism, and literature.

Even the politically conservative Slavophiles, such as the historian M. Pogodin, during their trips abroad not only maintained relations with such Czech scholars as Šafařík, V. Hanka and Purkyně, but also with such Polish emigrees as Mickiewicz. Gogol', who had been living mostly abroad since 1837, also had contact with Polish emigree circles (Mickiewicz, B. Zaleski, and Catholic-national circles). Slavists such as I. Sreznevskij and O. Bodjanskij also visited Slovaks. The efficacy of Czech Slavistics on the Polish and Russian was considerable.

V. Hanka's forged "old Czech" writings were also translated; however, they must be considered today only as the product of their creator's romantic enthusiasm, that is as romantic writings. Serbian folk literature also stimulated interest. Puškin reworked Merimée's mystification *Gouzla* and supplemented it with material from other sources including Slovakian. A. Vostokov, the founder of Russian Slavic studies and also a poet, tried to produce a more accurate rendition of the Serbian epic songs. Prince P. Vjazemskij translated Polish poetry. Ukrainian songs were translated into Russian by Del'vig and others. The mutual interest of the western and southern Slavs for one another also resulted in all sorts of translations and paraphrases. Čelakovský and Erben translated Russian songs and fairy tales.

The Slavic Congress that took place in Prague in 1849 was a characteristic undertaking even if it had little consequence for literary life.

Interest in Slavic literature was awakened in western literary circles during the romantic epoch. At that time, the first collections of Slavic folk and artistic literature appeared in West European languages.

Further information about Slavic literature was spread through public lectures. W. Küchelbecker held lectures on Russian literature in Paris as early as 1821. These, however, were discontinued at the demand of the Russian embassy. Mickiewicz lectured on Slavic literature in 1840 at the Collège de France. More was learned by students in lectures on Slavistics beginning in Breslau in 1842, and 1849 in Vienna.

The interest of the great West European writers of the time in Slavic literature was typical: the Slavic literature with which they became acquainted was primarily romantic.

Notable too were the numerous visits of Slavic authors to Goethe (W. Küchelbecker, V. Žukovskij, Tjutčev and others). Earlier the story that Goethe sent Puškin his pen with a dedication was considered legendary. The pen with Goethe's note has, however, been preserved.

Thus we are presented with a picture of lively relations among the Slavic literatures which, in their turn, also were gradually becoming better known to the West European world.

XI

REALISM

Russians

I. S. Turgenev (1818–1883)
F. M. Dostoevskij (1821–1881)
L. N. Tolstoj (1828–1910)
N. S. Leskov (1831–1895)
N. A. Nekrasov (1821–1877)
A. P. Čexov (1860–1904)
M. Gor'kij (1868–1936)

Ukrainians

Panas Myrnyj (1849–1920)
I. Nečuj-Levyćkyj (1838–1918)
I. Franko (1856–1916)—with tendencies toward modernism
M. Kocjubyńskyj (1864–1913)—with tendencies toward modernism
Several popular playwrights

Poles

B. Prus (ca. 1847–1912)
E. Orzeszkowa (1842–1910)
H. Sienkiewicz (1846–1916)

I must dispense with the necessarily long quotations in the treatment of prose works in this chapter. The works of the Slavic realists have, however, been translated into the West European languages in relatively large number, so that the reader may himself find "illustrations" for my assertions.

W. Syrokomla (1823–1862)
A. Asnyk (1838–1897)
M. Konopnicka (1842–1910)

Czechs

J. Neruda (1834–1891)
J. Arbes (1840–1914)
J. Vrchlický (1853–1912) with tendencies toward modernism

Slovaks

S. Hurban-Vajanský (1847–1916)
P. Hviezdoslav (1849–1921)
M. Kukučin (1860–1928)

Serbs

J. Ignjatović (1824–1889)
S. Sremac (1855–1906)
B. Nušić (1864–1938)
Laza Lazarević (1851–1890)

Croats

A. Šenoa (1838–1881)
I. Kozarac (1858–1906)
J. Leskovar (1861–1949)
S. Kranjčević (1865–1908)

Slovenes

J. Kersnik (1852–1897)
A. Aškerc (1856–1912)

Bulgarians

I. Vazov (1850–1921)
P. Slavejkov (1827–1895)—with tendencies toward modernism

1. Romanticism was superseded by realism. Perhaps a better word would be "ousted," since we are not dealing here with the unnoticeable

transition of two cultural movements, but rather with the violent struggle of one against the other. Realism was fighting romanticism at a time when the latter's literature had long since become a matter of the past. Later, attempts were even undertaken to disavow the very existence of romanticism and the affiliation of certain famous writers with this "reactionary" or even "pernicious" movement. The Western reader may in many cases wonder why works that he can conceive of only as totally romantic are designated "realistic" by Slavic scholars. Indeed, occasionally Western scholars and writers also succumb to the influence of such Slavic interpretations and apply to Western literature quite different criteria than to Slavic.

2. The vague definition of the concept "realism" lies more than anything else at the source of the difficulty involved in drawing a boundary between it and other literary movements. That "realism is the presentation of reality as it is" is, of course, a useless tautology: the presentation of reality as it is in reality. The mere presentation of reality cannot be considered a constructive element of a literary style. Depictions of the lives of peasants, artisans, industrial workers, or even of beggars and scoundrels appear at various times as "innovations," and indeed always so according to the manner in which any given period saw "reality." From this naive standpoint the comedies, satires, and even the travesties of classicism, the naturalistic portrayals of the renaissance and the baroque (see above), and even of all other epochs could be characterised as "realistic." Also "realistic" would then be every extension of artistic presentation into areas that, in general, one had never dared to put in front of the reader's eyes ("physiology" or bold erotic scenes).

The appeal was made for realism to take its forms, tones, and colors from reality. That is what every literary style does, however; the presentation of worlds lying beyond everyday life is only possible with the words that characterize the elements of our "Euclidian" world (Dostoevskij). Utopian and fantastic literature from antiquity to the present bears witness to our limited means of expression and powers of imagination. It is often only "negative hyperbole" that offers the poet an apparent possibility of exceeding the boundaries of the "Euclidian reality." It is merely necessary to recall the romantics' ironically used forms as, for example, "Beauty of a type never seen by the world," "my pen is not strong enough to present it," "with what words can I depict it." Or a manifestation or experience was characterized as "extraordinary," "unusual," expressions were used such as "a strange mood," "an indescribable feeling." Such means, of course, can create the illusion that they are leading us beyond the borders of reality into a "non-Euclidian world." Artifices such as these, however, are essentially foreign to realism.

In addition, metaphors, similes, and other stylistic means enable the poet to bridge the boundaries of reality. If a girl is called a flower, love a flame flaring in the human heart, the lover compared to a corpse, if a woman's eyes are as piercing as arrows, or if, having the intention of debasing reality, man is characterized as a wet poodle, as a "middle-sized bear," or even as a snapped twig or a watermelon, then metaphors and similes such as these also lead us away from everyday occurrences into a completely different sphere of being.

If we refrain from such literary games we remain faced with a "mono-planed" world where it is not a question of "above" and "below" but of "here" and "nearby." This is what defines the realistic style and its devices.

3. The means with which the consistent realist works are *not metaphoric* but *metonymic;* that is to say, a realistic presentation utilizes, above all, those literary possibilities that lead from the presented object to its environment, to "that which is located nearby." Roman Jakobson was the first to point out the significance of metonymic means in the poetics of realism. Whereas metaphoric means relate and, even more important, compare an object in various ways with objects of other spheres of being, metonomy depicts what is to be presented in relation to its own environment.

The reader is led to other objects found in the same sphere, adjacent to the presented object. We encounter these artificial means in romanticism as well.

See, for example, the heroine of Puškin's *Snow Storm* who "was educated with French novels," or the interior of Evgenij Onegin's study:

и груда книг . . .
. . . .
И лорда Байрона портрет,
и столбик с куклою чугунной,
под шляпой с пасмурным челом,
с руками сжатыми крестом (. . .)

And a pile of books. . . . And a portrait of Lord Byron
and a pillar surmounted with a cast-iron doll
with hat and sombre brow
with arms crossed upon its breast . . .
[Napoleon is meant!]

These surroundings, created by the hero himself, allow his essence to be discerned. The hero of *Dead Souls*, Čičikov, is characterized by the contents of his travel case that first of all bear witness to the absence of any intellectual interests.

The essential difference between the treatment of details in romanticism and in realism is found, however, in that in romanticism "bagatelles" of the hero's surroundings are symbols of his inner world, while the realists see in them only the origins of this inner world or the symptoms of its conditions.

Even though metonymic means of presentation were not unknown in other eras, nevertheless there was hardly any other style before realism that freed itself from metaphoric means to such an extent.

4. The names listed at the beginning of this chapter indicate that the number of Slavic writers who assumed an important position during the era of realism, at least in their own native literature, is extraordinarily large. There is no doubt, however, that only the realists of the two "great literatures," Russian and Polish, ever attained an especially far-reaching influence. The representatives of realism in other Slavic literatures are even less known beyond the borders of their native lands than the romantic poets. The relations among the individual Slavic literatures are, in part, strongly limited as a result of the fact that in the second half of the nineteenth century all the Slavic nations had too many of their own social and political problems.

It was the end of Nicholas I's reactionary regime and above all the easing of the strict censorship that opened to the Russians further possibilities of literary activity. The great—if not always consistently pursued—reforms, such as the liberation of the serfs, administrative and court reform, and the reorganization of the military, forced the writers in particular to take a stand in relation to the acute problems of the present. It was possible to discuss all these problems somewhat more freely in literature than in journalism. Then the bloodily repressed Polish Rebellion of 1863 brought an essential change to the, until then, "liberal" politics of the government and the radical mood of part of the intellegentsia. The division of the intellegentsia into two camps— the liberal and the socialistic—led to the isolation of some important writers: Tolstoj was often considered merely the portrayer of the narrowly limited aristocratic world, and only toward the end of the century, when his ethic and sociocritical works were published (*Folk Tales* and later the novel *Resurrection*), was he held in higher esteem. There was talk, however, of his two faces, and of his "right and left hand" (Lenin).

Dostoevskij received no recognition or understanding almost until his death. Several of Turgenev's novels were considered to be a "defamation of the younger generation," so that he even entertained the thought of ceasing further literary activity. It was even worse for the lyric poets whom no one any longer took seriously. The Polish reader was less radical and therefore hardly antipathetic to literature, while in the case of the other Slavic nations literature was highly estimated as a valuable component of the national culture that was just unfolding.

5. Some genres of romanticism and of the earlier periods were, of course, maintained in realism, however, their functions were now mostly different: this "commutation" (Russian, *pereključenie*) of literary genres was typical for the period. Thus we still find the *ballad tales*, which, however, were no longer designated as ballads. The themes too were no longer the same. Historical ballads were dedicated to the heroes of the struggles for freedom among all the Slavs who still had not attained or no longer possessed political independence. But the historical ballads were joined by ballad poems that dealt with modern social and political themes. As a result, the ballad frequently acquired a sharp, satirical note; the hero often remained nameless, only some representative of a particular, especially often of the "repressed," "lower" class. Plot was given up in favor of the presentation of an exciting *moment*, something that also happened in the romantic ballad which often depicted only the hero's demise. The author appeared only as the observer of a scene and left it to the reader to reconstruct the past and future of the characters and to the hero himself to relate his fate.

The Russian N. A. Nekrasov is master of the realistic ballad. He himself designated the poem in which he narrated the struggle of two brothers for the legacy at their father's deathbed, *Sekret—The Secret*, as *an attempt at a "contemporary" ballad*. His heroes are peasants who had been serfs, peasant wives, a mother whose only son returns home sick from the army and dies, a coachman, and a poor clerk. Some of the heroes are morally decrepit people, as the father in *The Secret*, no different from those heroes of the romantic ballads who sold their souls to the devil.

Nekrasov's *Vlas*, which was admired, though partly criticized, by Dostoevskij, is one of the most beautiful ballad poems. It tells of a man who is collecting money in order to build a church but who had previously been "a great sinner," an exploiter of the peasants, and a receiver of stolen goods. He recovered from a long illness by having taken a

vow that he fulfills by distributing his entire wealth among the poor
and becoming a collector of alms.

> 16. С той поры мужик скитается
>   вот уж скоро тридцать лет (...)
> 18. Полон скорбью неутешною,
>   смуглолиц, высок и прям,
>   ходит он стопой неспешною
>   по селеньям, городам.
>
>   ...
>
> 20. Ходит с образом и книгою,
>   сам с собой всё говорит
>   и железною веригою
>   тихо на ходу звенит (...)

> Since then the peasant wanders
> now almost thirty years . . .
> Filled with inconsolable sadness
> brown faced, tall and straight,
> he goes with measured step
> through the villages, through the cities.
>
> He carries an ikon and a book,
> and speaks with himself all the time,
> and with an iron chain shirt
> he clatters as he walks . . .

Often some realistic ballad poems are reminiscent of the "sketches"
of the "natural school." The Polish poet L. Syrokomla (Kondratowicz)
created a type of national ballad to which he gave the name *Gawęda*.

Ballads were written by realists of various persuasions: Hálek,
Ivan Vazov, and Konopnicka. The store of language and image is varied,
from epic-elevated to popular-vulgar, and from historic-serious to
everyday-prosaic. The fantastic ("numinous") ballad was preserved into
the realistic era by the utilization of fairy-tale motifs.

A typical ballad about such a nameless human that became popular
in Russia as well as in Poland was written by Konopnicka; its hero
Stach is merely the designation for an "unknown peasant soldier":

> 1. A jak poszedł król na wojnę,
>   grały jemu surmy zbrojne,
>   grały jemu surmy złote
>   na zwycięstwo, na ochotę...
> 2. A jak poszedł Stach na boje,
>   zaszumjały jasne zdroje,

zaszumjało kłosów pole
na tęsknotę, na niedolę...
4. ...
Stach śmiertelną dostał ranę,
król na zamek wracał zdrowy...
5. A jak wjeżdżał w jasne wrota
wyszła przeciw zorza złota
i zagrały wszystkie dzwony
na słoneczne świata strony.
6. A jak chłopu dół kopali,
zaszumiały drzewa w dali,
dzwoniły mu przez dąbrowę
te dzwoneczki, te liliowe...

When the King went to war
the battle-horns blew the way
the golden horns blew for victory and for joy.

And when Stach went to war
the clear streams roared
the cornfields rustled
of grief and calamity . . .

Stach received a mortal wound,
the King returned in good health to his castle . . .

And as he entered the bright gates
he was met by the golden dawn,
and all the bells began to resound to the sunny ends of the world.

And when they dug the peasant his grave,
the trees in the distance began to rustle,
for him pealed, through the oakwoods,
the bellflowers, the blue ones . . .

The antiheroic theme here is also characteristic.

Another genre, which, of course, completely altered its function, was the *fairy tale*. Naturally many realists maintained a serious interest in folklore. They did not, however, seek any deep metaphysical knowledge in it, but believed they were able to perceive the national character, the ethic, and social perceptions of the people from it. This belief led them astray; the fairy tale often had no function as far as the people were concerned, other than that of mere entertainment. Nevertheless, there were writers who used the fairy-tale form, on the one hand to express their own philosophy of life, and on the other hand as an imitation of the satiric folk fairy tale, or as a substitute for the fable that had almost died out by that time.

Leo Tolstoj in his *Folk Tales* had partly reworked genuine folk fairy tales, sometimes, however, only altering them slightly. He also wrote some excellent fairy tale imitations in order to set forth his new ideology in them. Occasionally a similar phenomenon is met in Dostoevskij and Turgenev. Some revolutionaries also used the fairy tale form in their propagandistic writings. In his satirical fairy tales, Saltykov-Ščedrin fashioned various types of folk fairy tales (even fantastic ones) as satires on the Russian present.

Shimmering through the actual satire, there are also general ethical thoughts to be seen in the work, as, for example, in the fairy tale about *The Idealistic Carp* who wanted to teach the concept of virtue to the pike, but who was swallowed by the latter without a second thought.

The utilization of fairy-tale motifs may be observed in the realists' ballads (see above) as well as on occasion in their short stories. We also encounter them in popular stage works. The use of fairy-tale materials often led to the employment of popular language.

The poetic song (*Kunstlied*), which had already experienced numerous transformations, finally became in the hands of the realists the expression of the people's lament over its fate. Particularly rich material was provided by the women's and prisoners' songs, while the revolutionary fighting songs that were beyond the limits of the folkloristic tradition employed motifs from robber-songs. All of these song forms were sometimes absorbed into folklore. Strangely enough, however, the people adopted the realistic songs less readily than the romantic. The fighting songs at first attained some dissemination among circles of the educated radical youth and the "freedom fighters."

Again it was the Russian N. A. Nekrasov who offered the prototype for the song-poems. The song of the wandering trader became a folk song: *Oj polna, polna korobuška . . . —Oh, thou full, full hamper.* Serious or humorous-pessimistic songs about the peasants' poverty and the women's tragic fate, despite their genuine popular key, found hardly any acceptance. Nevertheless, a few songs concerning prisoners and those exiled to Siberia did become folk songs.

The Ukrainian poets too adopted from the poetic songs (*Kunstlieder*) of that time, predominately the epigonous romantic poems. A similar phenomenon is seen in the other Slavic nations.

6. The diversity of literary forms during the period of realism is not easily overlooked, all the more so because of the artists' efforts to be not only charming but "useful" as well, and because of the appearance of numerous Slavic-language translations of famous works of world literature.

Typical were the translation activities of the Czech, Jaroslav Vrch-lický, who in the almost one hundred volumes of his poems imparted to Czech literature a knowledge of the classic poems of world literature.

At any rate, some typical forms of poetry became important: first of all, there were the reflective poems that had already been circulated during the late romantic period, the so-called Biedermeier: neither poet nor reader was frightened by extensive meditations or confessions. These were mostly the poet's reflections—rarely those of a ficticious narrator— on problems of his inner life that, in accordance with the spirit of the times, were frequently of a social and political sort. A demand for dedicated and selfless service to the people is mostly contrasted to in-dividual weakness and egoism.

The designation "thoughts" applied to the poems (no longer the tradi-tional "song") is associated with this. Short reflective poems in very interesting form are to be found in the work of Asnyk, Hálek, and oc-casionally Nekrasov and Vajanský as well.

Not far removed from reflective lyrics are the poetic tale, short story, or novel in verse. The most important Slovak poet, P. Hviezdoslav, wrote long, realistic novels in verse (*Hájnikova žena—The Forester's Wife, Ežo Vlkolinský*, and *Gabor Vlkolinský*, 1884–1899). Maria Konop-nicka's "chivalric," *Pan Balcer v Brazilij—Mr. Balcer in Brazil*, 1892– 1909, can probably also be considered a good example of a Polish novel in verse. Short verse stories spread and were often close to the ballads. The earlier verse tales of Turgenev and Nekrasov were closely linked to contemporary novels.

There were also attempts to introduce genres into poetry that were not otherwise taken seriously. In this category are included, above all, Varieté couplets, which had previously only been known in vaudeville, and imitations of bourgeois and gypsy songs. The late translations and reworkings of Béranger's songs were widely disseminated at this time.

N. A. Nekrasov was the master of the Russian couplets, the satirical seriousness of which remained hidden from the censor due to their ostensibly frivolous form. Asnyk's satiric and humoristic poems re-sound in a similar tone in Poland.

Many poems of the two epigones of the Biedermeier, Apollon Gri-gor'ev, and J. P. Polonskij, call Gypsy songs to mind.

There are numerous Russian translations of Béranger, whom Puškin knew and P. A. Vjazemskij imitated, that partially alter his songs with allusions to conditions in Russia (A. Mej and especially the otherwise insignificant V. Kuročkin).

These genres enriched the literary language by means of vulgarisms and prosaisms which were adopted from journalism and even from scientific literature.

Many poems are reminiscent of the themeless scenes of the sketches of the "natural school": nevertheless, they sometimes contain lyrical meditations.

Here again Nekrasov produced something remarkable, for example, his *Razmyšlenija u paradnogo pod'ezda—Thoughts before the Master's Entrance to a House*. Such individual scenes are also to be found in the works of Konopnika, Hálek, Ivan Vazov, and others.

Of course, the lyrical poems in the "old style" did not disappear; however, the poet adhered as much as possible to everyday speech intonations. Such intonation is typically found even in the love poems of the realists.

Russian romantic epigones such as A. K. Tolstoj and A. Fet long continued to write in the "old style." In Poland, as already mentioned, Asnyk and Konopnicka did not shy away from publishing poems that did not correspond to the spirit of the times. There are may good miniature poems in the work of Fet as well as among the poems, many often very weak, of Vazov, and in the work of the Ukrainian, Ivan Franko.

On the whole, however, poetry became considerably less prominent, for in "reality" one does not speak in verse. The reflections of the lackey Smerdjakov in Dostoevskij's *The Brothers Karamazov*, who rejects verse, are, of course, a caricature, however, not a coincidental one. For example, the two journals published in 1861–63 by Dostoevskij and his brother contained almost no poems. Turgenev, who began as a good poet, wrote only occasional poems during the rest of his life. In Poland, the novelist Eliza Orzeszkowa too published poems only as a novice. Poets as such were often not taken seriously. B. Prus doubted the possibility of verse's being able to present such plastic portrayals as is possible in prose, for verse "glistens and shines," and can blind the reader. Consequently, he considered the "poetic character" of realistic works "dangerous." In contrast to this it is interesting that Turgenev's favorably disposed German critic, Julian Schmidt, saw their shortcomings in the "too little poetic character" of the novels.

L. Tolstoj, according to the reminiscences of the actor P. Orlenev, *praises* a poem with the words: "No, this is not verse, but significant and deep prose"—*bol'šaja i glubokaja proza*.

Nevertheless, there was a considerable movement in poetics and verse composition that, at the very least, showed that problems of form were not foreign to the realists. Nekrasov appears here as well as an innovator.

The Puškinian tradition preferred the iamb, particularly the eight to nine syllable, or as the versification texts call them, the four-feet iambs, to all other meters:

> Деревня, где скучал Евгений
> была прелестный уголок ...

> The village where Evgenij [Onegin] was bored
> was a charming spot . . .

If we represent the unaccented syllables as "x" and the accented as "x́" we can diagram the rhythm of these lines as follows:

> x x́ x x́ x x́ x x́ x
> x x́ x x́ x x x x́

We see here that the long Russian words make the omission of some accents unavoidable as in the second line quoted above.

Opposed to this, Nekrasov's metrics are often trisyllabic, that is, normally every third syllable is accented. Compare,

> От ликующих, праздноболтающих,
> умывающих руки в крови
> уведи меня в стан погибающих
> за великое дело любви.

> From the rejoicing, vain gossips
> washing their hands in blood
> lead me into the camp of those who perish
> for the sake of great love.

> x x x́ x x x́ x x x́ x x
> x x x́ x x x́ x x x́
> x x x́ x x x́ x x x́ x x
> x x x́ x x x́ x x x́

The trisyllabic meter makes the use of longer words—participles, composita, and superlatives—possible for the poet. But even here some stresses must fall away, as for example in the line, *do svetoprestavlenija* (until world's-end).

> x x x x x x́ x x

Besides numerous vulgarisms and popular words, Nekrasov introduced journalistic words as, for example, *sozercajuščij*, *praktičeskij*, *ekonomičeskij*. The same thing, less decisively, was done by several other Russian poets.

Konopnicka, too, plays with numerous, partially new strophic forms. Her poems frequently tend to tonic meters, that is, to a regular alternation of stressed and unstressed syllables that contradicts the Polish tradition of syllabic verse and that demands great talent from the poetess in a language that normally stresses the penultimate syllable.

> W kolebce braterstwa słowiańskich narodów,
> w prastarej ziemicy Morawy...
>
> In the cradle of brotherhood of Slavic peoples,
> in the ancient, dear land of Moravia . . .

$$x \acute{x} x x \acute{x} x x \acute{x} x x \acute{x} x$$
$$x \acute{x} x x \acute{x} x x \acute{x} x$$

The Czech, Jaroslav Vrchlický, who later became professor of comparative literature, enriched Czech poetry through numerous new strophic forms, above all in his translations. I. Franko also attempted new forms and among others wrote poems in tonic imitation of ancient meters.

7. Metonymic style fosters and even demands extensive forms. It is not coincidental that the novel was the genre that acquired an international reputation for the Slavic literatures.

The Russian novelists, Turgenev, Dostoevskij, Lev Tolstoj, and Gončarov, attained particular significance in world literature. Their work was later continued by Maxim Gor'kij whose late autobiographical triology formed the zenith of his novelistic art.

Most noteworthy in Poland were Orzeszkowa, Prus, and Sienkiewicz. Their most important works appeared between 1878 and 1900. Among the foremost south Slavic writers belong Jaša Ignjatović with his novel *Vaša Rešpekt* (1875) and the Bulgarian Ivan Vazov with his successful novel *Pod igoto—Under the Yoke*. The Ukrainians Panas Myrnyj, beginning in 1880, and Ivan Franko also wrote realistic novels, Franko's having some modernist features. Even more strongly than Franko, Mikhaylo Kocjubynśky tended toward modernism. His novels appeared only in 1903–1911. The Slovakian novels of Martin Kukučin and Hurban-Vajanský are significant.

The novels were mostly quite extensive, mainly because the realistic writer was not able to forget his environment, what the Russians called *sreda*. New forms, however, began to appear: the short novel "Romanetto," the novel composed almost as a montage from historical sources—the historical *roman à clef*—and the realistic novel in verse, which, however, is fundamentally different from the romantic "Byronic epic."

The miniature novel was the invention of the Czech Jâkub Arbes. He also originated the name "Romanetto."

Historical *romans à clef* were written by the cultural historians Zygmunt Winter (1846–1912, Czech) and the Ukrainian Orest Levyćkyj (1849–1922). The latter adopted historical sources in his works almost *in crudo*. The novels in verse (see above, 6) introduced extensive milieu portrayals instead of the digressions characteristic for similar romantic works, as, for example, Puškin's *Evgenij Onegin*, Słowacki's *Beniowski*.

By means of realism's milieu portrayals, many secondary characters were drawn into the plot, the fates of whom exacted hundreds of pages from the author and the reader.

Sienkiewicz's historical trilogy taken from seventeenth-century Polish past comprised thirteen volumes! Tolstoj's novel *War and Peace* is similarly drawn out. Smaller novels also attempted to bring the social and political reality of the period being treated close to the reader.

In addition to Tolstoj's novels, we must mention those of Turgenev that give us a picture of the development of the Russian intellectuals from the forties to the seventies. The sociologically and psychologically oriented literary scholars D. Ovsjanikov-Kulikovskij and R. Ivanov-Razumnik, believed it possible to write a *History of the Russian Intellegentsia* on the basis of these novels. B. Prus' great novel *Lalka—The Doll*—portrays representatives of Polish society of that time. Higher and lower nobility, merchants, upper and lower middle class, and finally the artisans are depicted by their representatives in the novel, the theme of which is actually the story of a marriage. Sienkiewicz also included such extensive portrayals in his society novels. Ivan Vazov in *Under the Yoke* describes the situation of the Bulgarians under Turkish domination.

Almost all the significant novel writers of the time saw their most important task in "reporting."

Sometimes the portrayals were critical, satirical, and even caricature-like, for example, the Russian "reactionary" novels, such as Dostoevskij's *The Possessed*. Occasionally the hero is crowded entirely into the background by the milieu portrayal.

The historical novel is a genre that extensively continued the tradition of the romantic heroic novel in the new style.

In addition to Tolstoj's historical novels and Sienkiewicz's trilogy in which the author shines by the clever application of seventeenth-century vocabulary, there were novels replete with pomp from the past of other people, but superficial, as Sienkiewicz's *Quo Vadis* and a myriad of "naive" works by the Czech A. Jirásek, or novels by the Russian-Ukrainian author D. Mordovcev about whom the historian Kostomarov

wrote, "We reproach our historical romantics for their bad knowledge
of history. Mr. Mordovcev is an exception: he has no knowledge of it
at all."

The Slavic realistic novels are all too often tendentious. They are part
of the ancient Slavic literary genre of didactic novels (see chapter III, 4)
that are intended to suggest certain ideas to the reader. This is achieved
either by means of author's remarks, by the heroes' speeches, or by
extensive padding. Satiric or parodic works are effective in the same way.
They are able to serve not as rational, but as emotional arguments *sui
generis*.

Didactic material plays a large role in Dostoevskij's novels. In *The
Brothers Karamazov*, in addition to the Starets' Zosima's didactic remarks, we encounter in the same novel the brothers' conversations,
the appearance of the Devil in Ivan's hallucinations, and the *Legend of
the Grand Inquisitor*, attributed to Ivan. Prince Myškin's Slavophile
speeches in *The Idiot* were supposed to awaken sympathy; antipathy was
to be excited in *The Possessed* by Šigalov's socialistic project, the paro-
distic representation of Turgenev's (= Karmazinov) works, and of a
Romantic "mystery play." [1]

The tendentiousness is quite openly pronounced in all of L. Tolstoj's
novels as well as in his historical-philosophical remarks, or in the carica-
tured portrayal of Napoleon in *War and Peace*. Turgenev, on the other
hand, attempted to excite positive feelings in the reader toward certain
characters, as in the case of Bazarov in *Fathers and Sons*.

Orzeszkowa's novels are not free of didactic tendentiousness as witnessed by her novel *Meir Ezofowicz*, essentially a polemic against anti-
semitism. In her other works we encounter general humanitarian
tendentiousness.

In the case of most of the Slavic literatures of that time, popular and
nationalistic motifs are very strong and make their appearance in un-
disguised form.

The utilization of two given possibilities is characteristic for the
realistic novel: the *typifying* presentation of "average" representatives
of distinct nations, classes, and groups (see below, 10), and the often
simultaneous portrayal of unique critical cases in the most extremely
tense situations (11). A work having a theme bound by time and

1. A didactic, artistic work does not necessarily have to give *answers* to the
questions posed in it. It is far more essential for such a work to pose the *problems*
and to contribute to their clarification, leaving the solution to the reader, or
indicating various possible methods of solution. This occurs in most of Dostoevskij's novels.

place is often elevated through psychological analysis beyond these limitations to those works of universal significance. Questions applicable to men of all times are posed and answered in these works.

It was in the novels of Dostoevskij and L. Tolstoj that general validity in relation to man's ontological situation was first attained.

8. The heroes of realistic novels are in no way "heroic" as was mostly the case in romanticism. There had already been the desire, however, to "harness even scoundrels" into a work of literature: *priprjač'i podleca*, writes Gogol'. Now there were all too often "scoundrels" in the realistic novel who indeed, corresponding to "the truth of life," sometimes also possessed human traits, and who were depicted in a dynamic process of development in that they prove themselves to be at times worse, and at times better. In addition to the "scoundrels" there were also weak persons portrayed who succumb to external temptations or to their own inner assaults of either weakness of will, or the strength of an inhibiting reflex. The realists had to realize that the depiction of positive types, especially of those who are able to have a positive effect within their environment, is extraordinarily difficult. Further, the censorship placed unbridgeable obstacles in the way of presentations of revolutionary or national fighters. The "positive" types who appear in the background are often quite pale.

In addition to the negative types, the "unlucky characters" already known in romanticism played an important role. These are people who are always unsuccessful and whose demise is never heroic but plebean and prosaic.

A legacy of the "natural school" were the minor characters of many novels who were sketched in a caricaturizing and grotesque manner. This same method was sometimes applied to the drawing of the foreground as well in some satirical works.

I. Ignjatović's novel *Vaša Rešpekt* offers the best example of a negative hero. Vaša is an egotistical, clever, and unscrupulous person whose manner of life is bluntly depicted. Kalinovič, the hero of A. Pisemskij's novel (*Tysjača duš-A Thousand Souls*), stands on the border between consistent baseness and weakness of character. Most of the heroes in Turgenev's novels are weak men who alone are at fault for their unhappy fates. Even their hero's death, as in the case of *Rudin*, is no proof of their strength. Rajskij, the hero of Gončarov's novel *The Abyss*, is a many-faceted, talented man not capable of giving definite direction to his life, while the morally pure Oblomov in Gončarov's other novel perishes because of his passivity.

Turgenev's women are mostly drawn as positive types; however, he

does show seductresses and other negative types. Most detailed is the
negative, spiritually empty type of woman portrayed by Prus in his
novel *Lalka,* who is indeed depicted as a *Doll.* In the same novel, the
author sketches an entire spectrum of male characters of varying moral
qualities.

Dostoevskij also draws rapacious (*xiščnyje*) women who must play a
fatal role in the life of their surroundings. The criminals of his novels
also display positive human characteristics. The weakest portrayals of
humans are found in those novels that have as their subject peasant life
or national struggles. The dubiousness of the "positive" heroes of Turgenev and Gončarov is obvious, and it is only in Dostoevskij that there
occasionally appear characters bordering on the saintly, such as Zosima
in *The Brothers Karamazov.* Leskov's only important novel, *Soborjane—
Cathedral Folk,* depicts people who commit no heroic deeds but who
nevertheless can be characterized as positive heroes by virtue of their
moral steadfastness and their faithful performance of duty. We also
find similar types in many of Leskov's stories.

The authors of realistic novels always endeavored not to give a onesided picture of their characters. Only the historical novels of the far
and recent past often have figures that leave nothing further to be desired in terms of incredible heroic courage. Most of the heroes in Sienkiewicz's historical novels are of this sort.

9. The art of short story writing also bloomed in the era of realism.
The reason for this is partially a purely "practical" one. Poets were often
dependent upon the smaller journals for work, in addition to which
prose writing became for many the basis of their material existence, and
the short story was a ware more easily disposed of. This genre offered the
possibility—frequently in the tradition of the "natural school"—of
presenting individual slices of reality. Most novelists wrote short stories.

Short stories even make up the bulk of Turgenev's work. Sienkiewicz's
stories are important and of different structure from that of his other
works. The Czech Neruda, the Serb Matavulj, and others were story
writers in their artistic prose. There were also writers who wrote *only*
short stories. Later a school of short story writers formed itself taking
Maupassant and Čexov for its example. In the case of the later story
writers, a particular style developed which may be designated as impressionistic.

The language of the short stories was often closer to the everyday
language than was that of the novels. Humoristic elements frequently
became prominent. More space was devoted to the life of the people.

Perhaps the authors were not able to perceive of such exciting and complicated fates for the characters from the simple people as for the representatives of the intellectual class and the historical heroes.

10. As we have already mentioned, the realists often endeavored to present "typical" people, manifestations, and events. *Typifying* was not new in literature; in realism, however, it acquired a central importance such as it had probably never before had.

Precise literary figures and images were created that were able *to represent* entire groups of people, epochs, and relationships. The problem of "representation" gave rise to a series of questions, especially these of selection of "typical" traits from among the abundant elements of reality, and that of their union into an artistic whole.

The realists were for the most part not cognizant of these difficulties. One of the most interesting theoreticians of realism, the Polish novelist B. Prus, answered the question thus: one must "(a) select the most important points . . . (b) from them create a line that, according to its size and shape, would characterize the subject matter [to be presented]." In order to lend plasticity to a picture so created it is "good to give it a corresponding background," in front of which the character "can appear more sharply."

While selecting the traits considered "important" or "most important," certain criteria, varying with individual realists, had to be observed. Most of the writers did not realize that it was necessary to execute a judgment in this selection, and they often believed in the possibility of being able to ascertain the typical or characteristic traits by "observation." These problems were thoroughly discussed and elucidated later by Max Weber in his treatment of the "Ideal Type."

This idea was expressed by Prus and, in correspondence, by Turgenev and Gončarov as well.

No less difficult to answer was the question of the union of these individual traits into an artistic whole. That the views of the author played a significant role in this question was apparent in that the types created by various writers differed sharply one from another. Every author however, believed that it was precisely he who had created a type true to reality and that those authors who thought differently were mistaken. The literary and critical polemics over the "authenticity" of the individual types led, in some cases, to insurmountable differences of opinion.

The authors of historical works often only adopted the ideas already worked out by the scholars of that time. It was further believed that the *communis opinio* of the journalists and politicians offered a satisfactory guarantee for the selection of typical traits. The question of the sources of Sienkiewicz's historical novels demonstrates this difficulty of selection. Turgenev, L. Tolstoj, E. Orzeszkowa, and others, to judge by their statements, frequently believed they could let themselves be guided by personal experience or the "critical" utilization of contemporary opinion.

The combining of typical traits creates a concept, but no artistic picture. This picture can lend form to an image of a living personality through the fusing of "typical traits" with additional "human" traits. Exactly the same holds true of typical social relationships, landscapes, images of milieu, etc. And an enrichment of the abstract "typical" images by means of "coincidental" concrete material often resulted in the reproach that the artist himself did not understand the character he created.

Turgenev was reproached for this in the discussion over the "nihilist" type of Bazarov created by him in *Fathers and Sons*. It was, however, not only the critics and journalists, but the writers too, as, for example, B. Prus, who reproached each other for "not understanding" the characters they created.

In a word, an insolvable contradiction often developed between the typifying tendency of realism and the attempts at forming these types into concrete images.

11. Another manner of presenting reality consisted in the *description of special and extreme cases*, that is, portraying figures and situations that are never, or only rarely, found in reality. In such a manner the characteristic traits of reality are intensified and "raised to a higher power"; the heroes' psychic experiences and ideas are given in a form more pure and consistent than the one in which they can be met in life.

Such portrayals of extreme cases in Dostoevskij, and partly in Leskov, were particularly characteristic. Dostoevskij, as an enemy of the rationalistic "Enlightenment" of the 1860s in Russia, portrayed in Ivan Karamazov such a deep thinking and in Smerdjakov such a cruel representative of enlightened thought that were surely nowhere to be found in Russian reality.

This type of "magnification" of reality posed more problems than typifying: the writer while intensifying the characteristic traits of reality was not permitted to lend any traits to the "special case" he created that would "lead the portrayal astray." For in this way only a distorted picture could develop, one that deviated from reality and that was perceived merely as an "evil charicature." Only the satirists made conscious use of this right to "untrustworthiness," in Russian, *nepravdopodobje:* the justification was their right of portraying reality as it would be if man acted and thought consistently, and if relationships could develop unhindered.

We may consider, for example, the socialistic plans of Šigalev in Dostoevskij's *The Possessed* as a caricature. Saltykov-Ščedrin, a Russian satirist, believed himself able to go beyond the limits of truth into the region of fairy tales in his satires, for example, a mayor whose head is a pastry, another whose utterances are brought forth by a musical box (*organčik*) located in his head.

While typifying is threatened by the danger of presenting colorless character portraits in an artistic work, the portrayal of special and extreme cases runs the danger of drawing untrustworthy images.

12. The two systems of necessity led to a manner of portrayal that that can be designated as "Impressionistic." In both cases the presentation of reality is built upon *selection*, that is, upon an incomplete, inexhaustive collection of isolated elements of reality. I said "of necessity" because a presentation of reality in the entire fullness and diversity of its particulars is not possible. The character of the selection of the elements of reality is determined by various factors: (1) by the perspective in which the author is able to see reality—in addition to the restraints of time and space, there is above all his position within society to contend with; (2) by the author's personal qualities, such as his "talent," the sharpness of his perception, his interests; (3) by the influences of his environment, that is, the "spirit of the times," the demands placed upon him by literary conditions and by his readers. This may be identified with the recent conception of "social charge," Russian, *social'nyj zakaz*. The author can allow himself a certain degree of resistance, which can often determine his success with his readers, to this environmental influence. The most important thing is that the realistic writer depict his object *only fragmentarily*. The total picture is the synthesis of the individual features. If they are numerously and cleverly chosen the picture appears as a whole without any essential loopholes and "errors." Thus an "impressionistic" picture of fragmentary structure originates. In a certain sense, the attributive "impressionistic" can be applied to every work. The limits of a "realistic" presentation that is true to reality, however, are not clear to many realists; they do not notice the impressionistic—in this case, fragmentary—character of their depictions. Only individual authors—and these mostly in the later years of the realistic

epoch—*consciously* employed the impressionistic manner of style. It is difficult to lay out exact boundaries for such "impressionistic realism," especially because many authors only occasionally present impression- istic depictions.

Turgenev's observations on the impressionism of L. Tolstoj deserve particular attention. He maintains that certain passages that he found in *War and Peace* are only "little pieces of art" (*štučki*) which are "slyly observed" and "ingeniously expressed." Turgenev sees this as "rotten upon the broad pictorial expanse of the historical novel" (letter of March 16, 1865). Further, Tolstoj had "the old tendency of repeating the vacilations, vibrations of the same feeling or the same situation" (letter of February 26, 1868). The depiction of detail he contends is "only sleight-of-hand" (*fokusy*), the hammering-in upon the reader's eyes with the same fine details that are supposed to create the illusion of the author's omniscence. Turgenev sees Tolstoj's psychology as a "capriciously monotonous preoccupation with constantly the same sentiments that, in addition, lie beyond the normal world of experience" consequently Tolstoj's works, for example *Anna Karenina*, are "a chaos" (letters of March 22, 1875 and March 6, 1868).

The critics of that time judged Dostoevskij's novels similarly. Later in Čexhov's *serious* stories they were surprised by the lack of "ideology" and the "unclear" portrayals.

The impressionistic features of certain authors were the omens of the emerging modern literature. In the case of the Ukrainian Kocjubynśkyj, the continuation of the stylistic tradition of Čexhov was a direct transi- tion to modernism.

In short stories, impressionistic portrayals were often prevalent, although the realists attempted to conceal the fragmentary character of their presentations by varying means.

Turgenev frequently succeeded in this type of concealment by a narrowing of the presentation's limits, that is, by fewer participating characters, brevity of plot, or concentrating the presentation on a few points in time thereby making a report about the time in between unnec- essary. Artistic devices such as these are easier to employ in short stories than in novels.

Those authors who knew how to cyclize attempted to conceal the fragmentary nature of their short stories in another manner. The Czech Neruda, for example, proceeded in this way by uniting a series of sketches into the picture of the Prague *Malá Strana* under the general title *Povídky malostranské*.

It was Anton Čexov who from the end of the eighties more consistently than anyone else served himself of impressionistic stylistics (see his *The Steppe, A Boring Story, My Life,* etc.). He developed a special style based upon the presentation of "fragments" of inner life and the outer world. He soon found Slavic imitators.

The attention of the impressionists was directed toward isolated objects and colors of reality, toward the often unclear and indeterminant spiritual emotions, atmosphere, and moods. The works frequently lacked clearly discernible themes, or the plot was either not developed until the end or broken off. There was no return, however, to the themelessness of the "natural school." The experiences of the characters—their motivation, and their resulting expressions and actions—were inadequate and left behind the impression that the nature of the action was "unmotivated" or entirely coincidental.

In Čexov's case this is rooted in his insights as a physician into such sick disturbances of emotional life as neurasthenia, pregnancy, fever, effects of the subconscious.

Impressionism was further developed in "neoromantic" literature (see Chapter XII).[2]

13. Characteristic features of realistic style are primarily associated with the idea of the causal determination of all isolated elements of reality.

This conviction, which diminishes or even completely disappears only during the period of realistic impressionism, has several consequences: (1) attempts at genealogic explanations of the characters of the persons portrayed, (2) the motivation of their actions by means of motifs that are also presented in the work, or (3) the depiction of the milieu in which they live and act. All these stylistic means have, as is easily seen, metonymic character: they demand a far-reaching presentation of the circumstances under which the person has grown up and lived. This not only leads to an extension of the presentation's limits but also demands an extensive collection of materials as a precondition for the literary creation.

Consequently, the idea was almost general that literature presents in a certain sense a parallel to the other manner of perception, the scientific.

According to B. Prus, "science and literature" are two wings that "elevate man," that is, inform him of the truth, which is not fundamen-

2. Impressionism was also encountered among the romantic epigones during the realistic period. The lyric poetry of A. A. Fet was particularly typical in Russian literature.

tally different from scientific truth. With many Russian authors this "service to knowledge" went so far that they attached statistical tables to their artistic works, for example, Gleb Uspenskij. Consequently, the "utility" of literature as a source of knowledge seemed to be proven.

In order to characterize the "utility" of literature, Prus says that it should offer "potatoes instead of roses." Even more paradoxically, literature was spoken of as "bread."

Thus the preparation of literary works was to be based on the gathering of material, that is, the realistic writer often trod the path, characteristic for the scholar, of methodical observation, of the use of available sources of scientific and journalistic nature. Occasionally we meet Emile Zola's unhappily chosen term, "the experimental novel."

14. *Topicality* was a literary criterion for determining a work's value in realism. This term can also be understood in different ways, however, and the "transtemporal" problems in the novels of Dostoevskij or L. Tolstoj were surely considered "topical" in a higher sense by the authors as well as by many readers, and indeed more so than the treatment of the "current questions."

Naturally such works as *The Fruits of Education* by L. Tolstoj and Dostoevskij's *The Possessed* contained "topicality" in the sense of a treatment of the questions of the day, but in addition the latter work contained much that had "transtemporal topicality."

The realists were almost always able to lend a "topical" character to their works. It was the theatre that was especially ruled by the striving for "topicality." This was particularly true of the works of the "smaller" Slavic literatures. The Slavic stage, limited as its possibilities were by material grounds or censorship difficulties, now became a pulpit. This in turn determined many literary features of the stage works: their themes, the choice of their heroes, their style and, not least important, their "tendentiousness," for the stage was "didactic" in an even greater measure than was the case with the other genres (see 7).

15. During the realistic era the theatre played a particularly large role among the various Slavic nations: the stage addresses itself to a much broader spectrum than the rest of literature. But it is precisely this breadth of public that leads to a certain primitiveness in the works. The stages of almost all Slavic nations treated the "lower levels" of society. Here the task was first of all to show that these classes had an inner life that was just as complex and rich as that of heroes belonging to the educated or upper classes. Since the writer loses his right to speak himself on the stage, his heroes are alone with their primitive world.

Several theatrical works of Russian authors, as for example Leskov and Pisemskij, treated tragedies that arise from such primitive conflicts. A. Ostrovskij devoted the greater part of his plays to the uneducated merchant class, for which reason he was characterized by an epigram writer as "the Kotzebue of the department store."

The entire sizable Ukrainian stage literature of realism managed not to go beyond the borders of the peasant world. We find narrow limits in the work of the Serbian writer B. Nušić as well.

Another group of stage works was devoted to history. The tradition of romantic heroic literature is still strongly operative here, which in its turn narrows the problematic nature of the works. The authors often wound up on the path of false rhetoric and melodrama.

It was largely the works of authors bold enough to free themselves from historical reality that accounted for the exceptions, for example, Count A. K. Tolstoj whose *Tsar Feodor* gave masterful character portrayals—the absolutely insignificant Tsar who is close to feeblemindedness is presented as a sort of holy "pure fool"—and who was able to break through and treat deep ethical problems.

Thus the realistic theater was subject to the danger that purely artistic problems either disintegrate into "ethnographism" or false historicism. Nevertheless, realistic stage writing sometimes advanced to successful satiric presentations, and at the end of the realistic epoch Čexov created impressionistic stage works that pointed out new roads for theatrical literature (see above, 12).

So far as stage art was concerned, the element of pure "show" receded, so that the theater became "prosaic" and "everyday." Only historical and ethnographic works maintained variegated elements and attractive beauty—only in so far, however, as these works aspired to awaken interest and sympathy for the "simple people." Later the attempt was made to attain in these works as well a realistic exactness in the reproduction of life which often led to colorlessness of historical descriptions.

16. Among most Slavic nations, realism experienced a crisis around the end of the eighties. It developed from internal causes but was made more acute by outside effects, by the development of Western literatures. The crisis gripped the younger generation of creative writers, mostly those born after 1865, and it was only after some years that certain representatives of the older generation—in part such as had been until then passive observers of literary life—joined the newer one.

The immanent causes of the crisis were partly to be found in the gradual dying out of the older generation, above all in Russia, and

Russian realism was for the majority of the Slavic literatures a standard that pointed the way. The readers also lost interest with time—in the case of secondary writers—in the works that were continually becoming weaker and less exciting. If these reasons lay on the surface of literary life, then there were stronger causes at work in the depths, namely, a longing for beauty, something that certainly occupied no central position among the literary values of realism, and the awakening of interest in poetic form, which, in its turn, had been all too often neglected. For the word had been used and valued in poetry too, above all in its *communicative* function, and the representative function, in the broader meaning of the word, including the aesthetic functions as well, was overlooked and neglected.

Sociopolitical causes that varied in nature among the various Slavic nations also belonged to the causes of the recession of realistic endeavors.

The diminishing of the radical, revolutionary movement that had played a very important role, particularly in Russian intellectual history, was typical.

The leading Russian journalist N. Mikhajlovskij wrote, "For what is one to hope? In what is one to believe? What should one desire? Toward what should one aspire? Everything is broken into pieces and crushed." The satirist Saltykov-Ščedrin spoke of the domination of the "triumphant swine." The journalists were of the opinion that a new "Skeptical Generation" was appearing. "They did not let themselves be guided by the ideals of the fathers"; since the political struggle had brought forth too few results, one reconciled oneself to the everyday world.

The tensions between the older and younger generations arose from various and often hidden sources.

Surprisingly, similar descriptions of these tensions can be found in the presentation of the conflicts between the fathers and sons of the 90s in the memoirs of a representative of the Polish modernists, T. Boy-Żeleński, for example a description of Krakow in *Do You Know That Country?—Znasz li ten kraj?*, and in the memoirs of the Russian symbolist Andrej Belyj in his *On the Border of two Centuries—Na rubeže dvukh stoletij*, although the conditions of life in Krakow and Moscow were thoroughly different.

The external influences were, above all, of an artistic and literary nature: impressionism in painting, which the realists were not long able to withstand, the birth of arts and crafts in the works of W. Morris and Ruskin, and the ensuing *Jugendstil*, as it was called in German, art nouveau in England, and, above all the new West European literature.

The names of Ibsen, Oscar Wilde, and Maeterlinck must be mentioned. Next comes French poetry: Verlaine, Mallarmé, and Rimbaud. For some Slavic literatures German literature was of importance—George and the *Blätter für die Kunst*, Arthur Schnitzler, and even Gerhard Hauptmann; also the younger Scandinavians, as Hamsun. The turning of Western philosophy away from materialism and positivism, as well as the new scientific movements, and frequently a closer acquaintance with its older representatives, was not uninfluential.

17. Apparently, however, realism had not yet fulfilled its task in the intellectual history of the Slavic nations, so that it continued to find important representatives even within literary modernism. Several writers who had for a time gone along with modernism then turned back to an often stylistically renovated realism. Others employed only some of the new stylistic means while remaining, however, representatives and champions of "realistic" art.

The most important Polish realists were still effective at the beginning of the twentieth century: for example, B. Prus (died 1912) who only now produced a theoretical foundation for realism (see above, 10), Sienkiewicz (died 1916), and Orzeszkowa (died 1910). We see the same with the Slovaks: Hviezdoslav died in 1921, Hurban-Vajanský in 1916, Kukučin in 1928, the Bulgarian Vazov died in 1921, etc. (see the list at the beginning of this chapter). Literary animation among the Ukrainians, partly because of the easing of the censorship in Russia, came only at the beginning of the twentieth century.

For a time in Russia the most important new prosaists, Gork'ij and Bunin, followed modernism, and it was only years later that they took up a realistic style again. Even the less important followers of realism attempted at times to liken their style to modernism.

This strong epigonous realistic movement did not feel itself in any way to be epigonous, and the literary journals and publishing houses controlled by the movement were frequently able to repress the modernists.

XII

NEOROMANTICISM (MODERNISM)

Poles

K. Tetmajer (1865–1940)
A. Lange (1861–1929)
J. Kasprowicz (1860–1926)
Stefan Przybyszewski (1868–1927)
Stefan Wyspiański (1869–1907)
L. Staff (1878–1957)
B. Leśmian (1878–1937)
Stefan Żeromski (1864–1925)

Russians

I. Annenskij (1856–1909)
V. Brjusov (1873–1924)
K. Bal'mont (1867–1943)
Andrej Belyj (Boris Bugaev) (1880–1934)
A. Blok (1880–1921)
Vjačeslav Ivanov (1866–1949)
F. Sologub (1863–1927)

Ukrainians

O. Oleś (1878–1944)
M. Ryĺśkyj (1895–1964)
P. Tyčyna (1891)

White Russians

M. Bahdanovič (1892–1917)

Czechs

A. Sova (1864–1942)
O. Březina (1868–1929)
A. Procházka (1869–1925)
I. Karásek ze Lvovic (1871–1951)
K. Hlaváček (1874–1898)
Stefan K. Neumann (1875–1947)

Slovaks

I. Krasko (1876–1958)

Serbs

J. Dučić (1874–1943)
V. Ilić (1862–1894)

Croats

Ivo Vojnović (1857–1929)
V. Nazor (1876–1949)
M. Krleža (1893–)
I. Andrić (1892–)

Slovenes

D. Kette (1876–1899)
J. Murn Aleksandrov (1879–1901)
O. Župančič (1878–1949)
I. Cankar (1876–1918)

Bulgarians

P. K. Javorov (1877–1914)

Sorbs

J. Bart-Ćišinski (1856–1909)

1. Impressionism did not become the final path of the newer Slavic literature. In contrast, a "modern" trend that gave itself various labels among the Slavic nations had been developing in some Slavic literatures since the middle of the 1880s. The Poles called it "Young Poland" (*Młoda Polska*), in Russia it was "symbolism." The opponents of the movement called it "decadence," a name that the representatives of modernism themselves often used, partly for reasons of polemics. The Russian term "symbolism," in keeping with the extraordinarally strong influence Russian literature had enjoyed until this time, also penetrated into the other Slavic literatures. The term "neoromanticism," which literary historians more and more frequently use, is not quite applicable: Slavic modernism was, first of all, much less *philosophically* oriented than romanticism and considered the *aesthetic* value of literature in particular. The strong accentuation of aesthetic elements led many followers of the modern movement to a higher evaluation of various literary trends of the *pre*-realistic period.

2. The chief problem that moved the modernists was the limiting in realism of the word's functions to the purely *communicative* one. The *"realization"* of the word's other functions was the task set for themselves by the representatives of *Młoda Polska* and Russian symbolism, without, however, always consciously formulating this task. Realism's resulting weakening of the metaphorical function of the word, the neglect of its tonal side, of its emotional efficacy, led to the somewhat distorted conception of realism as a "making rational" of literature.

Also rejected was the "politicizing" of realistic literary criticism that often rejected important literature for social-political reasons and polemically labeled it "art for art's sake."

The pronouncements of the standard-setting Russian critic and "literary historian" M. Skabičevskij are typical: in his work he depreciated Fet and Tjutčev, the most important Russian poets after Puškin. About Tjutčev he wrote, "One can only read him with difficulty, and he is valued only by the zealous and inveterate aesthetes." Tolstoj's *War and Peace* reminded him of the "stories of a garrulous but simple-minded—*nedalekij*—noncommissioned officer in a remote village about his war experiences." Čexov seemed to him to belong to those authors who in old age "die drunk under a fence," etc. During the predominant radicalism of the sixties, Puškin was depreciated by D. Pisarev, and Lermontov by V. Zajcev. Dostoevskij experienced hardly any positive commentary during his lifetime, and at the turn of the century Čexov's plays were still not accepted for performance by the leading agencies which were supported by some influential literary historians.

The characterization "art for art's sake" was applied to the works of those writers whose Weltanschauung did not coincide with that of the leading critics.

The use of "unrealistic" metaphors became the object of venomous parodies.

The appearance of isolated "predecessors" announced the new period. They attempted either to attach themselves to the great writers of Slavic romanticism, or they succumbed to certain influences of Western literature. Through the study of philosophy, largely coincidentally selected works, they advanced to new aesthetic and literary-theoretical ideas.

In Poland we find among these predecessors some poets who lived abroad and who even wrote in foreign languages, as, for example, Stefan Przybyszewski in Germany and T. Rittner in Austria.

The representatives of late realism too came to the realization that the path of realism could only further lead to a dead end. The current literature was felt to be "ineffectual," and this ineffectuality was seen in the weakness of realistic form and in the lack of a deeper, ideological content.

In 1900, Gork'ij wrote to Čexov, "Do you know what you are doing? You are killing realism and will soon have killed it forever. This form has outlived its time, that is a fact. . . . Truly a time has come that has necessity of the heroic: everyone wants something exciting that would be not similar, but better, more beautiful than life." Gork'ij continues that the new literature can change life itself, "people are going to live more quickly, more brightly [*sic!*]." Čexov felt the same. He said that the literature of that time "contains no alcohol . . . that intoxicates and rules [the reader]." He felt that literature was leading to no "immediate or future goals." "He who wants nothing, hopes for nothing, and is afraid of nothing can not become an artist." A Polish contemporary, Artur Górski, wrote something similar; he addressed the writers: "Where are their heroic deeds? Where is their effect upon the reader?" "Have you ever screamed out from pain, you reader-Philistine?"

3. The influence of the newer West European literature mirrored itself first among those writers who hardly noticed the innovations in certain elements of their own creations. Among the Czechs, Poles, Russians, Ukrainians, etc. we find individual writers, primarily poets, whom we may characterize as predecessors of modernism.

A typical example is perhaps afforded by the Czech Jaroslav Vrchlický, whose translations and paraphrases of foreign forms led, of necessity, to his transmitting several new elements of Western literature as well. He translated Baudelaire and Verlaine, but also Rimbaud and Mallarmé.

Some Galician writers played a similar role in Ukrainian literature. The Russian K. Fofanov is an example of a completely unbiased writer who, without any interest in literary theory, independently discovered new impressionistic elements of style for his work. Modern French influences can be seen in the works of the prematurely deceased Serb, Vojislav Ilić.

Modernism made its appearance chiefly as a movement *consciously* opposed to realism. In Poland it happened in 1891 in the preface by Miriam (pseudonym for Z. Przesmycki) to a translation of Maeterlinck's works; in Russia it was 1893 in a brochure by D. Merežkovskij, *On the Current Condition and Decline of Russian Literature*. These manifestoes, although the modern reader is quite surprised by the *modestly retiring* tone in Merežkovskij's brochure, were accompanied by the appearance of the writers: in Poland the first volume of Tetmajer's poems had already come out in 1891, and from 1894 small collections of poems by Valerij Brjusov and his companions appeared in Russia. Several writers whose beginnings lay earlier quickly joined the new trends. There were already groups of modernists before the turn of the century who were joined around 1900 by representatives of the still younger generation, for example, in Poland L. Staff, in Russia A. Blok and Andrej Belyj (pseudonym of B. N. Bugaev), as well as by some older writers, in Russia F. Sologub (Teternikov), Vjačeslav Ivanov, and Innokentij Annenskij.

If the avant-gardists of Russian symbolism were predominantly interested in *aesthetic* problems and endeavored for the creation of new literary forms, which were probably considered literary experiments (*opyty*) more than anything else, then after 1900 several new writers also published whose points of departure were certain philosophical assumptions, and who aspired toward a total Weltanschauung. Blok and Belyj originally proceeded from Vladimir Solov'ev's philosophy; Vjačeslav Ivanov wanted to lay the foundations of a new philosophy of world and life. Later still, several writers who only admired the *new style* and who imitated or considered the innovations important as pure "fashion trends" also joined with the new movement.

From the beginning on there seems to have existed within *Mloda Polska* a unified *aesthetic* and *philosophical* trend. But in any case hardly any of the leading representatives of Polish modernism limited their work to purely aesthetic goals. In the beginning, perhaps, Tetmajer's poetry was only purely lyrical. Right from the start, however, Kasprowicz's lyrics were philosophically and religiously colored; the same may be said for Stefan Wyspiański's poetry and drama, while the prose works of Żeromski and Reymont were in no way averse to social, political, and intellectual historical themes. In Poland, however, a man played the role of the "fellow traveler" of Russian symbolism, at times of "ideologue," and assumed a strong, if also temporary influence on Russian and Czech literature: this was Stefan Przybyszewski who first appeared as a German poet, who thereafter became a Polish novelist, and who sounded a quite intensive "decadent" tone in his works.

In Czech literature it was perhaps the lack of a leading literary personality that explains the coexistence of various movements such as one still connected with the tradition of nationally oriented realistic literature, one disposed toward a world philosophy, and one inclined toward "decadence." In addition to A. Sova, who was still connected with the old tradition of Czech literature, there were at the other extreme, the mystic Otokar Březina and the group of "decadents," A. Procházka and J. Karásek ze Lvovic, while Stefan K. Neumann occupied a middle-of-the-road position.

A closed group was formed by the representatives of Slovene modernism; Ivan Cankar, the two prematurely deceased writers D. Kette and J. Murn Aleksandrov, who, incidently, were connected with Austrian literature, and the most important of all, O. Župančič.

The Croat Ivo Vojnović, primarily a dramatist who belonged to the older generation, frequently followed West European stimulae. The lyricist, prosaist, and translator Vladimir Nazor was more closely associated with modernistic development, while the Serbian writers were only able to separate themselves from the realistic tradition with difficulty. Nevertheless, the influence of modernism on Jovan Dučić and V. Ilić should be noted.

The works of such modernistic writers as the Slovak Ivan Krasko (J. Botto), who only first appeared in 1909 with the little volume of poetry *Nox et solitudo*, as well as (after many beginnings by P. Slavejkov) the Bulgarian P. K. Jovorov, for whom the collection of poems *After the Shadows* (*Podir senkite na oblacite*, 1910) is typical, were individually colored.

Modernism appeared quite early in Ukrainian literature too (see the list at the beginning of Chapter XI), but it was only at the beginning of the century that O. Oleś (Kandyba) assumed the leading position, and it was only in the second decade of the twentieth century that the most important writers, M. Pyl'skyj and P. Tyčyna appeared. M. Bahdanovič, who was strongly dependent on Russian symbolism (Blok), was a representative of White Russian literature.

4. The main task of all modernistic trends, regardless of the names un-

der which they appeared and of what programs they presented, was the
"realization" (Aktualisierung) of the poetic word, the restoration of its
non-communicative functions, above all the symbolizing. In this manner, literature was supposed to acquire its significance. The efficacy of
the beautiful word was obviously overestimated, and, as often happens
in the history of literature, it was first believed that the new literary
movement would renovate the whole of life. Even if this hope proved
itself misleading, it was nevertheless later seen that the new literature
left behind many deep traces in cultural life.

The characteristic aspect of modernistic literature is the attention
paid to the euphonic side of the language: alliterations and euphonies,
choice rhymes, harmonies within the lines, inner rhymes, and euphonies
in prose texts as well were the prime features of the new literary language.

For reasons incomprehensible to us today, some of Bal'mont's poems
belong to the first works of Russian modernism that excited indignation.
Here, for example, is a poem that in terms of content is nothing other
than a variation of the "eternal theme"—a boat (or a ship) in a storm;
the first lines run:

	Initial sounds
Вечер. Взморье. Вздохи ветра.	v--v--v--v
Величавый возглас волн.	v--v--v
Близко буря. В берег бьется	b--b--vb--b
чуждый чарам чёрный чёлн.	č--č--č--č
Чуждый чистым чарам счастья	č--č--č--sč
челн волненья, челн тревог.	č--v--č
Бросил берег, бьется с бурей,	b--b--b--sb
ищет светлых снов чертог (...)	šč--s--s--č

Evening. The shore of the sea. The sighs of the wind.
The majestic call of the waves.
The storm is near. Beating toward shore
is a black boat, a stranger to magic.

A stranger to the pure magic of happiness,
a boat of unrest, a boat of alarm.
It left the shore, fights with the storm,
seeks the palace of bright dreams.

Here is the beginning of a poem by Andrej Belyj, who was another
master of euphonic prose:

Кругом крутые кручи,   кру-кру-кру
смеется смехом смерть ...   сме-сме-сме

Steep slopes all about,
death laughs resoundingly . . .

Another variation was offered by poems made of short lines, often consisting of one word, that harmonized with one another. Almost all the poets of Slavic modernism wrote such poems. As a consequence, it became possible to uncover new choice rhymes (of foreign words, for example) in Slavic poetry whose rhyme poverty had been complained of since romanticism. Thus the probing representative of *Młoda Polska*, Anthony Lange, wrote a poem *Rhyme (Rym)* to "a lady who thought the rhymes of a poet too simple." The poem glitters with rhymes such as *zelaz-Anafielas, gongi-posągi, fandango-gidranga, koloryt-rifioryt, aksamit-piramid, abrakadabry-chrabry, Rizpah-wyspa, granit-Oceanid,* etc. But the poet found sufficient examples among Polish words as well: *brzeszczot-pieszczot, dzieląć-przeląć, posów-głosów, opól-topól, częstych-dwie z tych, czeladź-wcielać,* etc.

The symbolists demonstrated that in the Russian language, dactylic rhymes of the type encountered in romanticism, as well as hyper-dactylic rhymes with the accent on the fourth or fifth syllable or even further from the end are possible; V. Brjusov, for example, enjoyed making rhymes such as, *skóvyvajuščij-očarovyvajuščij, rasstilajuščimisja-zabyvajuščimisja, privjazannostjami-nedoskazannostjami.*

The introduction of "imperfect rhymes" was more significant in enriching the Russian store of rhymes. These were rediscovered by A. Blok after the romantic epigone A. K. Tolstoj had already used them and then defended them in his letters. Perhaps the first model was presented by the Ukrainian romantic Taras Ševčenko who most likely utilized them intentionally after the late baroque verses of Skovoroda (see Chapter VIII, 3). Blok's imperfect rhymes, such as *granic/caricu,* scandalized even his own literary adherents, but since that time they have become part of the stock of Russian poetic means; for example: *kúpol/slušal, búdet/ljúdi, láty/sžatyj, grívy/díva, vódy/pochódu, černi/svérgni,* and so on.

It must be noted that in Russian, because of the strong reduction of unaccented vowels, the devoicing of consonants when final, the special treatment of various consonant clusters, and the orthography taken over from Church Slavic (as the nominative singular, masculine of adjectives in -yj instead of -oj), many rhymes are only graphically imperfect, as, for example, *rod/rot, spokojna/strojno, burnyj/lazurnoj*, and even *vizža/doždja*, pronounced dožž'a, etc. However, Blok also used, as did his imitators, *true* imperfect rhymes.

Deviations from the traditional verse meters began to appear. In Polish syllabic verse there was the regular alternation of accented and unaccented rhymes, which, of course, had occurred earlier; the Russian symbolists frequently counted only stresses, and the number of unaccented syllables were paid no attention. This verse meter was often called *dol'niki*.

We encounter such lines in Blok's work, for example,

Девушка пела в церковном хоре	х́ х х х́ х х х́ х х́ х
о всех усталых в чужом краю,	х х́ х х́ х х х́ х х́
о всех кораблях уплывших в море,	х х́ х х х́ х х́ х х́ х
о всех забывших радость свою.	х х́ х х х́ х х х х́
Так пел ее голос, летящий в купол,	х́ х́ х х́ х́ х х х́ х х́ х
и луч сиял на белом плече,	х х́ х х́ х х́ х х х́
и каждый из мрака смотрел и слушал,	х х́ х х х́ х х х́ х х́ х
как белое платье пело в луче (...)	х х́ х х х́ х х́ х х х́

A girl sang in a church choir
of all the tired in foreign lands,
of all the ships far at sea,
of all who have forgotten their joy.

So sang her voice, flying to the cupola,
and a ray shone on [her] white shoulder,
and everyone looked from the darkness and listened
to the white dress singing in the ray.

This innovation, introduced very early in Blok's case, since 1901, equally found imitation and further development, as with the futurists.

Further innovations were concerned with form, and there was experimentation of the most varied sort. It may probably be said that since the baroque period such playing with form had only been met on occasion. It was often the work of dilettantes.

Brjusov's collection, *Experiments—Opyty*, 1918, belongs in this area. The book contained poems, however, that had previously been published. Once again versus cancrine, versus alphabetice, versus anacyclici, figure poems, etc. are encountered. Here is the beginning of one of Brjusov's alphabetical poems:

Алый бархат вечереет,
.горделиво дремлют ели,

жаждет зелень и июль
колыбельной лаской млеет (...)

Red velvet becomes evening,
proudly the firs slumber,
the greenness thirsts and July
melts away from lulling caresses . . .

Brjusov goes through all the letters of the Russian alphabet in this manner.

Acrostics were once again utilized in serious poetry. The sonnet became a favorite form; its Russian master was Vjačeslav Ivanov. The polish poet Jankowski wrote a sonnet in which every line consists of a single word, sometimes with a preposition. The lines are separated here by a slash.

W bój! / Z czuć / rzuć / zdrój!
Skuj / chuć! / Budź / Stój!
Drwij / z burz, / rwij
z róż, / żyj, / twórz!

To battle!/ From feeling/ let spring/ the source!/ Forge/ lust!/ Awaken!/ Mock/ the storms,/ tear/ from the roses,/ live,/ create!

This sonnet is also an example of how the semantic side of a poem can retreat in favor of form.

The Bulgarian modernist P. K. Javorov wrote an "anacyclic" poem, the second half of which repeats the same lines in the reversed direction. The first half,

Две хубави очи. Душата на дете—
в две хубави очи—музика—лъчи.
Не искат и не обещават те ...
Душата ми се моли,
дете,
душата ми се моли!
Страсти и неволи
ще фърлят утре върху тях
булото на срам и грях (...)

Two beautiful eyes. The soul of a child
in two beautiful eyes—music—rays.
They desire not and promise not . . .
My soul prays,
oh child,
my soul prays.
Passion and plights

> will tomorrow over you
> throw shame and sin . . .

Lemański lets the last words of every line rhyme with the first of the other lines:

> *Turyście*, łaknącemu, w skwar, w ogrodów *woni,*
> *ustroni* altan, zdrojów, ciekących *perliście—*
> *symfonii* boskich szmer rzucają palm *okiście*
> *i wnijście* kaktus mu wskazuje kolcem *dłoni.*

> To the tourist, thirsting, in the heat, in the scent of the gardens
> after the solitude of the arbour, of the springs, effervescently flowing—
> the palm branches cast the murmur of the divine symphonies,
> and a cactus shows him the entrance with the thorn of its hand.

All types of euphonic effects may be found in the works of almost all the modern poets.

See the poems of the Croat poet Vladimir Nazor, for example *Cvrčak,* or of M. Krleža who also clothes his works with sociopolitical tendentiousness in a euphonically original form, or of the Slovenians, O. Župančič in his *"Ciciban in še kaj"*—"Ciciban and Something Else," Kette, and Kosovel, of the Ukrainians H. Čuprynka and especially P. Tyčyna in his first collection of poems. All of them were able to present modern philosophical and political themes in exquisite "modern" forms.

Prose works, of course not by any means the works of all modernistic prose writers, also offer examples of euphonistic art. Again, euphony was in no way limited to purely belletristic prose, but was also employed in memoirs and even in theoretical writings.

Andrej Belyj is a master of euphony in his prose, which is also strongly rhythmic. See, for example, the description of the kitchen in his autobiographical novel *Kotik Letaev.* This language is found everywhere in Belyj:

1. Мы проходим на кухню—
2. шопоты, шумы, шипы, огни, пары, гари:
3. там на кухне стоит, там на кухне бурлит—
4. дымношипный котел; и огонь бьет в котел (...)
5. ломти мягкого мяса малиновеют на столике,
6. кровоусая кошечка с красным куском в зубах уже косится.

1. We go into the kitchen—
2. Whispers, noises, hissing, fires, steams, burnt smell:
3. There in the kitchen stands, there in the kitchen bubbles
4. a smoking, hissing kettle, and the fire beats on the kettle . . .

5. Slices of soft meat become raspberry-colored on the table,
6. the little cat with a red piece [of meat] between its teeth is already squint eyed.

Observe the rhythmic structure of these lines:

2. x́ x x / x́ x / x́ x / x x́ / x x́ / x́ x
3. x x x́ x / x x́ / x x x́ x / x x́
4. x x x́ x / x x́ / x x x́ / x́ / x x́

The euphony is rich, and by the use of the -š partly onomatopoetic:
1. Word repetition (lines 1, 3) *na kuxnju;* sound repetitions: x-x.
2. Sound repetitions: š-š-š-ary-ari.
3. Word repetitions: *na kuxne—na kuxne;* Sound repetitions: it-it.
4. Word repetitions: kotël—kotël; sound repetitions: š (to line 2).
5. Sound repetitions: m-mja-mja-ma.
6. Sound repetitions (considering Russian vowel reduction): kra-ko-š-ka-kra-k-ko-ka.

Even the "graphic" picture of a poetic work often became a stylistic means when, in connection with the required intonation the poet spread his verses among lines, contrary to all tradition, and shaped his prose texts in a sort of pictorial presentation as occasionally happened in baroque and as later became the rule among the futurists.[1]

5. The themes of modernistic literature are quite varied, no doubt because many authors laid the greatest value upon the formal side of their works and showed less interest in content. In addition, almost all the writers of the older generation were dependent upon the traditions of positivism or the Enlightenment of the eighteen sixties or, in their quest after a theoretical, philosophical foundation for their views, they built upon a superficial acquaintance with some theoretician or philosopher from the past or the present.

The positivistic elements of many writers of *Młoda Polska* have already been established, especially in the case of the movement's "theoretician," Stefan Przybyszewski (K. Wyka). The situation among the Czech modernists was similar. Influences of Schopenhauer and Ed. von Hartmann, and later of Darwinism and L. Feuerbach may be found even in the case of the Russian Christian mystical philosopher Vladimir

1. J. Tuwim's book *Pegaz dęba* (1950) offers a large collection of poetic play and bold experimentation. The new intensification of examples within modernism is striking. See D. Tschiževskij's discussion in *Zeitschrift für slavische Philologie*, XXII (1953).

Solov'ev who himself was very influential upon the younger generation of symbolists.

Among many modernists we encounter an intentional ambivalence in their declarations on fundamental philosophic questions, or confessions of such spiritual breadth that they are able to encompass their antitheses. The development of some writers later led them to views that stood in striking contrast to their earlier philosophy.

> W piersi naszej Chrystusy żyją i Nerony,
> w piersi naszej bogowie żyją i bydlęta...
> [A. Lange]

In our breasts dwell Christs and Neroes, in our breasts dwell Gods and beasts . . .

> Неколебимой истине
> не верю я давно,
> и все моря, все пристани
> люблю равно, равно.
> Хочу, чтоб всюду плавала
> свободная ладья,
> и Господа и Дьявола
> хочу прославить я (...)
> [V. Brjusov]

In an unshakable truth, I have long not believed, but I love all seas, all harbors equally. I wish that the free ship may sail everywhere, and I wish to glorify God as well as the devil . . .

Brjusov believed, "There are many truths. . . . My dream was always a pantheon, a temple to all Gods. Let us worship the day and the night, Mithras and Adonis, Christ and Satan."

Blok, who began as a mystic and admirer of Vladimir Solov'ev, later became not only a sceptic, but also wrote poems in which he employed a demonic symbolism, admitting that his Muse derided faith: *i kogda ty smeeš'sja nad veroj.* The fact that some Russian symbolists, among them Valerij Brjusov, in their later years became supporters of aetheistic communism may be a disguise or an honest conversion by the social thought of Communist Russia.

6. One tone of modernism, if not dominant, then certainly prevailing, was the despairing of the present and the conception of reality as a labyrinth in which man was hopelessly lost.

The labyrinth was already one of the continually reoccuring themes of Russian literature among the precursors of symbolism: we encounter the myth of Theseus and Ariadne in the work of Brjusov, Sologub,

Baltrušajtis, and Vjačeslav Ivanov where in most cases Ariadne's cord breaks or is not present. Blok writes about a person who goes astray in a forest thicket, for Bal'mont the large city with its "seven-storied coffins" is a symbol of the labyrinth.

Merciless, inevitable fate awaits man in the world. This conception was brought in graphic form to the stage in Maeterlinck's works.

Man is not born for victory over fate according to Tetmajer. A. Lange speaks straightway about the "Ananke." Brjusov also does not desire "to rule fate."

Maximilian Vološin takes over from Tjutčev the image of the "deaf-dumb demons" who are also blind and steer the world without a goal.

And therefore Death appears to be Man's liberator from the power of blind fate.

Death alone "will absolve us, he alone is our benefactor," says H. Hlaváček. F. Sologub is the poet of death among the Russian symbolists. For him death is "the tender friend," he liberates man. But the young Andrej Belyj who sees himself and his adherents as "Argonauts," can, at the same time, write,

> Нет ничего ... И ничего не будет ...
> И ты умрешь ...
> Исчезнет мир, и Бог его забудет ...

There is nothing . . . And there will be nothing . . . And you will die . . . The world will disappear and God will forget it . . .

Later this motif appears even more strongly in his work:

> ... Покоя нет.
> В покое только ночь. И ты её найдешь.
> Там ночь. Иди туда.

There is no peace. In peace is only the night. And you will find it. The night is there. Go there.

Similar thoughts are to be found in the works of several other Slavic writers.

7. The conception of the total and impregnable loneliness of every man, particularly the poet, belongs to the motifs of melancholy and despair. Perhaps mass as well has but an ostensible, illusory existence, as does the entire world. The theoretical cognitive scepticism was associated with the broadened conceptions of the time and was supported by Schopenhauer and the misunderstood Kant.

The poet flees to such far spheres as exoticism, India, Mexico, and

Africa, to the past—mostly seen only as a symbolic picture of threatened existence and finally into the distant worlds of the future, into utopias, but often "negative" or "pessimistic utopias." Images of future states consecrated to ruin were the favorite themes of modernistic literature.

Wyspiański's masterdramas are symbolic-historical stage works. A trilogy by D. Merežkovskij depicts the eternal struggle of the Antichrist against Christ at the time of "Julian the Apostate," at the time when the Renaissance brought paganism to new life, and at the time of the "Europeanization" of Russia under Peter the Great. He was followed by V. Brjusov in the portrayal of the dying of ancient paganism in his novel *Altar' pobedy*—Altar of Victory. In his novel *Ognennyj angel* (*The Fire Angel*), Brjusov also depicts the early Renaissance and in several stories presents the decline of the future states. Anthony Lange's stories have partially the same themes.

The modernists' positive utopias also strike a note of little hopefullness: the life depicted there takes place on other planets, under other suns.

Brjusov wrote short poems about life in such other worlds. F. Sologub created pictures of life in another solar system for himself and even wrote a large novel, the action of which takes place on another planet. The Pole Żuławski takes the moon and the earth as the places of action of a pessimistic utopia in his trilogy *The Silver Sphere*.

The right of transplanting themselves, at least in fantasy, to another world was claimed by the modernists on the basis of their "creation of new worlds" which was permitted and even required by creative fantastic invention.

8. The inconsistency of the poets' ambivalent declarations combine the portrayals of the thoroughly earthly and carnal excesses of vice and lewdness with pessimism; it is in order to be able to do this that the modernist demands the rights of a free man.

Stefan Przybyszewski was a master of amoralism: his philosophy of life derives human activity from sexuality, from blind libido, as it were. The heroes of his works are drunkards and libertines who fashion their lives while free from all inhibitions—or who let them flow unfashioned. His works influenced Czechs, Russians, and Ukrainians (Jackiv); their literary weaknesses, however, were soon recognized, a fact that did not prevent his influence, long extinguished in Poland, from becoming effective a second time, sometime after 1906, among the Czechs and Russians, mostly, however, affecting only the nominal members of literary modernism.

If a repetition of some romantic motifs may be seen in this, then the aesthetic amoralism was nevertheless—in Huysmans' style—now much more intensive, and it sought an ideological and historical foundation for itself. "Satanism" was spoken and written of outright.

A trilogy of Przybyszewski's was simply called *Children of Satan*. It was enthusiastically greeted with an essay, *Adveniat regnum tuum*, by the Czech Arnošt Procházka. Karásek ze Lvovic published a collection of poems under the title *Sodoma: Kniha pohanská (Sodom: A Pagan Book)*. This collection contained a chapter called "Priapea" and poems such as *Sexus triumphans* or a *Hymn to Priapus*, which was, however, quite harmless. Bal'mont wrote a poem *The Voice of Satan (Golos D'javola)* with the confession, "I hate all saints," "I've loved the serpent from childhood on." The melancholy dreamer Sologub reported of the course of his life:

> Когда я в бурном море плавал,
> и мой корабль пошел ко дну,
> я так воззвал: «Отец мой Дьявол,
> спаси, помилуй, я тону!»
> (...) «я власти тёмного порока
> отдам остаток чёрных дней»
> (...) И верен я, отец мой Дьявол,
> обету данному в злой час,
> когда я в бурном море плавал
> и ты меня от смерти спас (...)

> When I sailed the stormy sea,
> and my ship was sinking to the bottom,
> I prayed, "My Father, Satan,
> save me, have mercy, I'm drowning!"
> "... to the power of dark vice
> will I dedicate the rest of my black days."
> And true am I, my Father Satan,
> to my promise, given in an evil hour,
> when I sailed the stormy sea
> and you saved me from death ...

Nevertheless, Sologub's pessimistic works are far from any sort of "Satanism."

Only the Russian "fellow travelers of symbolism" such as Leonid Andreev directly attacked Christianity and wrote hymns to Judas or chose demons as heroes of their tragedies (*Anatema*) or novels (*Satan's Diary*).

9. Characteristic for the striking inconsistency of the modernists

were the beautiful nature lyrics of *Mloda Polska's* symbolism and of the representatives of related trends in the other Slavic literatures. Nature was often shown not as a concrete "landscape" but as elements, elemental forces, and spheres of existence. These are essences that lend a symbolic sense to concrete existence. Consequently, the images of the real world, as for example, of the sea, and indeed not only of the richly varying surfaces, but also of the dark depths, were favored as symbols of the soul.

In the same manner, fog and snow appeared as elements encompassing and enveloping visable existence. Finally, the light of the moon, which allowed reality to appear only vaguely, mysteriously, and mystically, was preferred to clear sunlight which permitted details to come forward. The night now appeared to have less significance. But dusk, which makes everything concrete in the landscape appear in a homogeneous, all-uniting opalescence, was also part of the preferred objects of the nature lyrics. Finally, the mountain ranges were also able to be presented as homogeneous existence where everything individual lost its individual nature in the Whole.

Tetmajer straightforwardly designated the objects of his nature lyrics as "symbolic," for example, the symbolic river. He depicts the nights in the mountains and the mountains (Tatra) themselves. Autumn also appears as a unifying natural element in Annenskij's poetry. We encounter autumn fog and polar landscapes with the ice and snow ruling all, while the iridescences or half-dark of the evening dusk are also frequently met. O. Župančič's miniature poems and especially L. Staff's early nature lyrics offer the best examples of landscapes ruled by elemental powers. In Staff's first volume of collected poems the landscapes are immersed in the half-dark of obscured vision by means of words such as "Something."

An outright symbolic presentation of such landscape elements are often met in Blok, Annenskij, etc. The influence of Tjutčev's nature lyrics—night, wind, night sounds—is strong with the Russian symbolists.

Much was contributed to synthetic presentations of nature by synaesthesia, favored by the writers of modernism. In spite of the gayness of the image the concrete details of the events are dissolved by the coloration.

There were numerous writers in modernism who had extraordinarily strong coloristic elements as, for example, Kasprowicz, Belyj, Blok, Annenskij, etc.

The vagueness of the nature scenes is frequently attained by impressionistic descriptions.

"Dark" poems in which the semantic side is weakened or completely absent make up a particular sort of modernistic poetry. They form a conspicuous parallel to the dark poems of the baroque, romanticism, and West European modernism, as, for example, those by Mallarmé, Apollinaire, etc. These poems are in no way in want of aesthetic efficacy, only they do not awaken definite, clear ideas in the reader, but rather unclear moods, and, in an oblique manner, thoughts as well.

A. Blok wrote his first "incomprehensible" poems as early as 1901–1902; they became continually more rare after 1910. At about this time he was followed, however, by I. Annenskij, the most important Russian representative of this genre who had even written an essay defending the eligibility of "incomprehensible literature." In Russia, the futurists (see 14) made further steps in this direction.

10. In their rejection of the traditions of realism and Enlightenment the representatives of modernistic literature in no way agreed with one another in their positive theses and demands. The individual hue of the work of individual modernistic writers was part of the esteemed values of the literature, and this individual tone is extraordinarily manifold. In addition to amoralism, Satanism, and atheism, we encounter all sorts of partially utopian plans; there is found the ideal of a synthetic culture that is supposed to have not only an aesthetic, but a national, social, and religious character as well. Religious seeking or a philosophy based upon religious traditions are not in the least rare.

National motifs break through among the representatives of those Slavic peoples who were still struggling for national-political independence. The heroes of prose works became national and social fighters who, nevertheless, often carried traits of the "modern man."

There were sufficient religious writers among the modernists (such as Kasprowicz in Poland, and Baltrušajtis in Russia), but there were even more of the religious seekers some of whom later went different ways from the established religious currents, as, for instance, Blok and Belyj. Belyj spent years involved with anthroposophy which he, however, deserted in the last years of his life. Blok ended in "areligious mysticism" *sui generis*, the content of which consisted of visions of forthcoming, worldwide catastrophes.

11. The prosaic and poetic themes of Slavic modernism are extraordinarily manifold. I have already mentioned some of the typical themes. Also typical was, among other things, the preference for distant-

lying objects of presentation. There were also paraphrases of the old works as, for example, the *Alexandreis*. But in these paraphrases the writers sometimes utilized modern language and modern style. Even more characteristic, however, were the "stylization experiments," the imitation of foreign and particularly old language and style, or, at any rate, how a given author imagined these elements to be.

The Russian symbolist A. Remizov was a master of stylization. He retold the old Russian chapbooks of the seventeenth century and the old Russian novels of pre-Tartar times. The Czech romancer Julius Zeyer and many others reworked old narratives. Folkloristic stylization also appeared, as Lucjan Rydel's *Betleem polskie* and the ballad *O Kasi i Królewiczu*. Bal'mont attempted to imitate the songs of the Russian sectarians.

The preference for unusual, even "paradoxical" themes is thoroughly understandable. Cruelties and crimes appeared—perhaps more often among the nominal members and imitators who perceived the new literature as a fashion. In this atmosphere Demons, Satan, Judas, Nero, Catilina, and Caligula often appeared as heroes.

Mythology is one of the most interesting themes of modernism. To some extent, the ancient myths and, in association with this, the ancient narrative structures reappeared; some figures out of Germanic mythology turned up; partially in connection with the admiration for Richard Wagner, exotic mythology also made an appearance, such as Indian and Mexican. Slavic mythology seems to be the most weakly represented. Original mythological creations of individual authors were frequent, however.

The vaguely depicted "monsters," the symbols of the misanthropic powers of fate, of course including the eternal mythological figure of Death, were already in evidence among the precursors of modernism. The beginnings of Russian symbolism were accompanied by the figures of Centaurs, also favored in West European *Jugendstil*, and of unicorns, which were placed into Russian everyday life (see Belyj and Brjusov). During the same period, figures from Germanic and ancient mythology turned up. The Polish poet B. Leśmian presented interesting, original creations in his Russian and Polish poems.

The thematic oddness of the works or collections of poems was often alluded to by the titles.

Karásek ze Lvovic wrote a collection of stories entitled *Lásky absurdné*, and a collection of poems, *Sodoma*. "Incomprehensible" titles, a sort of self-protection from "superfluous" popularity, intended to prevent the uneducated or half-educated from reading the works were also typical.

V. Brjusov's first volumes of poetry all carry titles in foreign languages: *Chef d'oeuvres, Me eum esse, Tertia vigilia,* and *Stephanos.* The latter title was even printed in Greek letters. The literature of *Młoda Polska* and its followers utilized such titles as: *Anima lacrymans, Circines,* and unusual combinations of Polish words. The Slovak Krasko gave his work Latin titles (*Nox et solitudo*). The journals carried just as "shocking" titles, for instance, the Polish *Sfinks* and *Chimera,* just as did the presses of the Russian symbolists, for example, *Skorpion, Grif,* etc.

12. Naturally the recasting of the literary language played a considerable role in the literary movements, the origins of which were so closely connected with endeavors to renovate language and style. As in all new stylistic epochs, there at first took place an enrichment of the literary language from old and new lingual sources that were as yet unexhausted by literature. Popular speech, archaisms, jargons, and "prosaisms" are often connected with stylization. New creations were a further source of linguistic enrichment that eclipsed every epoch since the baroque. As always, now too there were authors who possessed a special talent for the creation of neologisms.[2] Other authors created unusual word combinations. Finally we meet all kinds of morphological daring. All roads led to a true enrichment of the language which in turn has left considerable traces behind in today's Slavic literary languages.

Many Polish writers used borrowings from the popular language. They were already present in the work of Tetmajer, in his depiction of Tatra and its inhabitants, in the works of S. Wyspiański, and W. Reymont, in his *Peasants,* etc. Historical themes call for archaisms that were, however, more boldly used than ever before. In Russian literature it was Remizov who was the master of dialectal vocabulary. He was also no stranger to neologisms; however, they played a special role in the work of Andrej Belyj in whose work more than 2,000 can be found. A. Blok employed unusual word combinations from his earliest works on, something which brought him reproaches of poor language because it did not comply with school rules. See such examples as

> Высоко бегут по карнизам
> улыбки, сказки и сны (...)
> белое платье пало в луче (...)
> печаль о невозвратном море
> проходит утлой чередой (...)
> груз тоски многоэтажной (...)

2. Even in antiquity, Laberius was famous as the creator of numerous neologisms (see Aulus Gellius, XVI, 7); in Russian romanticism, Jazykov and Benediktov (see above, X, 10) also filled this role.

ог: петли веков, завывающая стужа, мой ангел вчерашний, тьма бродила, поникла мгла ...

> High above along the cornices run
> smiles, fairy tales, and dreams . . .
> The white dress sung in the ray of light . . .
> Sorrow about the irretrievable sea
> passes by in frail succession . . .
> The burden of multistoried grief . . .

Or: the nooses of centuries, the screaming cold, my yesterday's angel, the gloom groped about, the fog bowed, etc.

Examples of morphological boldness are the use of the singular in cases of "pluralia tantum" and, reversed, the use of ungrammatical plurals, particularly in Bal'mont's work.

These features are also making their way into the work of contemporary writers who have little or nothing to do with modernistic literature.

13. It was primarily the still numerous and not insignificant realists who were among the writers who had nothing to do with "modernism": the most important Polish positivists were still living during the full bloom of Polish modernism. The new Russian realists, above all Gor'kij and Bunin, joined with symbolism in the nineties stylistically and, to some extent, thematically as well. Čexov immediately perceived the symbolists to be allies. Only Korolenko continued to hold fast to the traditions of realism.

In other literatures there were numerous hybrid figures, even among Ukrainians and Yugoslavs, while the Bulgarian modernist P. K. Javorov slipped off to the realistic plane. Yet more indicative remains the fact that even the Polish prose writers Żeromski and Reymont, who can with certainty be counted among the "neoromantics," nevertheless sometimes wrote works which, not too unjustly, may be designated "realistic."

At the crossroad stand the later Russian writers who indeed began as thoroughly neoromantic, such as L. Leonov, partly Babel', and Pil'njak, who was decidedly influenced by Andrej Belyj, and all then found the way to the new realism, later designated as "socialist."

14. Already there were modernists in Russia who before the First World War had considered themselves opponents of symbolism and who gave to their closed groups names such as "acmeists," and especially "futurists." In the last years, when individual writers were dedicating

works to the futurists—the two most important among them, V. Majakovskij and V. Xlebnikov, and recently B. Pasternak too, are mostly
treated without any connection with the entire movement which they
created or from which they proceeded—one often came to the realization
that they indeed presented a certain uniformity with symbolism. The
tasks they had set themselves were frequently the same, as, for example,
the realization of the literary word; and the methods with which they
solved these problems were also partly the same, even if they did lead
to ostensibly different appearing results. A great deal connects Blok
and particularly Belyj to the futurists; it is perhaps also not exaggerated
to characterize Andrej Belyj as the "first futurist" in the words of
Vladimir Markov. It is thoroughly possible too that in a more distant
perspective of the future all the modernistic "unrealistic" movements
in Russian literature between 1895 and 1925 will be conceived of as one
great—though differentiated—unity. This problem, however, can only
be alluded to here.

Similar questions may be posed in relation to the Polish literary
movements after the retreat of *Młoda Polska* when one thinks of the few
Polish futurists such as Titus Czyżewski and the influential group, the
Skamandrites, Julian Tuwim and others.

The important contemporary Croatian writer M. Krleža stands close
to modernism too, something that may also be shown by his earlier
published critical essays on modernistic West European literature.

XIII

IN CONCLUSION

1. We have no doubt shown that the Slavic literatures have generally experienced identical or similar periods of development in the course of the last thousand years, even if individual literatures have occasionally gone their own ways and have at times dissolved their otherwise almost continually present mutual bonds. It can not be denied that the Slavic literatures stand largely within the broader community of European intellectual and literary development.

Unfortunately, it must be admitted that research in literary history, and indeed Slavic research as well as West European, has devoted less attention than might be desired to the problems of connections between the Slavic East and the European and American West. This, of course, has been partly the result on both sides of interests entailed by the times.

In the West, much less interest has been devoted to the Slavic world —and it is still so today—than to the Near and Far East. There are a few exceptions, as, for example, in the area of fairy tale and folk epic research. It is to wonder that the West European literary historians only seldom reach for Slavic scholarly literature, even when it is a case of books and journals that appear in West European languages. Conditions have recently become less conducive to the use of Slavic scholarly literature because this literature, in so far as it stems from East European countries, speaks a language that is completely foreign to West European scholars with their concepts and terminology. Even the West European Marxists such as G. Lukácz do not fully understand it.

Literary study in the Slavic countries is also not without blame for the lack of contact with that of Western Europe, and indeed not only in the last decades. There are a number of works on the influences of West European and American literature upon Slavic literature that, however, almost exclusively limit themselves to determining the identity or similarity of plots and motifs. This collection of individual works has frequently directly prevented insight into the deeper intellectual associations. This seeking after "influences" has for some fifty years been considered| an obsolete and unfruitful method of investigation. But recently we have even experienced a period in which even the most obvious bonds between West European and Slavic literature have been intentionally concealed. It was permitted, or required, that a history of eighteenth-century Russian literature be written that almost completely ignored the effects of the West. An attempt was even made to deny the huge extent to which Old Slavic literature and the literary language was dependent on the Byzantine and Latin. But even more important are the attempts to reject concepts that are valid for West European literature in relation to Slavic literature. This is what happened, for example, with the concept "romanticism" and, to an even more significant extent, with the concept "baroque"; even the use of this term was for a time taboo and point-blank prohibited.[1]

Modern "socialist realism" naturally sought, as does every literary trend, after its ancestors in literary history, and, without thorough investigation, explained almost all important writers of the past—from the Greek tragedians up to the Renaissance poets and even William Blake—as "realists."

In the West, it was only natural that there was no desire to consider seriously studies in literary history that worked with such primitive concepts. But with time, even in the West—without being a Marxist or a proponent of "socialist realism"—people began to follow faithfully East European scholarship, or to reproduce its content. Since, in the meantime, the "orthodoxy" of literary study in the East seems to have been strongly shaken, the danger exists that while in the East the methods of literary scholarship are changing, it will only be in the West that there are authors who continue to juggle with these tendentious, fully unscholarly concepts.

2. This being the situation of West-East relations, it appears that many literary historians when treating such purely Slavic themes as Huss, the False Demetrius, Peter the Great, even take quite insignificant

1. In regard to the concept "baroque literature," the caution among the Czech and Polish investigators will soon have been overcome; recently the standpoint of Soviet research also seems to be shaken.

works of Western origin into account but do not find important Slavic works, sometimes translated into "comprehensible" languages, worthy of mention.

The Slavs as well bear the blame, at least partially; if such an important literary movement as Russian symbolism is passed over in silence in Russian works, if the works of the symbolist poets—regardless of how they are judged—are not reissued, then they are being injurious to their own culture.

There constantly appear translations from the Slavic languages abroad that, because of their poor quality, make any real acquaintance with the authors impossible.

3. There are, however, important problems for investigation. We have, at least allusively, named them on the various pages of our book. Among these problems, above all, belongs a careful examination of the innovations introduced by the Slavic literatures during various literary epochs; also sources of influence, which until now have been almost entirely neglected, should be thoroughly investigated, for example, those of English and American literature: Washington Irving knew Puškin, Bret Hart quoted Leskov, Feodor Sologub took over topics from the newer English-language writers. Or an investigation of the influence of such remote countries as Mexico upon such poets as Bal'mont, later Majakovskij who visited it should be undertaken. Such influences are often treated without learning more about the countries and their literatures. The influences of the Scandinavian (Hamsun) or Belgian (Maeterlinck, Verhaern) writers should also be more thoroughly examined.

One of the most important problems is that of the possible role of go-between of some Slavic literatures for others: in the case of baroque literature, this problem has been at least briefly treated.

Naturally one may no longer proceed, as has already been stressed, along the old paths which originated from the conception of often imaginary adoptions of isolated elements from foreign literary works. Rather, the fundamental stylistic influences must be investigated, in the case of the important writers, not the details of their works respectively, but their general attitude toward reality and a certain fundamental literary intuition.

4. The general pattern of development and its "basic laws," as far as these may be spoken of at all, will surely undergo important modifications. The alternating, "undulatory" course of development (see Chapter I, 8ff.) will in many points most likely appear different after such

an examination, or it will at the least experience essential corrections of detail, particularly so in relation to modernistic literature (Chapters XI and XII).

The necessity, repeatedly stressed in the last decades, for the treatment of writers of secondary and less importance will surely help to create a clearer and more unified picture of many epochs. Good examples of this are the treatment of the "natural school" in Russian literature (Chapter X, 13), the awakening of interest in the less representative members of *Młoda Polska*, or the treatment of the "nationalized" Czech literature (*zlidovelá literatura*).

Also of note are the problems of the overlapping of different literary movements among the individual Slavic nations at various times; for example, the countereffects of the Hussite movement and the Renaissance among the Czechs, of the radical reformational trends, especially anti-Trinitarian, and of the baroque among the Poles. Also of importance are the deep rifts effected by political events in various countries during given stylistic epochs, as the successes of the nationalist movement among the Southern Slavs in the nineteenth century. There were similar rifts elsewhere: the Petrine period ripped Russian baroque into two culturally and lingually different segments.[2] Later, late classicism was separated from early classicism by the renovation of the language of the so-called Karamzinian school.

The heydays of various Slavic literatures played a special role in that they also impressed their stamp upon quite differently disposed styles of art. In this way, baroque art was influential in Ukrainian literature, according to A. L. Boehm, and even upon Gogol', a Ukrainian who wrote in Russian. In a like fashion, Gogol' and Puškin effected the lingual and literary development of Russia right up into our time as two almost diametrically opposed stylistic forces. The baroque tradition was mainly defined stylistically; however, it also determined the essential consistency of the Slavic type.

In particular, the extraordinarily penetrating and far-reaching tradition of romanticism with its conception of Slavic rebirth among all the Slavs should not be left out of consideration. A great deal was adopted from romantic ideology—even disregarding the completely illusory ideas of the so-called Slavophilism—by the most decided opponents of romanticism and continued to remain effective in a "pseudomorphic" form. Other, older traditions long maintained their efficacy

2. See footnote 1, Chapter Eight.

just as long with different Slavic peoples, as the Hussite movement among the Czechs.

Furthermore, the numerous, and quite often disguised, conscious and unconscious imitations of ancient literatures are of importance. Just as important however is the very nearly neglected question of biblical influences and the even less obvious suggestions of "ecclesiastical literature," that is, of the Mass and liturgy. Such undertones are everywhere to be found.

Finally, our previously mentioned question concerning folkloric elements in the store of images, metaphors, and vocabulary in artistic literature and, on the other hand, concerning the influences of artistic literature—above all of the baroque and romanticism—on folklore, which in its turn had secondary reflexes in later artistic literature, has hardly been touched.

The influences of those languages and literatures lying outside of European cultural spheres (see in this regard Chapter I, 16), which in recent times have been taken increasingly more into consideration, should also be thoroughly investigated.

5. Of exceptional importance is the investigation of the "transitions" between various epochs of literary history, the persual of the quiet and modest beginnings of new stylistic features and the gradual preparation and development of the new movements which push back and replace the old traditions. Just as significant are the disintegration processes of the old "schools" and dominant trends, even though these processes often continue much more slowly and unnoticeably and are frequently associated with reactions and "pseudomorphic" transformations. One further important object of future investigation should be the survival of epigonous groups in the new historical epoch. Also, "lone wolves" deserve particular attention.

Only the treatment of all of these problems, for which there was almost no place in this book, will make the development of a genuine, profound, comparative history of the Slavic literatures possible. This book offers only modest preliminary observations for such a history. Not a few works have been dedicated to the main topic of this book— the relations of the Slavic literatures with each other. Rarely, however are these questions treated within the context of intellectual history, the only context within which these relations can be clarified.

With this reference to the problematic nature of intellectual history, which we have sometimes only allusively mentioned, we would like to close our survey.

BIBLIOGRAPHY

Editor's note: This Bibliography was compiled by Professor Čiževskij. Some recent important books have been added to the list, especially those published in the United States or England. Since these are integrated into the original bibliography prepared by the author, they are listed in the manner of the original entries. For English translations of Slavic literary texts, the reader is advised to consult the following: *The Literatures of the World in English Translation,* Volume II (New York Public Library); Richard Lewanski, compiler, *The Slavic Literatures— Beginning to 1960* (1967) (New York Public Library).

Abbreviations:

SPb, L	St. Petersburg, Leningrad
M	Moscow
W	Warsaw
P	Prague
Lpz	Leipzig
C	Cracow
B	Berlin

CHAPTER I

1. LITERARY HISTORIES

The first list is of general reference works. One should bear in mind that few of these works go into stylistic analyses, and in those cases in which they treat various literatures they do not deal with their stylistic similarities. One should be particularly careful in using literary histories published in recent decades since they often present only officially recognized, tendentious points of view.

Since most books dealing with literary periods are pertinent to several chapters of the present book, they are listed here.

Editions of selected literary works are noted only in so far as they contain older works that are otherwise hard to find.

a) General Outlines:

Aničkov, E. *Zapadnye literatury i slavjanstvo.* 2 vols. P, 1926. (Goes through the eighteenth century.)

Georgiev, E. *Očerki po istorija na slavjanskite literaturi.* 2 vols. Sofia, 1958–63. (A strong Marxist bias, particularly in the second volume.)

Karásek, J. *Geschichte der slavischen Literaturen.* 2 vols. B-Lpz, 1906 (Sammlung Göschen, 277–278).

Krejčí, K. *Heroikomika v básnictví slovanů.* P, 1964. (Especially on the eighteenth and nineteenth centuries.)

Máchal, J. *Slovenské literatury.* 3 vols. P, 1922–29.

Pypin, A., and V. Spasovič. *Geschichte der slavischen Literaturen.* 2 vols. Lpz, 1880–84. (Antiquated.)

Wollman, F. *Slovesnost slovanů.* P, 1928.

Die osteuropäischen Literaturen und die slawischen Sprachen. Die Kultur der Gegenwart, part one, Section 9. B-Lpz, 1908. (A number of authors are represented.)

b) Russian Literature:

Gudzij, N. G., ed. *Xrestomatija po drevnej russkoj literature XI–XVII vekov.* M. (Any edition; the most recent edition, the seventh, appeared in 1965.)

———. *Istorija drevnej russkoj literatury.* Most recent edition, 1966.

Istorija russkoj literatury. 11 vols. M-L; AN SSSR, 1941–56. (The treatment is very biased; the first two volumes, the second in two parts—the literature through the seventeenth century—and volume five, on late classicism, can be recommended.)

Lettenbauer, W. *Russische Literaturgeschichte.* 2d ed. Wiesbaden, 1958.

Lixačev, D. S. *Poetika drevnerusskoj literatury.* Leningrad, 1967. (English translation in preparation.) (A highly technical scholarly discussion of Old Russian poetics.)

Luther, A. *Geschichte der russischen Literatur.* Lpz, 1924. (A useful treatment of the nineteenth century and an interesting bibliography.)

Mirsky, D. S. *Contemporary Russian Literature.* New York: Alfred Knopf, 1927.

———. *History of Russian Literature.* New York: Alfred Knopf, 1926.

———. *A History of Russian Literature,* edited by F. J. Whitfield. New York: Alfred Knopf, 1960. (A slightly abridged edition of the two previous volumes.)

Pypin, A. *Istorija russkoj literatury.* 4th ed., 4 vols. Spb, 1911–13. (The treatment of the older literature is still useful.)

Stender-Petersen, A. *Geschichte der russischen Literatur,* translated from Danish by W. Krämer. 2 vols. Munich, 1957.

Tschiževskij (Čiževskij), D. *History of Russian Literature from the Eleventh Century to the End of the Baroque.* The Hague, 1960.

Zenkovsky, S. A. *Medieval Russia's Epics, Chronicle's and Tales.* New York: Dutton, 1963. (Old Russian Texts in English translation; historical introduction, commentaries.)

c) Ukrainian Literature:

Bilećkyj, O. I., ed. *Xrestomatija davňoji ukrajinśkoji literatury.* Kiev, 1949. 2d rev. ed., 1952.

Hruševskyj, M. *Istorija ukrajinśkoji literatury.* 5 vols. Kiev-Lvov, 1923–27 (or

2d ed., New York, 1959–60). (To the beginning of the seventeenth century; vols. 3 and 4 deal with folk poetry.)

Tschižewskij, D. (Čiževskij). *Istorija ukrajinśkoji literatury: Vid počatkiv do doby realizmu.* New York, 1956.

——. *Kurze Geschichte der ukrainischen Literatur (16.—20. Jahrhundert).* (In progress.)

Voznjak, M. *Istorija ukrajinśkoji literatury.* 3 vols. Lvov, 1920–24. (To the eighteenth century.)

d) Polish Literature:

Brückner, A. *Geschichte der polnischen Literatur.* 2d ed. Lpz, 1922.

Chmielowski, P. *Historia literatury polskiej.* 6 vols. W, 1899–1902.

Kleiner, J. *Die polnische Literatur.* Handbuch der Literaturwissenschaft, ed. O. Walzel. Wildpark-Potsdam, 1929.

Krejčí, K. *Dějiny polské literatury.* P, 1953.

Kridl, M. *Literatura polska na tle rozwoju kultury.* New York, 1945.

Kridl, M. *A Survey of Polish Literature and Culture.* New York: Columbia University Press, 1956.

Krzyżanowski, J. *Historia literatury polskiej.* W, 1964.

Milosz, C. *The History of Polish Literature.* New York: Macmillan, 1969.

Pollak, R. and others. *Literatura polska w perspektywie światowej.* Wrocław-W-K, 1963.

——. *Polskie życie literackie przed rozbiorami.* Poznan, 1948.

Most of the older histories of Polish literature include extensive excerpts from the early literary texts.

e) Czech Literature:

Havránek, B., ed. *Výbor z české literatury od počátků po dobu Husovu.* P, 1957.

Jakubec, J. *Dějiny literatury české.* 2 vols. P, 1929–34. (Antiquated, but useful bibliography.)

Jungmann, J. and K. Erben, eds. *Výbor ze starší české literatury.* 2 vols. P, 1845–68.

Jungmann, J. *Historie literatury české.* 2d ed. P, 1849. (Primarily a bibliography.)

Novák, A. *Die tschechische Literatur.* Handbuch der Literaturwissenschaft, ed. O. Walzel. Wildpark-Potsdam, 1931.

Selver, P. *Czechoslovakian Literature.* London, 1942. (A short and rather superficial survey.)

Škarka, A. *Nástin dějin české slovesnosti období před rozkladem feudalizmu.* 1st vol.: do sedmdesatych let 15. stol. P, 1955.

Šváb, M., ed. *Antologie ze starší české literatury.* P, 1964.

Novák, V. J. and A. *Přehledné dějiny literatury české od nejstarších dob až po naše dny.* 4th ed. Olomouc, 1936–39.

Vlček, J. *Dějiny české literatury.* 2d ed., 4 vols. P, 1931.

Dějiny české literatury. Various authors. 3 vols. P, 1959–61.

f) Slovak Literature

Mráz, A. *Die Literatur der Slovaken.* B-P-Vienna, 1943.

——. *Dejiny slovenskej literatúry.* Bratislava, 1948.

Pišút, M., ed. *Dejiny slovenskej literatúry.* Bratislava, 1960.
Vlček, J. *Dejiny literatúry slovenskej.* Turčanský sv. Martin, 1933 (3d ed.) and 1953.
Dejiny slovenskej literatúry. Various authors. 2 vols. Bratislava, 1958–61.

g) Sorbian Literature:

Frinta, A. *Lužičtí Srbové a jejich písemnictví.* P, 1955.
Gołąbek, J. *Literatura serbsko-łużicka.* Kattowitz, 1938.
Jenč, R. *Stawizny serbskeho pismowstwa.* 2 vols. Bautzen, 1954–60.
Mětšk, F., ed. *Chrestomatija dolnoserbskego pismowstwa.* 2 vols. B, 1956–57.
Páta, J. *Úvod do studia lužickosrbského písemnictví.* P, 1925.
Zmeškal, V., ed. *Lužičtí básníci.* P. 1935.

h) Bulgarian Literature:

Angelov, B. *Bulgarskata literatura.* 2 vols. Sofia, 1923.
Angelov, B., M. Genov, and M. Arnaudov. *Istorija na bulgarskata literatura v primeri i bibliografia.* 2 vols. Sofia, 1922.
Istorija na bulgarskata literatura. Various authors. 1st ed. Sofia, 1962. (2d vol. in progress.)
Manning, C., and S. Stokij. *The History of Modern Bulgarian Literature.* New York: Bookman, 1960.

i) Serbo-Croatian Literature:

Barac, A.: A History of Yugoslav Literature, Belgrade, 1955 [a concise survey].
Bogdanović, D. *Pregled književnosti hrvatske i srpske.* 3 vols. Zagreb, 1933–35.
Cronia, A. *Storia della letteratura serbo-croata.* 2d ed. Milan, 1963.
Gavrilović, A. *Istorija srpske i hrvatske književnosti.* 4th ed. Belgrade, 1927.
Gesemann, G. *Die serbokroatische Literatur.* Handbuch der Literaturwissenschaft, ed. O. Walzel. Wildpark-Potsdam, 1930.
Ježić, S. *Hrvatska književnost od početka do danas.* Zagreb, 1944.
Kadić, A. *Contemporary Croatian Literature.* The Hague: Mouton, 1960.
———. *Contemporary Serbian Literature.* The Hague: Mouton, 1964.
Kombol, M. *Povijest hrvatske književnosti do narodnog preporoda.* 2d ed. Zagreb, 1961.
Novaković, S., ed. *Primeri književnosti i jezika staroga srpsko-slovenskoga.* 3d ed. Belgrade, 1904. (And other editions.)
Stanojević, M. S. *Early Yugoslav Literature, 1000–1800.* London, 1922.
Trogrančić, F. *Storia della letteratura croata dall'Umaninesimo alla rinascita nazionale.* Rome, 1953.
Vodnik, B., and V. Jagić. *Povijest hrvatske književnosti.* 1st ed. Zagreb, 1913. (Selected texts.)

j) Slovenian Literature:

Grafenauer, I. *Kratka zgodovina slovenskega slovstva.* Ljubljana, 1919.
Kidrič, F. *Zgodovina slovenskega slovstva: Od začetkov do Zojsove smrti.* 5 vols Ljubljana, 1929–38.

Janež, S. *Zgodovina slovenske književnosti.* 2d ed. Maribor, 1957.

Rupel, M. *Zgodovina slovenskego slovstva.* 1956.

Slodnjak, A. *Geschichte der slovenischen Literatur.* Grundriss der slavischen Philologie und Kulturgeschichte, No. 13. B, 1958.

k) Macedonian Literature:

Lunt, H. G. *A Survey of Macedonian Literature.* Harvard Slavic Studies, 1953.

2. Slavic Linguistics

[Editor's note: Check also E. Stanke and D. Worth, *Selected Bibliography of Slavic Linguistics* (The Hague: Mouton, 1966).]

Bräuer, H. *Slavische Sprachwissenschaft.* 1st vol.: Einleitung, Lautlehre. Sammlung Göschen 1191/1191a. B, 1961. (Vols. 2 and 3 in progress.)

Bulaxovskij, L. A. *Russkij literaturnyj jazyk pervoj poloviny XIX veka.* 2 vols. M, 1954 f.

Lehr-Spławiński, T. *Język polski: Pochodzenie, powstanie, rozwój.* W, 1947.

Levin, V. D. *Istorija russkogo literaturnogo jazyka.* M, 1957.

Nachtigal, R. *Die slavischen Sprachen: Abriss der vergleichenden Grammatik.* Wiesbaden, 1961.

Pauliny, E. *Dejiny spisovnej slovenčiny.* Slovenska vlastiveda, diel 5, sväzok 1. Bratislava, 1948.

Vaillant, A. *Grammaire comparée des langues slaves.* 3 vols. 2d ed. Lyon-Paris, 1950 ff.

Vinogradov, V. V. *Očerki po istorii russkogo literaturnogo jazyka XVII–XIX vv.* Leiden, 1949.

———. *The History of the Russian Literary Language from the Seventeenth Century to the Nineteenth.* Translated by Lawrence J. Thomas. Madison: The University of Wisconsin Press, 1969.

Československá vlastivěda. Díl 3: Jazyk. P, 1934. (Especially the articles by O. Hujer, F. Oberpfalcer, J. Mukarovsky, and R. Jakobson.)

3. Literary Relations with Eastern Languages and Literatures (Selected Works)

Jahn, K. E. O. "Turken en ost-slaven: Enkele beschouwingen over hun onderlinge betrekkingen." Inaugural lecture. Leiden, 1950.

Knežević, A. *Die Turzismen in der Sprache der Serben und Kroaten.* Meisenheim-Glan, 1962.

Menges, K. H. *Influences altaïques en Slave.* Académie royale de Belgique, Bulletin de la classe des lettres, 5e série, t. XLIV, 1958.

———. "The Oriental Elements in the Vocabulary of the Oldest Russian Epos." *Word*, supplement 7, 1951.

Miklosich, F. *Die türkischen Elemente in den südost—und osteuropäischen Sprachen.* Denkschriften der Wiener Akademie, Nos. 34, 1884, 35, 1885, and 38, 1890.

Škaljić, A. *Turcizmi u narodnom govoru i narodnoj književnosti Bosne i Hercegovine.* 2 vols. Sarajevo, 1957. (2d ed., Sarajevo, 1963.)

Vernadsky, G., and M. Karpovich. *History of Ancient and Medieval Russia*. New Haven, 1952. (Much doubtful material.)

Československo-mad'arské literární vstahy. Various authors. P, 1964.

4. BIBLIOGRAPHIES:

Estreixer, K. *Bibliografia polska XIX stulecia*. 2d ed. K, 1959. (To be continued.)

————. *Bibliografia polska*. 36 vols. K, 1872–1934.

Korbut, G. *Literatura polska od początków do wojny świaitowej*. 2d ed., 4 vols. W, 1929–31. (Bibliography!)

Muratova, K. D., ed. *Istorija russkoj literatury konca XIX–načala XX veka*. Bibliografičeskij ukazatel'. M-L, 1963.

————, ed. *Istorija russkoj literatury XIX veka*. Bibliografičeskij ukazatel. M-L, 1962.

Nowy Korbut. 3 vols. W, 1963 ff. (To be continued; arranged in bibliographical form.)

Rizner, L. V. *Bibliografia písomníctva slovenského na spôsob slovníka od najstarších čias do konca r. 1900*. 6 vols. Turčanský sv. Martin, 1929–34.

Simonič, F. *Slovenska bibliografia*. Vol. 1: Knjige (1550–1900). Ljubljana, 1903–05.

Sopikov, V. S. *Opyt rossijskoj bibliografii*. 2d ed. SPb, 1904–06 (reprint, London, 1962). (Deals with the eighteenth century.)

Tobolka, Z., and F. Horak, eds. *Knihopis československých tisků od doby nejstarši az do konce XVIII. století*. P, 1925 ff. (Soon to be completed.)

Zenkovsky S. and D. Armbruster *Guide to Bibliography of Russian Literatures*. Nashville: Vanderbilt University Press, 1970.

CHAPTER II

Dvorník, F. *Les légendes de Constantin et de Méthode vues de Byzance*. P, 1933.

Grivec, F. *Konstantin und Method: Lehrer der Slaven*. Wiesbaden, 1960.

Grivec, F., and F. Tomšić, eds. *Constantinus et Methodius Thessalonicenses: Fontes*. Radovi Staroslavenskog Instituta, IV, 1960. (German edition, Wiesbaden, 1963.)

Il'inskij, G. *Opyt sistematičeskoj Kirillo-Mefodievskoj bibliografii*. Sofia, 1934.

Lavrov, P., ed. *Kyrylo ta Metodij*. Kiev, 1928. (Texts.)

————. *Materialy po isotorii vozniknovenija drevnejšej slavjanskoj pismenosti*. The Hague, 1966.

Murko, M. *Geschichte der älteren südslawischen Literaturen*. Lpz, 1908. (Antiquated.)

Pauliny, E. *Slovesnost' na Vel'kej Morave*. Bratislava. (Now being printed.)

Popruženko, M., and S. Romanski. *Bibliografski pregled na slav. kirilski istočnici za života na Kirila i Metodija*. Sofia, 1953.

————. *Kirilometodievska bibliografija za 1934–1940 g*. Sofia, 1942.

Radovi Staroslovenskog Instituta. 5 vols. Zagreb, 1952–64. (To be continued.)

Ratkoš, P., ed. *Pramene k dejinám Vel'kej Moravy*. Bratislava, 1964.

Slovanské studie. Sbírka statí, věnovaných . . . J. Vajsovi P, 1948.

Stanislav, J., ed. *Rísá Vel'komoravská: Sborník*. 2d ed. P, 1935.

Tschiževskij, D. *K voprosu o liturgii sv. Petra*. 2d ed. Zagreb: Slovo, 1953.

————. "Neue Lesefrüchte." *Zeitschrift für slavische Philologie*, XXIV (1955).

Vašica, J. "Slovanská liturgie sv. Petra." *Byzantinoslavica*, VIII (1939–46).
Vavřínek, V. *Staroslověnské životy Konstantina a Metoděje*. Rozpravy ČSAV.
Řada společn. věd., LXXIII, 7, 1963.
Cyrillo-Methodiana: Sammelband. Cologne, 1965.
Groß-Mähren. P, 1964. (Exhibition catalogue.)

CHAPTERS III AND IV

See also the bibliography to Chapter I and the general histories of the individual Slavic literatures.
Černý, V. *Staročeská milostná lyrika*. P, 1948.
Daničić, D. *Rječnik iz književnih starin srpskih*. 3 vols. Belgrade, 1863–64. (Reprint, Graz, 1962.)
Hafner, S., ed. *Serbisches Mittelalter: Altserbische Herrscherbiographien*. Graz-Vienna-Cologne, 1962.
———. *Studien zur altserbischen dynastischen Historiographie*. Munich, 1964.
Istrin, V. *Očerk istorii drevnerusskoj literatury domongol'skogo perioda (11–13 vv.)*. Petrograd, 1922.
Jakobson, R. "Význam ruské filologie pro bohemistiku." *Slovo a slovesnost*, IV (1938).
Kralík, O. *K počátkům literatury v přemyslovských Čechách*. Rozprazy ČASV. Řada spolčen. věd., LXX, 6, 1960.
Lixačev, D. S. *Nekotorye zadači izučenija vtorogo južnoslavjanskogo vlijanija v Rossii*. M, 1958.
Lilienfeld, F. v. *Nil Sorskij und seine Schriften*. B, 1963.
Sobolevskij, A. I. "Cerekovnoslavjanskie teksty moravskogo proisxoždenija." *Russkij Filologičeskij Vestnik*, XLIII (1900).
Tschiževskij, D. (Čiževskij). "Anklänge an die Gumpoldslegende des hl. Václav in der altrussischen Legende des hl. Feodosij." *Wiener slavistisches Jahrbuch*, I (1950).
———. *Geschichte der altrzussischen Literatur im 11., 12. und 13. Jh. Kiever Epoche* Frankfurt/Main, 1948. (The material discussed pertains to the prehistory of Ukrainian and White Russian literature.)
———. "Über den Stil der Galizisch-Volynischen Chronik." *Südost-Forschungen*, XII (1953).
———. "Zwei čechische geistliche Lieder." In the author's book *Aus zwei Welten*. The Hague, 1956.
Večerka, R. *Slovanské počátky české knižní vzdělanosti*. P, 1963.
Vilikovský, J. *Písemnictví českého středověku*. 1948.
———, ed. *Staročeská lyrika*. P, 1940.
Weingart, M. *Československý typ cirkevnej slovančiny*. Bratislava, 1949.
Acta of the Cyrill-Methodius Congress in Salzburg, 1963. Papers by Havránek and Tschiževskij. (Now being printed.)
Das Igor'-Lied: Eine Heldendichtung; der altruss. Text m. d. Übertr. v. R. M. Rilke u. d. neuruss. Prosafassung v. D. S. Lixačev. Insel-Bücherei, No. 689. Lpz, 1960.
Na úsvitu krest'anství. P, 1942.
Trudy otdela drevherusskoj literatury, XIX (1963). (Articles by O. Králik and V. Mareš.)

CHAPTER V

Presnjakov, A. E. *Moskovskoe carstvo*. Petrograd, 1918. (Reprint, Düsseldorf, 1966.)
Istorija russkoj literatury. 11 vols. M-L: AN SSSR, 1941–56. (Vol. 1, Pts. 1 and 2).

CHAPTER VI

Bučar, F. *Povijest hrvatske protestanské književnosti za reformacije*. Zagreb, 1910.
Havránek, B., J. Hrabák, and J. Daňhelka, eds. *Výbor z české literatury doby husitské*. 2 vols. P, 1963–64.
Heck, R., and E. Maleczyńska, eds. *Ruch husycki w Polsce*. Wrocław, 1953. (Collection of texts.)
Jakobson, R. "Úvahy o básnictví doby husitské." *Slovo a slovesnost*, II (1936).
Kubala, L. *St. Orzechowski i wpływ jego na rozwój i upadek reformacji w Polsce*. Lemberg-W, 1906.
Maleczyńska, E. *Ruch husycki w Czechach i Polsce*. W, 1959.
Mirković, M. *Matija Vlačić (Flacius Illyricus)*. Belgrade, 1957.
Svejkovský, F., ed. *Veršované skladby doby husitské*. P, 1963.
Völker, K. *Kirchengeschichte Polens*. B-Lpz, 1930.
Reformacja w Polsce (ed. until 1945: St. Kot). Vol. 1 (1921)—Vol. 12. (1953–55).

CHAPTER VII

Alekseev, M. P. *Javlenija gumanizma v literature i publicistike drevnej Rusi (16–17 v.)*. M, 1958.
Backvis, C. "Quelques remarques sur la bilinguisme latino-polonais dans la Pologne du seizième siècle." Paper read before the Moscow Slavistic meeting in Brussels, 1958.
Barycz, H. *Historia Uniwersytetu Jagiellońskiego w epoce humanizmu*. K, 1935.
Budzyk, K. *Przełom renesansowy w literaturze polskiej* . . . . W, 1953.
Cronia, A. "Marco Marulic: Ein Vertreter und Deuter der christlichen Renaissance in Dalmatien." *Wiener slavist. Jahrbuch*, III (1953).
Goleniščev-Kutuzov, I. *Gumanizum u vostočnyx slavjan (Ukraina i Belorussija)*. M, 1963.
———. *Ital'janskoe vozroždenie i slavjanskie literatury 15–16 vv*. M, 1963.
Hejnic, J. "Dva humanisté v roce 1547." Rozpravy ČSAV, 1957, (rada společn. věd, No. 7.
———, and J. Martínek. *Rukověť humanistického básnictví v Čechách a na Morave od konce 15. do začátku 17. století*. P, 1964.
Körbler, D. *Taljanske pjesništvo u Dalmaciji 16. vijeka*. Rad Jugosl. Akad., No. 137, 1911.
Kombol, M. *Dinko Ranjina italijanski petrarkisti*. Gradja za povijest književnosti hrvatske, No. 9, 1932.
Kopecký, M. *Daniel Adam z Veleslavina*. P, 1962.
Krzyżanowski, J. *Proza polska XVI wieku*. W, 1954.
Łempicki, S. *Renesans i humanizm w Polsce*. W, 1952.
Maver, G. "La letteratura croata in rapporto alla letteratura italiana." In *Italia e Croazia*. Rome, 1942.

Medini, M. *Povijest hrvatske književnosti u Dalmacii i Dubrovniku.* Zagreb, 1902.

Nowicki, A. *Grzegorz z Sanoka.* W, 1958.

Pražák, E. *Řehoř Hrubý z Jelení.* P, 1964.

Šmahel, F. *Humanismus v době poděbradské.* Rozpravy ČSAV, No. 73, 1963.

——. "Základní problematika renesance a humanizmu." *Československý časopis historický*, No. 7 (1959).

——. "Přehled českého bádání o renesanci a humanismu." *Československý časopis historický*, No. 9 (1961).

Torbarina, J. *Italian Influences on the Poets of the Ragusan Republic.* London, 1951.

Truhlář, J. *Počátky humanismu v Čechách.* Rozpravy ČAV, Class II, 1, 3, 1892.

——. *Humanismus a humanisté v Čechách za Krale Vladislava II.* Rozpravy ČAV, Class II, 1, 4, 1894.

Tschiževskij, D. (Čiževskij). *Die Renaissance und das ukrainische Geistesleben.* Abhandlungen des Ukrainischen Wissenschaftlichen Institutes in Berlin, No. 2, 1929.

Vaněček, V. *Mistr Viktorin Cornelius ze Všehrd.* Rozpravy ČSAV, rada společn. věd, No. 9, 1960.

Vodnik, B. *Pregled hrvatsko-srpske književnosti.* Zagreb, 1923.

Winter, Eduard. *Frühhumanismus: Seine Entwicklung in Böhmen und deren europäische Bedeutung.* B, 1964. (With bibliography)

Odrodzenie i reformacja w Polsce. Vol. 1 (1956)—Vol. 9 (1964). (To be continued.)

Pamiętnik Zjazdu naukowego imienia Szymona Szymonowicza. Zamoście, 1930.

Stari pisci hrvatski. To date 32 vols. Zabreb, 1869 ff. (Especially the introductions to the various volumes.)

CHAPTER VIII

See also the general works given for Chapter VII and the entire series *Stari Pisci Hrvatski* (above).

Angyal, A. "Die Barock-Epoche in der slavischen Literatur—und Kulturgeschichte." In *Blick nach Osten.* Vienna, 1949.

——. *Die slavische Barockwelt.* Lpz, 1961.

Backvis, C. *Some Characteristics of Polish Baroque Poetry.* Oxford Slavonic Papers, No. 6, 1955.

——. "Dans quelle mesure Derzhavin est-il un baroque." *Studies in Russian: Festschrift fur W. Lednicki.* The Hague, 1962.

Bitnar, V. *O českém baroku slovesném.* P, 1932.

——. *Postavy i problemy českého baroku.* P, 1939.

Brauner, Helga. *Friedrich Bridel: Ein Beitrag zur tschechischen Literaturgeschichte des 17. Jhs.* Diss., Heidelberg. (Now being printed.)

Brťáň, R. *Barokový slavismus.* Lipt. sv, Mikuláš, 1939. (Very unreliable; see review by D. Tschiževskij in *Zeitschrift für slavische Philologie*, XVIII [1942]).

Dürr-Durski, J. *Daniel Naborowski.* Tódź, 1966.

Eremin, I. *Poètičeskij stil' Simeona Polockogo. Trudy Otdela dreverussk. lit.,* No. VI, *1948.*

Fischerówna, R. *Samuel Twardowski jako poeta barokowy.* K, 1931.

Jagić, V. *Život i rad J. Križanića.* Zagreb, 1917.

Kalan, F. *Baročna kultura v srednji Evropi in izvori slovenskega gledališča.* Rad Zagreb, No. 326, 1962.

Kalista, Z. České baroko. P, 1941.

Krzyżanowski, J. *Widnokręgi barokowe.* Przegląd humanistyczny, No. 4, 1960.

——. *Od sredniowiecza do baroku: Studia naukowoliterackie.* W, 1938.

——. *Historia literatury polskiej: Alegoryzm—preromantyzm.* W, 1964.

Lachmann-Schmohl, R. *Ignjat Djordjić: Eine stilistische Untersuchung zum slavischen Barock.* Cologne-Graz, 1964.

——. *Einführung zu I. Bunić-Vučićević: Gedichte.* Munich, 1965.

Maraković, L. "Gundulić u okviru baroka." *Gundulićev Zbornik* in *Hrvatska Revija,* XII (1938).

Pelc, J. *Liryka polska XVII wieku.* Przegląd humanistyczny, No. 1, 1967.

——. Zbigniew Morsztyn, arianin i poeta. Wrocław-W-K, 1966.

Porębowicz, E. *J. A. Morsztyn.* K, 1893.

Prohaska, D. *I. Djordjić i Antun Kanižlić: Studija o baroku u hrvatskoj književnosti.* Rad No. 178, 1909.

Pavlović, D. *Marinizam u ljbavnoj lirici Ivana Bunića: Iz književne i kulturne istorije Dubrovnika.* Sarajevo, 1955.

Šalda, F. X. "O literárním baroku." In *Zápisník,* 1936.

Setschkareff, W. *Die Dichtung Gundulićs und ihr poetischer Stil: Ein Beitrag zur Erforschung des literarischen Barock.* Bonn, 1952.

Škarka, A. *Einführung zu den Werken von Adam Michna z Otradovic.* Munich, 1967.

Tschižewskij, D. "Aus den neuen Veröffentlichungen über die čechische Barockdichtung." 5 installments. *Zeitschrift für slavische Philologie,* XI (1934)—XIX (1945).

——. "Ke kompozici Bridelovy básně 'Co Bůh? člověk?' " *Akord,* XI (1943–44).

——. "Slavistische Barockforschung." *Welt der Slaven,* I (1956).

——. *Ukrajinśkyj literaturnyj barok.* 3 vols. P, 1941–44.

——. *Poza mežamy krasy: Do poetyky ukrajinśkoho barokko.* New York, 1952.

Vašica, J. *České literarńt baroko.* P, 1938.

Weintraub, W. O niektórych problemach polskiego baroku. Przegląd humanistyczny, No. 4, 1960.

——. "Barok sarmacki i jego bisurmanskie koneksje." *Wiadomości,* I, May 14, 1946.

Wollman, F. "Některé projevy vědomí sounáležitosti a součinnosti slovanské humanisticko-barokníhu rázu." *Slavia,* XXVI, 1 (1957).

CHAPTER IX

Berkov, P. *Vvedenie v izučenie istorii russkoj literatury 18 veka.* L, 1964. (To be continued.)

Borowy, W. *O poezji polskiej w wieku XVIII.* K, 1948.

Brang, P. *Studien zu Theorie und Praxis der russischen Erzählung.* Wiesbaden, 1960.

Gukovskij, G. *Russkaja literatura 18 v.* M, 1939. (Texbtook)

——. *Russkaja poezija 18 veka.* L, 1927. (Reprint: Ann Arbor, 1964.)

Jirát, V. *Lyrika českého obrození.* P, 1940.

Pietraszko, S. "Introduction." in Dmochowski, F. K. *Sztuka rymotwórcza*. Wrocław, 1956.

Schröder, H. *Russische Verssatire im 18. Jahrhundert*. Cologne-Graz, 1962.

Striedter, J. *Der Schelmenroman in Russland*. Wiesbaden, 1961.

Tschižewskij, D. *Istorija ukrajinśkoj literatury* (see above).

Vlček, J. *První novočeská škola básnická*. P, 1896.

Wojciecechowski, K. *Wiek Oświecenia*. Lwów, 1926.

Zerov, M. *Nove ukrajinśke pyśmenstvo*. K, 1924. (Reprint: Kiev, n.d.)

Russkaja literatura XVIII veka i slavjanskie literatury. M-L, 1963.

Russkaja literatura 18 veka: Èpoxa klassicizma. M-L, 1964.

XVIII vek: Sbornik. 4 vols. M-L, 1935–62.

CHAPTER X

Beleckij, A., ed. *Russkij romantizm. Sbornik statej*. Leningrad, 1927.

Belyj, A., L. Èllis-Kobylinskij, B. Sadovskij, and V. Brjusov. Articles on Gogol in *Vesy*, IV (1909).

Djilas, M. *Njegoš: Poet, Prince, Bishop*. New York: Harcourt, Brace, & World, 1966.

Èjxenbaum, B. *Lermontov*. Leningrad, 1924. (Reprinted, Munich 1967.)

Gippius, V. *Gogol'*. Leningrad, 1924. (Reprinted, Ann Arbor: The University of Michigan Press, 1962.)

Gregg, R. A. *Fedor Tiutchev: The Evolution of a Poet*. New York: Columbia University Press, 1965.

Jakobson, R. "Poznámky k dílu Erbenovu: O mythu. O versi." *Slovo o slovesnost*, I (1935).

Kawyn, S., ed. *Walka romantyków z klasykami*. Biblioteka narodowa, I, 183. Breslau, 1960.

Matuszewski, I. *Słowacki i nowa sztuka*. Warsaw, 1902. (2nd ed., 1904.)

Mejlax, B. *Puškin i russkij romantizm*. Moscow and Leningrad, 1937. (A Marxist interpretation.)

Mersereau, J. *Mikhail Lermontov*. Carbondale: Southern Illinois University Press, 1962.

Mickiewiwz, A. *The Forefathers*. London, 1968.

———. *Pan Tadeusz*. London, 1964.

Mukařovský, J. *Máchův Máj. Estetická studie*. Prague, 1928.

Murko, M. *Deutsche Einflüsse auf die Anfänge der slavischen Romantik*. Vol. I: *Die böhmische Romantik*. Graz, 1896.

Nebel, H. M. *M. Karamzin—A Russian Sentimentalist*. The Hague: Mouton, 1967.

Nejegoš, P. P. *Der Bergkranz*. Translated with an introduction and commentary by A. Schmaus. Munich, 1963.

Njegoš, P. P. *The Ray of Microcosm*. Cambridge: Harvard University Press, 1957.

Pigarev, K. *Žizn' i tvorčestvo Tjutčeva*. Moscow, 1962.

Pišút, M. *Počiatky básnickej školy štúrovej*. Bratislava, 1938.

Proffer, C. *The Simile and Gogol's Dead Souls*. The Hague: Mouton, 1967.

Sakulin, P. *Iz istorii russkogo idealizma. Knjaz' V. F. Odoevskij*. Vol. I, 1–2. Moscow, 1913.

Šamraj, A. *Xarkivśka škola romantykiv*. 3 vols. Xar'kov, 1930.

Setchkarev, V. *N. V. Gogol': His Life and Work.* New York, 1965.

Skublanska, T. *Neologizmy w polskiej poezji romantycznej.* Krakow, 1964.

Straszewska, M. *Romantyzm.* Warsaw, 1964. (With texts.)

Tscheževskij, D. (Čiževskij, Chyzhevskyj) "Besprechung des Sammelbandes *Urania.*" *Zeitschrift für slavische Philogie,* VII (1930).

———. *"Einige Aufgaben der slavistischen Romantikforschung."* *Welt der Slaven,* I (1956).

———. *On Romanticism in Slavic Literatures.* Musagetes, 1. 's-Gravenhage, 1957.

———. *Russische Literaturgeschichte des 19. Jahrhunderts.* Vol. I: *Die Romantik.* Munich, 1964.

———. "Gogol'-Studien," in the anthology *Gogol'-Turgenev-Dostoevskij-Tolstoj.* Munich, 1966.

———. *"Tjutčev und die deutsche Romantik."* *Zeitschrift für slavische Philologie,* IV (1927).

———. *A History of Nineteenth Century Russian Literature,* translated by Richard Noel Porter and Martin Rice. Nashville: Vanderbilt University Press (forthcoming).

Tynjanov, Ju. *Archaisty i novatory.* Leningrad, 1929. (Reprinted, Munich, 1967).

Weintraub, W. *The Poetry of Adam Mickiewicz.* 's-Gravenhage, 1954.

Welsh, D. *Adam Mickiewicz.* New York: Twayne, 1966.

Wyka, K. *Historia literatury polskiej.* Vol. I: *Romantyzm.* 2nd ed. Warsaw, 1953.

Zamotin, I. *Romantizm 20-x godov 19 stoletija v russkoj literature.* 2nd ed. 3 vols. St. Petersburg, 1911–1913. (Weak).

Zeńkovskij, V. *N. V. Gogol'.* Paris, 1961.

Žirmunskij, V. *Bajron i Puškin.* Leningrad, 1924. (Abridged in *Zeitschrift für slavische Philologie,* III [1926] and IV [1927].)

Torso a tajemství Máchova Díla. Anthology, Prague, 1938. (Contains essays by R. Jakobson, J. Mukařovský, D. Čiževsky, and others.)

CHAPTER XI

Baxtin, M. *Problemy poetiki Dostoevskogo.* 2nd ed. Moscow, 1963.

Bicilli, P. *Tvorčestvo Čexova. Opyt stilističeskogo analiza.* Sofia, 1942. (German translation, Munich, 1965.)

Cejtlin, A. *Masterstvo Turgeneva-romanista.* Moscow, 1958.

Čukovskij, K. *Masterstvo Nekrasova.* Moscow, 1952. (3rd ed., 1959.)

———. *O Čexove.* Moscow, 1967.

Dolinin, A. *Poslednie romany Dostoevskogo.* Moscow and Leningrad, 1963.

Èjxenbaum, B. *Lev Tolstoj.* Leningrad, 1928.

Èjxenbaum, B. *Morodoj Tolstoi.* Petrograd, 1922. Reprinted, Munich, 1968.

Èjges, I. "V. A. Žukovskij." *Sofija, Žurnal iskusstva i literatury,* IV (1914).

Fanger, D. L. *Dostoevsky and Romantic Realism.* Cambridge: Harvard University Press, 1965.

Gerigk, H.-J. *Versuch über Dostoevskijs "Jüngling."* Munich, 1965.

Giergielewicz, M. *Henryk Sienkiewicz.* New York: Twayne, 1968.

Grossman, L. *N. S. Leskov: Žizn'-tvorčestvo-poetika.* Moscow, 1945.

Gukovskij, G. *Realizm Gogolja.* Moscow and Leningrad, 1959.

———. *Očerki po istorii russkogo realizma.* Vol. I: *Puškin i russkie romantiki.*

Saratov, 1946. (Republished, Moscow, 1965.) Vol. II: *Puškin i problemy realisti-českogo stilja*. Moscow, 1957.

Heidenreich, J. *Ruské zaklady srbského realismu*. Prague, 1933.

Jakobson, R. "O realismu v umění." *Červen*, IV (1921). (The same work in Ukrainian in *Vaplite*, II (1927), and in Russian in *Michigan Slavic Materials. Readings in Russian Poetics*. Ann Arbor: The University of Michigan Press, 1962.)

Jackson, R. L. *Dostoevsky's Quest for Form*. New Haven: Yale University Press, 1966.

Kombol, M. *Hrvatski pripovjedači osamdesetih i devedesetih godina*. Sto godina hrvatske književnosti, 1. Zagreb, 1935.

Kott, J., ed. *Kultura okresu pozytywizmu. Wybór tekstów i komentarzy*. Vol I: *Mieszczaństwo*. Warsaw, 1949. (Onesided.)

Kulczycka-Saloni, J. *Henryk Sienkiewicz-krytyk i teoretyk literatury*. Pamiętnik literacki, 4. 1956.

Máchal, J. *O českém romanu novodobém*. 2nd ed. Prague, 1930.

———. *Dějiny českeho dramatu*. 2nd ed. Prague, 1929.

Melkowski, St. *Poglądy estetyczne i działalność krytycznoliteracka Bolesława Prusa*. Warsaw, 1963.

Merežkovskij, D. *L. Tolstoj i Dostoevskij*. 2 vols. St. Petersburg, 1901. (German translation, 3rd ed., Berlin, 1924.)

Mochulsky, K. *Dostoevsky: His Life and Work*. Princeton: Princeton University Press, 1967.

Najder, Z., ed. *Orzeszkowa, Sienkiewicz, Prus o literaturze*. Warzaw, 1956.

Neruda, J. *Kritické a smísené spisy*. Prague, 1921.

Orzeszkowa, E. *Pisma krytycznoliterackie*. Edited by E. Jankowski. Breslau, 1959.

Pržák, A. *Literární Slovensko let 50 až 70*. Prague, 1932. (Many inaccuracies.)

Trypućko, J. *Język Władysława Syrokomli*. Uppsala and Wiesbaden, 1955.

Tschiževskij (Čiževskij, Chyzhevskyj) "What is realism?" In Russian in *Novyj Žurnal*, LXXV (1964).

——— (Čiževsky). *Outline of Comparative Slavic Literatures*. Boston: American Academy of Arts and Sciences, 1952.

——— (Tschiževskij). *Russische Literaturgeschichte des 19. Jahrhunderts*. Vol II, 1: *Realismus*. Munich, 1967. (English translation in progress, to be published by Vanderbilt University Press.)

———. "Čechov und die russische Literaturentwicklung." In *Anton Čechov 1860–1904*. Edited by T. Eekman. Leiden, 1960.

———. *A History of Nineteenth Century Russian Literature*, translated by Richard Noel Porter and Martin Rice. Nashville: Vanderbilt University Press (forthcoming).

Setschkureff, V. *N. S. Leskov: Sein Leben und sein Werk*. Wiesbaden, 1959.

Turey, K. *Bolesław Prus i romantyzm*. Lemberg, 1937.

Vlček, J. *Češti spisovatele 19. věku*. 1904–1916.

Wasiolek, E. *Dostoevsky: The Major Fiction*. Cambridge: Harvard University Press, 1964.

Winner, Thomas. *Chekhov and his Prose*. New York: Holt, Rinehart and Winston, 1966.

Zamotin, I. *Sorokovye i šestidesjatye gody.* 2nd ed. St. Petersburg, 1915.
Aškercev Zbornik. Celje, 1957.
Program a styl českého realizmu v 19. století. Prague, 1964.

CHAPTER XII

Boy-Żeleński, T. *Znasz li ten kraj?* Warsaw, 1931. (3rd ed., Krakow, 1955; also in Boy-Żeleński, *Pisma.* Vol. II. Warsaw, 1956.)
———, ed. *Młoda Polska. Wybór poezji.* Lemberg, 1939. (Reprinted, Breslau, 1947.)
Bowra, C. M. *The Creative Experiment.* London, 1949. (About Majakovskij and Pasternak.)
———. *The Heritage of Symbolism.* London, 1947. (About Blok.)
Donchin, G. *The Influence of French Symbolism on Russian Poetry.* 's-Gravenhage, 1958. (Much doubtful information.)
Feldman, W. *Współczesna literatura polska.* 8th ed. Warsaw, 1930. (About late realism and modernism.)
Hindley, L. *Die Neologismen Andrej Belyjs.* Munich, 1965.
Holthusen, J. *Feodor Sologubs Roman-Trilogie.* Musagetes, 9. 's-Gravenhage, 1960.
———. *Studien zur Ästhetik und Poetik des russischen Symbolismus.* Göttingen, 1957.
———, and D. Tschižewskij, eds. *Versdichtung der russischen Symbolisten. Ein Lesebuch.* Heidelberger slavische Texte, 5 and 6. Wiesbaden, 1959.
Hönig, A. *Andrej Belyjs Romane. Stil und Gestalt.* Munich, 1965.
Humesky, A. *Majakovskij and his Neologisms.* New York, 1964.
Jakubowski, J. Z., ed. *Zarys literatury polskiej. Wraz z antologią poezji i publicystyki.* Vol. I: *1887–1918.* 7th ed. Warsaw, 1957.
———. *Młoda Polska, Antologia i materialy.* Warsaw, 1958.
Krzyżanowski, J. *Neoromantyzm polski. 1890–1918.* Breslau, Warsaw, and Krakow, 1963.
Máchal, J. *O symbolismu v polské a ruské literatuře.* Prague, 1934.
Markov, V. *The Longer Poems of Velimir Xlebnikov.* Berkeley, 1962.
———, ed. *Manifesten der russischen Futuristen.* Munich, 1967.
———. *Russian Futurism: A History.* Berkeley: The University of California Press, 1968.
Maslenikov, Oleg A. *The Frenzied Poets: Andrey Biely and the Russian Symbolists.* Berkeley: The University of California Press, 1952.
Močul'skij, K. *Andrej Belyj.* Paris, 1955.
———. *A. Blok.* Paris, 1948.
———. *Valerij Brjusov.* Paris, 1962.
Poggioli, R. *The Poets of Russia: 1890–1930.* Cambridge, Mass., 1960.
Reeve, F. *Alexander Blok: Between Image and Idea.* New York: Random House, 1962.
Šalda, F. X. *Moderní literatura česká.* Prague. 1909. (Reprinted in, Šalda, F. X. *Soubor díla.* Prague, 1961.)
———. *A. Sova.* Prague, 1924.
Schmidt, A. *Valerij Brjusovs Beitrag zur Literaturtheorie.* Munich, 1963.
Soldan, F. *Karel Hlaváček, typ české dekadence.* Prague, 1930.
Tschižewskij, D. *Russische Literaturgeschichte des 19. Jahrhunderts.* Vol. II, 2: *Der Spätrealismus: Symbolismus und Futurismus.* (In preparation.)

——, ed. *Anfänge des russischen Futurismus.* Heidelberger slavische Texte, 7. Wiesbaden, 1963.

Václavek, B. *St. K. Neumann.* Prague, 1955.

Vinokur, G. *Majakovskij-novator jazyka.* Moscow, 1943. (Reprinted, Munich, 1967.)

Wyka, K. *Modernizm polski.* Krakow, 1959.

CHAPTER XIII

1. PROBLEMS OF COMPARATIVE SLAVIC LITERARY HISTORY

Bąbala, J. *Zagadnienie łącznego badania literatur słowiańskich,* Warsaw, 1938.

Bittner, K. "Methodologisches zur vergleichenden germanisch-slavischen Literaturwissenschaft." *Germanoslavica,* III (1935).

Brückner, A. "Geschichte der slavischen Literaturen." *Slavische Rundschau,* IV (1932).

——. *Zarys dziejów literatur i języków słowiańskich.* Lemberg, 1929.

Deržavin, V. "Problemy kljasycyzmu ta systematyka literaturnych styliv." *Mysteckyj ukrajinśkyj ruch. Zbirnyky,* II (Munich and Karlsfeld, 1946).

Georgiev, Emil. *Obšto i sravnitelno slavjansko literaturoznanie.* Sofia, 1965.

Gołąbek, J. "Zagadnienie łączności literatur słowiańskich." *Ruch słowiański,* II (1929).

——. *Literatury słowiańskie. Rozważania o metodzie.* Marchołt, 4. Warsaw, 1938.

Hruševśkyj, M. "Istorija slovjańskyx literatur-fikcija čy neobxidnyj naukovyj postuljat?" *Sveslavenski Zbornik.* Zagreb, 1930.

Jakobson, R. "The Kernel of Comparative Slavic Literature." *Harvard Slavic Studies,* I. Cambridge, Mass., 1953.

——. "Comparative Slavic Studies." *The Revue of Politics,* XVI, 1 (1954).

Krzyżanowski, J. *Od średniowiecza do baroku.* Warsaw, 1938. (Especially pp. 1–53: "Barok na tle prądów romantycznych.")

Lednicki, W. "Existe-t-il un patrimoine commun d'études slaves?" *Le monde slave,* IV (1926).

Mazon, A. "Le patrimoine commun des études slaves." *Revue des études slaves,* IV (1924).

Tschižewskij, D. *Kul'turno-istoryčni epoxy.* Augsburg, 1948.

—— (Čiževsky). *Outline of Comparative Slavic Literatures.* (See Chapter XI).

Wollman, F. *Slovesnost Slovanů.* Prague, 1928.

——. "Vom Geiste des literarischen Schaffens bei den Slaven." *Slavische Rundschau,* IV (1932).

——. *K metodologii srovnávaní slovesnosti slovanské.* Brünn, 1936.

——. "Dvě polské polemiky o slovanských literaturách." *Slovo o slovensnost,* V (1939).

2. A SELECTION OF WORKS ON MUTUAL SLAVIC LITERARY INFLUENCES

American Contributions to the Fifth International Congress of Slavists. Vol. II: *Literary Contributions.* The Hague, 1963. (Particularly articles by W. B. Edgerton, V. Erlich, M. Giergiebewicz, William Harkins, and T. G. Winner.)

Florovskij, A. *Čechi i vostočnye slavjane.* 2 vols. Prague, 1935–1947.

Festschrift for M. P. Alekseev. Moscow and Leningrad, 1966. (In Russian.)

Festschrift for P. N. Berkov. Moscow and Leningrad, 1966. (In Russian.)

Heidenreich, J. *Vliv Mickiewiczův na českou literaturu přebřeznovou.* Prague, 1930.

Krhoun, M. "Češi a počátky běloruského národního literárního hnutí v prvním desetiletí 20. století." *Sbornik Praci Filos. fakulty Brněnské Univers.* Řada literárněvědna, 13. 1964.

Lednicki, W., ed. *Adam Mickiewicz in World Literature.* Berkeley: The University of California Press, 1956.

Magnuszewski, J. *Stosunki literackie polsko-czeskie w końcu XIX i na początku XX wieku.* Breslau, 1951.

Pervol'f, I. *Slavjane, ix vzaimnye otnošeniaja i svjazi.* 2 vols. Warsaw, 1888–1890. (Out of date.)

Ševčenko, F. *Rol' Kyjiva v mizslov'janskyx zv'jazkaw u 17–18 stol.* Kiev, 1963.

Szyjkowski, M. *Polska účast v českém národním obrození.* 3 vols. Prague, 1931–45.

Zabolockij, P. *Očerki russkogo vlijanija v slavjanskix literaturax novogo vremeni.* Vol I: *Russkaja struja v literature serbskogo vozroždenija.* Warsaw, 1908.

Živanović, D. *Srbi i poljska književnost (1800–1871).* Belgrade, 1941.

INDEX

Adrianova-Peretc, V., 107
Aeneas Silvius. *See* Piccolomini
Afanas'ev, A., 128
Aksakov, A. S., 14
Aksakov, Konstantin, 14, 144
Alekseev, M. P., 87
Aleksej Mixajlovič, Tsar, 64
Alexander Nevskij, Prince, 41, 44
Amartol. *See* Hamartolos
Andreev, Leonid, 191
Andrić, I., 177
Angelus Silesius, 15, 111, 132
Annenskij, Innokentij, 176, 180, 192, 193
Appolinaire, G., 193
Arbes, J., 151, 163
Aristotle, 66, 75, 77, 87, 104, 113
Asnyk, A., 151, 159, 160
Aškerc, A., 151
Auerbach, Erich, 19
Aulus Gellius, 195

Baader, F., 132
Babel', I, 196
Bach, J. S., 123
Bahdanovič, M., 177, 181
Bakvis, C., 109
Balbín, B., 93
Balimont, K., 20, 176, 182, 189, 191, 194, 196, 200
Baltrušajtis, Jurgis, 189, 193
Balzac, H., 146
Baraković, Juraj, 80
Bart-Ćišinski, J., 177
Bartoš, F. M., 71
Basilius the Great, 35
Baudelaire, P., 179

Bebel, Heinrich, 81
Beethoven, L., 123
Bél, Matthias, 89, 93
Belinskij, V. G., 23
Belyj, Andrej, 24, 174, 176, 180, 182, 186–187, 189, 192, 193, 194, 195, 196, 197
Benediktov, B., 139, 195
Benešovský, M., 85
Benisławska, K., 111
Bentham, J., 138
Béranger, P. J. de, 159
Berynda, P., 86
Bestužev-Marlinskij, A. A., 118
Bielski, Marcin, 73, 81, 82
Bitnar, Vilem, 89
Blahoslav, Jan, 12, 73, 84–85
Blake, William, 199
Blok, A., 20, 176, 180, 181, 183, 184, **188**, 189, 192, 193, 195, 197
Blumauer, J. A., 115
Boccaccio, G., 76, 87
Bodjanśkyj, O., 86, 148
Boehm, A. L., 201
Boehme, Jacob, 15, 132
Boileau, 113, 114
Bonaventura, 56
Boratynskij, E. A., 127, 139
Boris, St., 31, 37
Borovykovskyj, 131
Bošković, R., 93, 94
Botto, J. *See* Krasko
Boy-Żeleński, T., 174
Bräuer, H., 36, 42
Bridel, B., 88, 89, 92, 96, 98, 101
Brjusov, Valerij, 20, 176, 180, 183, 184–185, 189, 190, 194, 195